Editor
Eric Migliaccio

Managing Editor
Ina Massler Levin, M.A.

Editor-in-Chief
Sharon Coan, M.S. Ed.

Illustrator
Bruce Hedges

Cover Artist
Denise Bauer

Art Coordinator
Denice Adorno

Imaging
Alfred Lau

Product Manager
Phil Garcia

Take Five Minutes

Fascinating Facts and Stories for Reading and Critical Thinking

Grades 4-8

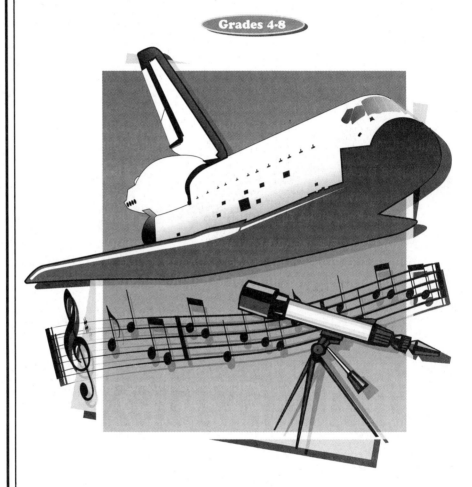

Author:

Ruth Foster, M. Ed.

Publishers:
Rachelle Cracchiolo, M.S. Ed.
Mary Dupuy Smith, M.S. Ed.

Teacher Created Materials, Inc.
6421 Industry Way
Westminster, CA 92683
www.teachercreated.com
ISBN-1-7439-3050-9
©2001 Teacher Created Materials, Inc.
Made in U.S.A.

Table of Contents

Introduction

Fact: Harry Houdini was born right-handed, but he forced himself to use his left hand until he could use both hands equally well. Because of his continuous rigorous training, Houdini could use his toes as well as most people could use their fingers.

Fact: Beethoven is considered a musical genius. His compositions are hailed today as masterpieces. Yet Beethoven composed some of his greatest work while he was deaf. Also, Beethoven could not multiply.

Take Five Minutes: Fascinating Facts and Stories for Reading and Critical Thinking sparks interest. The information reported above is contained in lesson units of this book, and it is this type of information that gets students sitting up in their seats and paying attention. Spanning centuries, from Cleopatra to living heroes of today, *Take Five Minutes: Fascinating Facts and Stories for Reading and Critical Thinking* provides factual information about people and events. It was not written as "test material," where one is expected to memorize facts. It was written so that a teacher can generate class discussion, reinforce geography skills, and present people and history in a less stilted manner than is typical of academic textbooks.

The lessons and activities in *Take Five Minutes: Fascinating Facts and Stories for Reading and Critical Thinking* are short and fun. They supplement and add to classroom learning.

Using this Book

What You Have

It is early morning, and the school bell has just rung. Your students cannot seem to focus or settle in their seats. There is no class unity; everyone is off in his or her own separate world.

You have five minutes before the bell rings at the end of the day. You have only seven minutes before you will be leaving for your field trip. Your students are bored, but by the time they take out a piece of paper and a pen, it will be time to put them away.

It is after lunch, and you need to rein your students in, channeling and redirecting their energy once again into the classroom. You do not want to waste your students' valuable instructional time at school with idle waiting and down time. You want every minute to count.

You want your students happy and entertained, but you also want them learning. You want them engaged in intellectually stimulating activities that promote learning, that reinforce what has been covered, and that also sparks your students' interest. You want your students so eager to know more that they pepper you with questions and talk amongst themselves about what was or what could be.

You have *Take Five Minutes: Fascinating Facts and Stories for Reading and Critical Thinking*. What exactly is *Take Five Minutes: Fascinating Facts and Stories for Reading and Critical Thinking*?

It is a book for teachers that is filled with short activities and stories that take about five minutes of class time. The stories vary greatly in what they discuss, but they are written to get students thinking and involved in classroom discussion.

Each story is followed by a section called "Questions to Ponder." Usually one of these questions has a geographical component that reinforces a student's recall of physical geography. For example, if the person described was born in New York, some questions might be "What is the capital of New York?" or "New York borders which ocean: the Pacific, Atlantic, or Indian?"

Take Five Minutes: Fascinating Facts and Stories for Reading and Critical Thinking also contains some fun short quizzes (matching quotes to people, putting rivers with countries, finding missing words in proverbs, etc). If the instructor desires to use one of the quizzes, copies can be made and distributed to each student. If the instructor prefers, the quizzes can be prepared for an overhead projector. Answers are always provided.

Using this Book (cont.)

How Far Can One Go?

There is no set way that this book has to be used. Some instructors may use it every morning as a first activity. Others may choose to save it for those spare minutes before leaving on a field trip or waiting for a bell to ring. Some teachers may find it a valuable resource for substitutes. Indeed, professional substitutes may find it useful to own their own copy.

Some instructors may choose to go further than a five-minute discussion. They may want to involve the students when it comes to choosing who or what is discussed next, and some inculcators may even use the selection process as a reinforcement of math facts. Ideas for this are discussed under the "Choosing the Name or Topic for Daily Instruction" section on page 6.

For those teachers who are looking for novel ways to develop the writing skills of their students, a special writing section (page 8) is included with instructions and ideas on how this book can be used to promote writing.

Speeding Up the Car Trip:

A Note to Parents and Home Schoolers

Learning takes place everywhere. Learning is not and should not be confined to the four walls of a classroom, nor should it be limited to school days. *Take Five Minutes: Fascinating Facts and Stories for Reading and Critical Thinking* provides a format for intellectual development. It promotes stimulating discussion while introducing facts and stories about the world we live in.

As parents, we are instrumental in opening our children's minds. At the same time, we too often do not have facts at our fingertips. *Take Five Minutes: Fascinating Facts and Stories for Reading and Critical Thinking* provides entertainment. It can be read not for the memorizing of facts but as something that provides fun glimpses into worlds that are different from those of our immediate families.

Keep a copy of this book in your car! Someone can read a page of it out loud to the rest of the passengers. Ask your children how that person would feel if they had your automobile to travel around in, or if they would like where it is you are traveling to.

Rest assured that the game in which one thinks up a person, place, or thing and the others have to figure out who or what it is using only "yes" or "no" questions is about to get much more interesting. Yes, the drive can seem shorter!

Dinner Conversation

For the first time in months, the entire family is sitting down to dinner at the same time. It may well be at a fast-food restaurant rather than your own kitchen table, but you are all together. An amazing feat, considering the chunks of time allocated for soccer and gymnastic practice, the miles driven to extra curricular activities, the necessary preparation of school assignments, and work.

Yet, despite this family time, there is no conversation. Everyone concentrates on eating (some using better manners than others!), and the only comment one may hear besides "Pass the salt" may be "I'm done. Can you drive me now?"

Just as we teach our children proper etiquette, we must teach them proper dinner conversation. *Take Five Minutes: Fascinating Facts and Stories for Reading and Critical Thinking* can be a valuable instructional aid.

◆ "Float like a butterfly, sting like a bee," that's what Muhammad Ali said.

◆ Mawson went from 15 stone to less than eight. That means he lost over 100 pounds. His feet and hands were rotting at the ends; and when he finally made it back, the man who reached him first cried, "My God, which one are you?"

◆ The first submarine was used in the War for Independence, and it looked like a wooden barrel. There was enough air in it for 30 minutes, and when it began to fill up with water, you had to stop turning the propeller shaft or stop steering it and pump with both hands. The pumps sort of looked like our bicycle pumps. It was made by a farmer who didn't even live by the sea!

◆ Morgan—who invented the gas mask—was the son of a former slave, and no one would believe that his invention worked. Then there was a terrible fire in a tunnel 250 feet below Lake Erie, and even the firemen couldn't do anything. Morgan and his brother, using the masks, went in and saved 32 people. The next thing you knew, police departments all over were sending in orders.

Make a comment like one of these, and there will be more things to say than "Can I go now?" Insist that your children make a comment. Have them practice the art of lively and sparkling conversation. It will pay off later on in life, socially and professionally.

Fit *Take Five Minutes: Fascinating Facts and Stories for Reading and Critical Thinking* into your family dynamics. Will it be better for you to pick the topic, or can you delegate a different child each week? Children often list their chores to friends or on fact sheets in school. Can you imagine the interest your child will generate when he or she says or writes, "I have to provide stimulating conversation every Tuesday?"

Using this Book *(cont.)*

Choosing the Name or Topic for Daily Instruction

Instructors have the right to have some fun here! There is no correct order when it comes to using the pages of this book. Because each lesson is an individual unit that does not rely on any other unit, teachers have flexibility when it comes to choosing what particular lesson to use for instruction on any particular day. A teacher might . . .

- Read out five names, simply picking them out by random. Students choose a name, even if they don't recognize any of the ones called out. Thus the element of surprise augments the lesson.

- Have a student arbitrarily choose a page number. The instructor could couple this method of choosing a topic with math reinforcement.

  ☞ The student may choose a page number that is odd.

  ☞ The student may choose a page number that is even.

  ☞ The student may choose a number that is prime.

  ☞ The student may choose a number that is a multiple of two, three, four, five, etc.

- Make up a math problem in which the solution is the page to be discussed for the day. For example, the teacher might say, "Who can tell me what page we will be discussing today? The answer is the solution to [a mathematical problem]." In this way, the teacher can supply problems that assist in reinforcing the following mathematical skills:

  ☞ **Addition with Carrying Basics**
  Example: $65 + 48 = x$

  ☞ **Order of Operations**
  Example: $(16 \times 2) + 7 \times 6 - 3 = x$

  ☞ **Elementary Algebra**
  Example: $100x - 40 = 160$

- Take into consideration what is being taught on a particular day and at a particular time. For example, a teacher might want to discuss a unit that deals with exploration (Sir Ernest Shackleton, Henry Stanley and David Livingston, Roald Amundsen and the South Pole, etc.) or the Civil Rights Movement (Marian Anderson, Rosa Parks, Martin Luther King, Jr., etc.) simply because the class is already working on that particular part of the world or instructional unit. The mini lessons in *Take Five Minutes: Fascinating Facts and Stories for Reading and Critical Thinking* would thus supplement and aid in starting discussion for the primary classroom unit.

As the instructor becomes more familiar with the lessons and activities in *Take Five Minutes: Fascinating Facts and Stories for Reading and Critical Thinking*, he or she will discover some personal favorites.

Using this Book (cont.)

They Are Missing!

There are people who are not in this book who helped change the world. Their presence created an impact. If a student approaches his or her teacher with the words, "Why isn't this person in the book?" the teacher should explain that *Take Five Minutes: Fascinating Facts and Stories for Reading and Critical Thinking* is not a typical textbook: it is a supplemental text written to encourage thinking outside of straight memorization of facts. It was written to spark interest and to generate comments exactly like "Why isn't this person in the book? I think this person should be in the book." A teacher might . . .

◆ Encourage his or her students to keep a class list that they can add to throughout the year. Every time students read or learn about someone interesting, the names of the people they discover can be added to the "list of people who should be in the next edition of *Take Five Minutes: Fascinating Facts and Stories for Reading and Critical Thinking*."

◆ Use the writing instructions on page 8 as an aid to help teach his or her students how to write their own page. Depending on class interest, the teacher might have the class write a book that deals specifically with particular ethnic groups, people living during the time of the American Revolution, or current politicians and athletes. A class edition may also focus exclusively on animals or fellow students and their families.

The Blank Page Solution

As every teacher knows, it is easy to assign writing topics. Yet when the students actually sit down to write, they cannot start the process: they are intimidated and then immobilized by the blank page. Facts and anecdotes about the subject may be whirling around in the student's mind, but the student does not know how to sort them or put them down on the paper in an organized manner.

An aid for these students can be found on pages 167 and 168. Page 168 provides a solution for those students who need a clear visual format. The blank lines and paragraph indentations enable the writer to "see" how his or her writing should look. It provides a framework for organization. The student knows beforehand what his or her output needs to be. The student does not have to worry that he or she will show inadequate or not enough work. In addition, this visual format can provide comfort for many students—the task is not overwhelming and intimidating because there are clear boundaries. It is manageable.

Page 167 provides hints that students will find useful while composing their writing sample. It gives specific suggestions for the first sentence, along with tips on where information should be placed in paragraphs. In addition, unambiguous and precise suggestions are given for the writing of the "Questions to Ponder" section of the student's writing sample.

Depending on the class and the student, the instructor may choose to use both of these pages, only one of them, or neither.

Using this Book *(cont.)*

Writing Practice

Students need to write. Every instructor knows this. Yet for too many students, writing is to be avoided. It is a painful exercise that is best kept to the 40 or 50 minutes that are allocated to the subject English during the school day. *Take Five Minutes: Fascinating Facts and Stories for Reading and Critical Thinking,* though by no means a full writing instructional book, can be used to supplement writing practice. After class discussion, a teacher might request students to . . .

♦ Write out one sentence about the person the class just discussed. It might be suggested that the sentence be compound or complex.

♦ Write out one sentence that answers one of the questions verbally discussed. This can provide practice for more technical writing, where questions are asked and answered in the same sentence. For example, if one of the questions to ponder was "Which ocean borders California?" the student would be expected to write out something like, "The Pacific Ocean borders the United States on its western coastal state of California."

♦ Create a sentence that uses a particular vocabulary word that can be used to describe the person or something he or she did.

♦ Write a wish list for the person discussed.

♦ Write as if you were the particular person discussed. Enter notes in your private journal.

As the year progresses and the student becomes more familiar with the *Take Five Minutes: Fascinating Facts and Stories for Reading and Critical Thinking* lessons, a teacher might want to request that a student write a page that would "fit" in the book. The teacher could . . .

♦ Have each child interview and then write about a fellow student in the class.

♦ Have each child interview someone outside of the classroom—perhaps even another family member.

♦ Choose an animal or event.

♦ Allow the students complete freedom of choice in picking their own subject.

♦ Request that the child find information by means other than an interview, perhaps by using resource books or accessing the Internet.

Using this Book (cont.)

Reading a Biography and Report Blues

Students are often asked to read a biography and then report on the person about whom they read. It is up to the student to use several reference sources, some of which may be a bibliography as well as encyclopedias or information from the Internet.

Many students flounder when it comes to choosing the report topic. To the adult, they often seem to be unfocused, but in reality, it may be that the student is not sure exactly about whom it is he or she wants to write. The library and all of its reference section seems to overwhelm them, and the number of books they can choose from are too many. The names that they do recognize are too familiar and boring.

Teachers may then suggest a name with which the student is unfamiliar, but often it appears as if the student is still unmotivated. It may be, instead, that the child does not trust the teacher. Someone or something interesting to the teacher does not necessarily spark interest with the child.

A student may actually go to the library and look up a source the teacher has suggested. Yet after finding the book or article and reading through it, the student may realize that it holds no interest for him or her. At this point, many students feel frustrated and angry that they have expended what they consider to be needless energy. They feel behind, and they haven't even put pen to paper!

Bring into play *Take Five Minutes: Fascinating Facts and Stories for Reading and Critical Thinking!* This book can be used as an aid for those students who need a quick reference. They can leaf through the book, reading snippets, until something catches their interest. Perusing the paragraph about separating conjoined twins (page 60) may be enough for the student to decide that he or she wants to find out more about Ben Carson. Reading about Neil Armstrong's first steps on the moon (page 59) may spur a student's interest enough for him or her to read up on the history of space travel and exploration.

Names abound, all at the students' fingertips. The students will enjoy the search—and the find!

Using this Book (cont.)

The End of Writing One's Name on the Board 500 Times

Even with the best teachers and the greatest students, there are times when a student has crossed required and expected school behavior. Assigning a child to write "I will treat others with respect" 500 times may seem like an appropriate response at the time. This type of assignment is often just a very time-consuming, mindless exercise. Viewing it as pointless, students and parents become even more distanced from the teacher. An alternative is needed.

With *Take Five Minutes: Fascinating Facts and Stories for Reading and Critical Thinking*, a teacher may combine disciplinary measures with an educational task. Instead of copying a particular sentence over and over, a teacher may require a student to read a particular page of *Take Five Minutes: Fascinating Facts and Stories for Reading and Critical Thinking*. The child may then be asked to write down the answers to some or all of the questions.

As teachers become familiar with the individual stories in *Take Five Minutes: Fascinating Facts and Stories for Reading and Critical Thinking*, they may find particular stories that they feel are particularly relevant to an individual student or the situation in which the student has found him- or herself. Assigning the story to a child may turn a disciplinary task into one that sparks interest and educates.

Extra Credit Ease

Extra credit can be a powerful teaching tool that can be used to increase a student's motivation and confidence. A student may have a grade point average of 79 percent, or the equivalent of a "C+." To a student—and indeed with many schools when it comes to calculating grade-point average—a "C" is a "C" whether it is a "C-," "C," or "C+." If students see that despite all their work and effort, their 79 percent is the same as a 70 percent to school authorities, they may feel that their work was to no avail. Why try? Extra credit can deal with this problem without promoting grade inflation or lenient grading.

Teachers are already fully engaged with creating innovating and stimulating class lessons. Often they do not have the time to create worthwhile and instructional extra-credit assignments. Yet, with this book, a teacher can devise extracurricular assignments that are meaningful and instructional.

- ◆ After class discussion, students may be given the option of further answering a question on paper.
- ◆ A teacher may assign a page to a student. The student can earn extra points by writing out the answers or being ready to discuss them at a convenient time for the teacher.
- ◆ A student may write out his or her own page that would fit into the book *Take Five Minutes: Fascinating Facts and Stories for Reading and Critical Thinking*. (See page 7.)

Many students feel that they do not have any control over their grades. By allowing a student the opportunity of performing extracurricular assignments, a teacher can succeed in showing a child that the child does indeed exercise some control. By carefully choosing the extracurricular assignments, a teacher can provide highly motivating and rewarding instruction. Teachers can help students learn that "going the extra mile" pays off.

People, Places, and Events

Sir Ernest Shackleton

(1874–1922)

A sea leopard, a vicious seal that feasts on other seals, jumped onto an ice floe and began a deadly chase. The prey, one of Shackleton's men, screamed as he ran as fast as he could across the rotten ice. The 12-foot (3.6 m) creature suddenly dove off the ice floe and back into the water. Seconds later, the head of the sea leopard lunged out of the water in front of the man on the other side of the ice floe, its mouth snarled open, its huge, saw-like teeth exposed. The sea leopard had tracked the man's shadow through the thin ice! It was shot just in time.

Ernest Shackleton was a British explorer who had come to lead an expedition across the entire continent of Antarctica via the South Pole. The year was 1914. Before reaching land, their ship was trapped in pack ice—ice floes packed against each other because of the ocean currents pushing them against the land. Ten million tons of ice crumpled their ship as if it were a toy. They were alone and adrift in a world of white ice, freezing air, and frigid winds. Beneath them lurked the dark freezing Arctic Ocean.

Shackleton changed his goal. Instead of wanting to be the first across the Antarctic continent, Shackleton was determined to keep his men alive and bring them safely back home. Living off of penguins and seals, Shackleton never allowed his men to think that they would not succeed in making their way home. One night, the floe on which they were sleeping cracked in two. A man fell in, and Shackleton pulled him out of the icy water, still in his sleeping bag, just seconds before the ice pieces closed over. All night, the wet man was walked around the floe—there were not any dry clothes for him, and if the man had stopped moving, he would have froze to death.

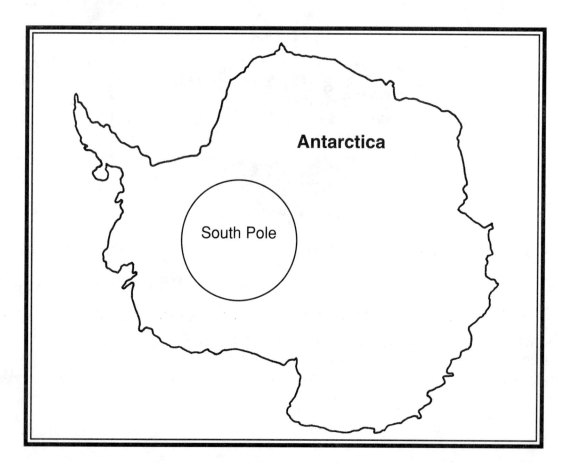

Sir Ernest Shackleton (cont.)

After 497 days on ice and water, Shackleton and his men, using the three tiny life boats they had saved from the ship before it went down, finally made it to Elephant Island, a tiny uninhabited piece of land. The boats were in such poor condition and some of the men so ill that Shackleton knew that he would have to leave some of his men if he were to save them all. With just five others, he took one boat and headed to South Georgia Island, where there was a whaling station. He was attempting the impossible, for the journey was over 1,000 miles (1609 km) across the stormiest ocean in the world.

Despite almost dying of thirst, losing the sea anchor, and suffering through gale winds, Shackleton made it to South Georgia Island. But they were on the wrong side! The island had never been crossed: it was too unsafe and steep. Yet Shackleton crossed it with nothing but a rope. At one point, blinded by a fog, knowing they had to climb lower if they were to survive, Shackleton tied his men together, and sitting on their rope, they slid over 2,000 (610 m) feet down the mountain! It has been said that when Shackleton reached the whaling station, men wept in disbelief when they realized who he was. It took four attempts and three months before Shackleton could save the men he had left on Elephant Island. Shackleton never let his men down.

Questions to Ponder

❏ Can you find Elephant Island and South Georgia Island on a map?

❏ Can you find a picture of a sea leopard?

❏ Was Ernest Shackleton a failure?

❏ Could you live 497 days on an ice floe?

❏ The words *floe* and *flow* sound the same, but they aren't the same at all. For this reason, they are *homophones*—words that sound exactly alike but have very different meanings. Can you name other homophones?

Jackie Robinson

(1919–1972)

"Mr. Robinson, I'm looking for a ballplayer with the guts enough not to fight back." These words were spoken to Jackie Robinson in 1945 by Branch Rickey, the president of the Brooklyn Dodgers baseball team. At that time, teams were segregated: white baseball players and black baseball players played in different leagues. Many people knew that this was wrong. Rickey knew that it would take a very strong man to break the barrier. The man would have to have the courage to bear verbal and physical abuse. Rickey knew that if the man fought back, people would use that as a reason why people of all different colors should not play together. Jackie Robinson told Rickey that he had the courage.

Robinson's difficulties started as soon as he was placed on the Montreal Royals, a minor league team affiliated with the Brooklyn Dodgers. On route to Florida, Robinson and his wife landed in New Orleans, where they were supposed to board a connecting flight. They were not allowed to get on the flight or eat in the cafeteria. When they took a bus, they were forced to sit in the back. When they finally arrived in Florida, Robinson's teammates avoided him, and he wasn't even allowed to play in an exhibition game because it was against the law in Florida for blacks and whites to play together. At the first real game though, more than 51,000 fans filled the 25,000-seat stadium. Robinson's playing was stupendous; and on April 9, 1947, the Dodgers issued a press release stating that Robinson had just been called up to play in the majors.

Robinson proved himself all over again. Despite hate mail, pitchers throwing at him, cleats raised to puncture his skin, and teammates who told him that they didn't like him, Robinson never gave up. During one game, when the other team and its fans were especially cruel and relentless in their taunts, one of Robinson's teammates finally screamed at them, "Why don't you yell at someone who can answer back?" This was a turning point, because the man who yelled these words at the crowd had been open in his dislike of Robinson being a teammate. Robinson's dignity and athletic ability had come to mean more than the color of his skin.

On July 23, 1962, Robinson accomplished another first: he became the first African American to be voted into the Major League Baseball Hall of Fame.

Questions to Ponder

❑ Robinson was born in Cairo, Georgia, on the same plantation on which his grandparents had been forced to work as slaves. What is the capital of Georgia, and does Georgia share a border with Florida or Mississippi? (*Atlanta is the capital. Georgia shares a border with Florida.*)

❑ When Robinson was only six months old, his mother and the rest of his siblings moved to California. What is the capital of California, and does California border the same ocean as Georgia? (*Sacramento. Georgia borders the Atlantic; California, the Pacific.*)

❑ Robinson used to say, "A life is not important, except in the impact it has on other lives." What did he mean?

❑ Robinson demonstrated throughout his life the ability to work hard and persevere—two traits he learned from his mother's example. What is perseverance? (*To persevere is to be steadfast and to not give up.*)

Louis Pasteur

(1822–1895)

Every time you drink milk, you need to thank Louis Pasteur. All of the milk we buy has been pasteurized. Pasteurized milk has been heated up to about 161.6° Fahrenheit (72°C) for 15 seconds. The heat sterilizes the milk, and all the harmful microorganisms and bacteria that make one ill and make the milk go sour are killed. Many foods one buys in the store are pasteurized, not just milk!

Pasteur also developed the first rabies vaccine. Rabies is a disease that is usually transmitted to humans by an animal bite. Before we vaccinated our dogs against rabies, people often contracted rabies when they were bitten by dogs. Pasteur first tried his vaccine on a human before he was really ready. What happened was this: on July 4, 1885, a nine-year-old boy named Joseph was attacked by a dog with rabies. He was bitten at least a dozen times, and the boy was almost certainly going to die. Joseph's mother and the dog owner brought Joseph on the train to beg Pasteur to help them. Pasteur decided to try his vaccine only after two other doctors said that Joseph was going to die. It took many painful shots, but the boy survived! Today, because of medical research, the vaccine has been improved. Fewer shots are needed, and the shots are less painful.

There is a famous story about Pasteur's wedding day. He went to his lab to work on the day before the wedding, and he got so involved in what he was doing that he had to be reminded to go to the church!

Before a doctor operates on you, he or she washes his or her hands carefully, making sure to not spread any germs. Everything that can be disinfected and sterilized in the operating room is. This careful procedure is partly due to Pasteur. Dr. Lister, the man who is often considered the father of modern surgery, was quick to admit how much he had learned from Pasteur's writings.

Questions to Ponder

❑ Pasteur was born in France. What is the capital of France? (*Paris*) Can you find it on the map?

❑ Note the similarity between Pasteur's name and the word *pasteurized*. Do you think *pasteurized* is a new word, made up because of Pasteur? (*It is. Pasteur invented this method of keeping foods safe, and so the process has been named after him.*)

❑ Can you think of some new words that have come about in your lifetime? (*New words appear in dictionaries each year. Scholars get together and decide what should be added. Many computer terms that are now in dictionaries were not there even 20 years ago. Some relatively new words and phrases are "Internet," "chat rooms," and "call waiting." Even "groovy" is relatively new!*)

❑ Pasteurization kills germs or microbes. Are there some microbes we do not want to kill? (*Yes, some bacteria do helpful things, such as turning cider into vinegar.*)

❑ Pasteur showed no sign of being a scientific genius when he first went to school. He didn't start to shine until he was a teenager. Do you know anyone like that?

Sarah Winnemucca

(1844–1891)

How are you at public speaking? Would you be able to walk out on a stage in front of a crowd of elegantly dressed people that you have never seen before and start speaking fluently—in their native language, not yours?

Sarah Winnemucca, a Northern Paiute Native American, was once terrified of the new settlers who had entered her lands. Yet, eloquently and passionately—but with humor—she learned to speak before crowds, asking for understanding and better treatment of her people. "We Indians are the little fish," Winnemucca would tell her white audiences, "and you eat us all up and drive us from home."

Life for the Northern Paiute began to change the year Winnemucca was born. An expedition of explorers, led by John Fremont and guided by Kit Carson, met Winnemucca's grandfather at what is now known as Pyramid Lake. (Fremont named this lake.) The Native Americans greeted the explorers with the Paiute words, "Truckee, truckee," meaning "good" or "all right." Fremont then began to call Winnemucca's grandfather Truckee; and Truckee acted as a guide for Fremont, traveling to California with him. Fremont named a river after Truckee, and the river goes by that name today.

Though Truckee felt that the whites could be trusted, Winnamucca's father was not so sure. After hearing tales of whites killing Paiutes, Winnamucca's father took his band to the mountains for the summer. They returned in the fall to gather their winter supplies, burying their fish and seeds as they usually did under a large dome of grass and mud that they then sealed off. Just as they finished sealing their precious dome, someone detected the presence of outsiders. Everyone took off in terror, but Wimmamucca and her cousin could not keep up. The two fearful mothers buried the children in the dirt, covering their bodies completely, leaving only their faces exposed. Using branches of sage to hide their faces and protect them from the sun, the adults told the girls not to make a noise. The two children lay in terror, almost afraid to breathe. Finally, when it was dark, their mothers came back, weeping in relief that the two girls were still alive. The girls were unharmed, but their dome, with its crucial food supply, had been burned.

For years after, just thinking about that day was enough to make Winnemucca tremble. Yet Winnemucca conquered her fears and refused to hide from the injustices that her people were suffering. She spoke out everywhere, even traveling to Washington, D.C., to speak to the president. Winnemucca also wrote a book about Paiute life.

Questions to Ponder

❏ Winnemucca was born in what is today Nevada. What is the capital of Nevada, and can you name the states that border Nevada to the west and to the north? (*Carson City. California borders Nevada on the west; Washington and Idaho border it on the north.*)

❏ Can you find the city of Winnemucca on the map? (*It is in Nevada.*) Can you locate the Truckee River and the city named Truckee in California on this river?

❏ Which is braver: having no fears, or doing something in spite of your fears?

❏ Winnemucca wanted all the Paiute to learn English, but she did not want them to lose their tribal identity. Is this a common wish of many immigrants? How can it be done?

Chuck Yeager

(1923–)

Sound travels at 761 miles per hour (1,225 kph) at sea level. Sound travels slower in cold air, though, and thus the speed of sound decreases to 660 miles per hour (1,062 kph) above 45,000 feet (13,716 m). Mach 1 is the term that means a speed equal to the speed of sound. Mach 2 would be twice the speed of sound, and Mach 3 would be three times the speed of sound.

No airplane had ever flown faster than the speed of sound. Was it even possible? And if it were ever done, could a pilot control the violent battering the plane and pilot would suffer from the shock waves that resulted from traveling at such incredible speeds?

After years of secret research, the Air Force was ready to try. Yeager was the man chosen to fly the Bell X-1. On October 14, 1947, Yeager did fly faster than sound. He smashed the invisible sound barrier, and the first man-made sonic boom was heard on Earth. A sonic boom is a sound resembling an explosion that is produced by shock waves produced by the object moving through the air at supersonic speeds.

Over the years, Yeager has been promoted up to general. Not only has Yeager studied hard and worked long hours, he has continually remained calm and clear-thinking in tense situations. Once, a pilot was suddenly blinded by the sun shining directly in his eyes. It was impossible for him to see his instrument panel. Yeager was flying chase, which means that Yeager was flying alongside the pilot who was testing the plane. The person flying chase does not get the glory that comes from testing the new plane, but he or she is there to provide help if something goes wrong. Yeager, paying close attention, not only realized that the pilot was in trouble, but within an instant, figured out what to do. He immediately piloted his plane to where he could dip his wing in front of the sun, and thus shade the pilot's eyes.

Another time when Yeager was flying chase at 20,000 feet (6,096 m), he noticed that the other pilot's plane was weaving and flying sloppily. Yeager figured that the pilot was suffering from hypoxia. *Hypoxia* occurs when there is not enough oxygen in the body. Yeager concluded that the pilot's oxygen hose had somehow become disconnected. Yeager got the pilot to respond by pretending that he was the one in trouble. Known for always being cool and collected, Yeager roared out, "Follow me down!" Later when the cockpit was examined, an oxygen tube that had pulled loose was found. Yeager's analysis of the problem, quick thinking, and solution saved both the pilot and the plane.

Questions to Ponder

❏ Yeager was born in West Virginia. What is its capital? (*Charleston*)

❏ Yeager flew his Bell X-1 at the Muroc (now Edwards) Air Force Base in California, located in the Mojave Desert. Can you find the Mojave Desert on the map, and why would a desert be a good place for an Air Force base? (*Despite the heat—up to 120 degrees in the daytime—there was privacy and ideal terrain. Rogers Dry Lake, a lake bed seven miles long and five miles wide, was solid clay, smooth, level and hard; and it made for a perfect landing field.*)

❏ Yeager had to keep his successful flight a secret: our government did not want other countries to know what we could do. Would you have been able to keep quiet?

❏ The sound barrier was an invisible wall, as was the four-minute mile. Once a man ran a mile under four minutes, it seemed that everyone could do it. Why do you think it is easier to do something once it has been done?

Alexander Fleming
(1881–1955)

In 1922, Alexander Fleming blew his nose and changed the world. It's true! Fleming was engaged in some bacterial research in his gloomy, tiny laboratory when he blew his nose. He looked at the mucus on his handkerchief, and, just out of curiosity, put some of it in a dish containing a culture jelly in which colonies of microbes were breeding. The next day, Fleming found that the microbe colonies were smaller. With further examination and experimentation, Fleming found that his bodily secretions contained an antiseptic that provided a natural protection against germs. Fleming called this germ-killing substance lysozyme.

At that point in time, we had no antibacterial drugs. We had antiseptic drugs—drugs that could kill germs on the outside of the human body—but none that could attack germs on the inside of our bodies. Our blood is a mass of red and white cells called corpuscles. The red cells carry oxygen, and the white cells attack and destroy invading microbes. For humans to have an effective antibiotic drug, they needed one that would not harm the white corpuscles. If the white corpuscles were killed, the drug would do more harm than good.

Fleming began to look for a lysozyme in other substances that perhaps could be used to help humans fight internal infections. After six long years, it just so happened that when he took the cover off of one of his dishes, some mold from a plant blew in through the open window and settled on the jelly. Instead of seeing his experiment as ruined and throwing the dish away, Fleming decided to see what happened. Thus, with mucus and an open window, penicillin was discovered!

Great as this achievement was, Fleming was unable to purify and concentrate the drug into a state that made it practical for humans to use. Fleming was not a chemist, and he knew that this problem needed a chemist. Nine years went by, and then two men—Professor Florey and Dr. Chain—took up the task. In 1941, after four years of intensive research and experimentation, they succeeded. All three men shared a Nobel Prize for ushering in a new era of medicine.

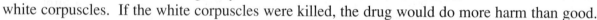

Questions to Ponder

❑ Fleming was born in Scotland. What language do they speak in Scotland, and what is the capital? (*The official language of Scotland is English. The capital is Edinburgh.*)

❑ Before antibiotics, people died from infections much more often. Have you taken antibiotics? (Note: Antibiotics do not necessarily have the word *penicillin* in their name.)

❑ Today, many office buildings and schools are being built with windows that do not open. Do you think this is a good idea? Why or why not?

❑ When penicillin first came out, during World War II, there was a black market for it. What does that mean? (*The demand was greater than the supply. People could not get enough of it through normal means, like in a drug store. Therefore, if someone had some, they could sell it illegally at higher prices. Much of the penicillin first produced went to our wounded soldiers. This drug saved countless lives during the war and has continued to do so even today.*)

❑ Do scientific breakthroughs happen quickly?

Lynne Cox

(1957–)

On August 7, 1987, Cox had to jump into the water feet first. If she jumped head first, the sudden impact of hitting water at a temperature of 44 degrees (think of a glass of ice water) might be enough to stop her heart. Cox also had to worry about the walruses and 15-foot (4.5 m) sharks that were common in the Strait. Yet, Cox jumped on purpose; and she did not swim in a shark cage (a strong metal basket that is attached to a crane on a ship that moves at the same rate of the swimmer), nor did she wear a wetsuit or grease her skin with lanolin. (Lanolin is used by many long distance swimmers because it acts as a protection from the cold water, and thus the body stays warmer.) Cox was only accompanied by two *umiaks* (walrus-skin canoes). Where was Cox, and what in the world was she doing?

Cox was in the frigid Arctic Ocean. She was swimming from the United States to Russia. She swam from Little Diomede Island to Big Diomede Island. These islands are between Alaska and Siberia, and the International Date Line bisects the channel between them. Strictly guarded, the strait had not been open to boats since 1948; and it had never been swum.

Though the islands were only 2.4 miles (3.9 km) apart, because of the strong currents, Cox would have to swim over twice that far. Winds would vary abruptly from periods of calm to gale force. The water (which freezes over in the winter months) would vary in temperature from 34°–44°F (1.1°–6.7°C). Water this cold would kill most humans in under 30 minutes, but Cox was swimming in nothing but a one-piece swimsuit.

While Cox was swimming, a dense fog descended, and Cox could not see where she was going. Several times the umiaks, which had started leaking from the beginning and were being bailed out with a soda can, got lost. Cox had to shout back through the mist to make sure that she was swimming in the right direction. Seals rose to the surface to get a better look at her.

When Cox finally made it to shore, the Soviets met her with blankets, seal skin slippers, and flowers. Cox walked to the recovery tent but, once there, her body temperature dropped to 94°F (34.4°C)— borderline hypothermia—and she began to slur her words, before slumping to the ground. Once she was warmed up and had regained her health, the Soviets throw her a tea party—chef in white uniform, tables with white cloths, and all!

Questions to Ponder

❑ One can probably not find the Diomede Islands on a map because they are so small, but can you find the International Date Line and see where it crosses between Alaska and Siberia?

❑ Cox is the only person in the world to swim across the Strait of Magellan, one of the most treacherous stretches of water in the world. Many ships have gone down in this strait. Where is the Strait of Magellan? (*It is near the bottom of South America.*)

❑ Cox has swum through Lake Baikal, one of the deepest, longest, and coldest lakes in the world. Where is Lake Baikal? (*It is above China in Russia.*)

❑ The worst jellyfish Cox ever encountered were in the waters off Sweden. The tentacles slammed into her and burned her. Have you ever seen a jellyfish?

❑ Why didn't Cox freeze to death?

Nat Love

(1854–1921)

Nat Love was a former slave who became known as one of the best all-around cowboys of the Old West. Before heading west, Love spent most of his time sharecropping to support his sisters and widowed mother. His life changed in 1869 when Love won a horse in a raffle. Love sold the horse, and after splitting the money with his mother and paying his debts, he took off for Dodge City, Kansas, to become a cowboy.

Because he was already an experienced horse trainer, it was easy for Love to learn how to herd cattle, brand them, and use a gun. Love became known by his nickname Deadwood Dick when in 1876, at a big Fourth of July celebration held in Deadwood, South Dakota, he competed in and won several contests. Cowboys had come from all over the territory hoping to show off their skills, but it was Love who won the rifle and handgun matches. He also set records in the rope-throwing and bronco-riding contests.

Being a cowboy meant that over the years Love worked as a gunfighter, scout, range boss, and rodeo driver. A tough man, he survived outlaw attacks, being captured by Native Americans, and 14 gunshot wounds. Love left the range after the West became settled and worked on the railroad.

One of the things Love had to watch out for while out on the range was being caught in a stampede. If cattle became "spooked" by a loud noise, the herd could very easily go out of control, charging across the prairie and running wild. The cowboys would have to try and ride their horses around the edges of the panicked herd, driving them back together and in the direction that they wanted. If a cowboy was thrown from his horse, it often meant death. A cowboy also had to watch for the horns of the angry steers if he did not want to get slashed.

Questions to Ponder

❏ Love was an ex-slave from Tennessee. What is the capital of Tennessee, and what range of mountains runs through the eastern part of the state? (*Nashville is the capital of Tennessee. Ranges of the Appalachian Mountains, including the Great Smoky Mountains, run through the eastern part of Tennessee.*)

❏ Deadwood is in South Dakota. Is Bismarck or Pierre the capital of South Dakota? (*Pierre is the capital of South Dakota. Bismarck is the capital of North Dakota.*)

❏ Love originally supported his family by sharecropping. What is sharecropping? (*A sharecropper is someone who is given seeds, tools, living quarters, and food on credit. They then farm the land and give back to the owners what they owe. Often sharecroppers could never get ahead, and they would be forced to continue to sharecrop because they could not pay their debts.*)

❏ Rodeo clowns have been around since the first rodeos. Why do they wear short pants? (*Being a rodeo clown is a very dangerous and intense job. Often, they attempt to do the same events as the competing cowboy, but they deliberately look incompetent. Their pants have to be short for safety reasons. They do not want to trip or get their legs and feet tangled in them as they use themselves as a diversion when a cowboy has fallen from a ferocious horse or bull.*)

Dorothea Lange

(1895–1965)

When Dorothea Lange was seven years old, she came down with a paralyzing disease called polio. (These days, we vaccinate young children for polio.) Lange's right leg, from the knee down, was afflicted, and for the rest of her life Lange limped. Children called her "Limpy," and it hurt her feelings horribly. What was worse than the name-calling, though, was the attitude of Lange's own mother. When Lange and her mother encountered someone they knew, Lange's mother would whisper to her, "Now walk as well as you can!"

Lange learned not to be afraid of what other people would think. She learned that if one wanted to do something, then one must act; and that is what she did. At the age of 17, she graduated from high school. Her mother asked her what she wanted to do with her life. Lange replied with assurance, "I want to be a photographer." Lange had never taken a picture in her life or even picked up a camera!

Lange's mother made her attend a teacher college, but Lange found work on her own. She got her first job simply by walking into the upstairs studio of one of the greatest American photographers (he was famous, in part, for his pictures of the 1906 San Francisco earthquake) and asking him directly for a job. From Genthe, the photographer who hired her, she learned that great pictures often reveal hidden truths about their subjects.

After learning what she could by working for other photographers, Lange went out on her own, starting her own studio. She moved to San Francisco, California, and from there she started to take a different type of picture. Instead of portraits, she took documentary pictures. The Latin root of the word documentary is *docere*, which means "to teach," and good documentary photographs do inform us; but they also have the power to move us. Lange traveled all over the United States documenting migrant workers, people in bread lines, steel mill workers, ex-slaves working the land, and dust-bowl victims. She also documented Japanese Americans who were cruelly and unfairly held in internment camps during World War II. Lange's pictures have been shown all over the world. They are a powerful and moving documentary of American life during her time.

Questions to Ponder

❏ As a child, Lange lived in small towns in New Jersey, but she went to school in New York. Lange's mother had a job as a librarian in New York City on the lower east side of Manhattan, and Lange went to the school near the library. What are the capitals of New York and New Jersey? (*Albany is the capital of New York; Trenton is the capital of New Jersey.*)

❏ Lange once said that polio was the most important thing that happened to her: it formed her, instructed her, helped her, and humiliated her. What are some of the events in your life that have affected you?

❏ When you look at a newspaper, what catches your eye first? (*Often, photographs catch your eye first. Editors will often use them to hook you into reading stories.*)

❏ Lange traveled around the world taking photographs. Some of her pictures were taken in Egypt, Ecuador, Nepal, and Venezuela. Which two of those countries are in South America? (*Ecuador and Venezuela*)

Ellison S. Onizuka

(1946–1986)

Over 8,000 candidates applied for NASA's space-shuttle program; 210 were interviewed. Out of these 210, only 35 were chosen. Onizuka was one of them.

Onizuka worked hard to be selected. The grandson of Hawaiian plantation workers, Onizuka was born and raised in Hawaii. He won a scholarship to the University of Colorado, where he majored in aerospace engineering and participated in the Air Force ROTC program. After earning a master of science degree, he won acceptance into the very competitive Air Force Test Pilot School at Edwards Air Force Base in California's Mojave Desert. There, he was invited to apply for the astronaut program.

In 1982, when Onizuka flew on the space shuttle *Discovery*, he became the first Asian American to fly into space.

The United States is a great and unique country because it is made up of many diverse cultures and people. Think of our money, with *"e pluribus unum"* ("from many, one") printed on it. People from all over the world have immigrated to the United States and made it their home. At first everything is new, but slowly the new immigrants get accustomed to American ways. Onizuka was a third-generation Japanese-American, and he married a fellow third-generation Japanese-American Hawaiian. Yet both Onizuka and his wife were the first in their families to choose their own marriage partners!

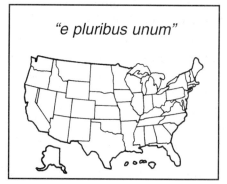

"e pluribus unum"

Onizuka's second mission into space ended in tragedy. Onizuka was a crew member on the doomed *Challenger* mission. Along with Onizuka was a schoolteacher named Christa McAuliffe. Just 73 seconds after lift-off, a malfunction on the rocket booster caused the *Challenger* to explode and fall into the Atlantic Ocean. None of the crew aboard *Challenger* survived.

When we think of Onizuka, instead of thinking of the tragedy of the *Challenger* disaster, we should remember the words Onizuka spoke to a high-school graduating class in Hawaii: "Every generation has the obligation to free men's minds for a look at new worlds . . . to look out from a higher plateau than the last generation. . . . Make your life count—and the world will be a better place because you tried."

Questions to Ponder

❑ What is the capital of Hawaii? Can you find it on the map? (*Honolulu*)

❑ Was Hawaii the 49th or 50th state to join the U.S.? (*On August, 21, 1959, Hawaii became the 50th state to join the union.*)

❑ American and European traders introduced devastating infectious diseases that greatly reduced the native Hawaiian populations. Would the vaccinations we have today have helped stop this tragedy? (*Yes. If vaccinated, fewer traders would have been ill when they came to trade. Vaccinating the native Hawaiians would have insured that, even if diseases were carried to the island, the Hawaiian's immune systems would have built up antibodies.*)

❑ Will you choose your own marriage partner?

Marco Polo

(1254–1324)

A tiger screamed. In the distance, another tiger screamed. The sounds began to come closer. There were not any homes to find sanctuary in or people to help protect them. In order to defend themselves, Marco Polo and his guide cut bamboo canes. Of course, a bamboo cane would not keep them safe from a massive tiger if they used it directly, but what if they threw it on the fire? Bamboo canes grow in jointed segments and are hollow inside. As the air in the hollow spaces expands because of the heat from the fire, the canes explode. The result is a very loud but harmless explosion producing a barrage of pops and bangs. The bamboo kept Polo safe.

Marco Polo has been called the Father of Geography. He was a Venetian explorer who left Venice in 1271 to travel with his father and uncle to China. It took four years, but they finally reached the court of Kublai Khan in the city of what is now known as Beijing. Polo became a favorite of Khan's, and he traveled throughout China, India, and Southeast Asia while in service to him. He did not return to Venice until 1295. When Polo returned, many people did not believe it was he. It wasn't until he showed all the jewels he had sewn into the seams of his ragged clothes that they believed him.

Polo wrote of his travels in the book *The Travels of Marco Polo*. Many people did not believe what Polo had written. They thought it was a fantasy. Yet, with the passage of time, people realized how truthful Polo had been. Mapmakers used his book, traders followed his routes, scholars learned about Buddhist and Hindu faiths, and historians learned about the Mongol Empire.

At the time that Polo journeyed to China, Europeans did not bathe very often. Polo was amazed to see that the Chinese bathed almost every day, and that they soaked in hot water. The bath water was heated up with what Polo described as "black stones existing in veins in the mountains, which they dig out and burn like firewood." By reading Polo's book, many Europeans learned about coal for the first time.

There is a legend that even as Polo lay dying, a priest asked him if he wished to take back some of his stories so that he would not die with lies on his conscience. Polo replied, "I did not tell half of what I saw, for I knew I would not be believed."

Questions to Ponder

❏ Is Venice the capital of Italy? What is the capital of China? (*No, Rome is. Beijing.*)

❏ What geographical oddities make Venice different from most cities? (*Venice is built on 118 islets (little islands) within a lagoon in the Gulf of Venice. It is joined to the mainland by bridges, and canals and bridges connect all the islands. The houses are built on piles, and gondolas and other boats are used to travel from place to place. Piles are long columns made out of lumber, steel, or concrete that are driven into the ground so that they can carry a vertical structure.*)

❏ Can you find Venice and Beijing on a map? Think about traveling to those places when they were still unknown and without any modern-day conveniences.

❏ Marco Polo described a unicorn he saw on the island of Sumatra as having "feet like those of an elephant, and a horn in the middle of the forehead which is black and very thick. . . . 'Tis a passing ugly beast to look upon, and is not in the least like that which our stories tell of." What animal was Polo seeing? (*Polo was probably seeing a species of rhinoceros that is still found in Sumatra today.*)

Mark Twain

(1835–1910)

To make sure that he went to school instead of going swimming, Mark Twain's mother used to sew a thread attaching both sides of his collar together in the morning before she sent him off to school. When he would come home from school, she would check to see if the thread was still attached.

When Twain wrote *The Adventures of Tom Sawyer,* he used this part of his life to build his story. In the story, Tom is found out because someone points out to Tom's Aunt Polly that though the thread is still there attached to both sides of the collar, it is a different color thread!

Mark Twain is actually the pen name for Samuel Clemens. Clemens was a Mississippi River pilot for some years. When navigating the Mississippi, the pilot had to keep a constant and careful watch. He had to look out for shifting sandbars, submerged trees that created underwater hazards, and eroding banks; and he needed to learn the signs of a possible sunken wreck (dimpled water), a new snag (a silver streak), and a dangerous shoaling or shallow part (a slick). The water level also had to be constantly monitored, and to do this, a man in the bow of the ship would drop a line with a lead attached to it so that it would sink to the bottom.

Every six feet, or fathom, the line was marked. The number of fathoms measured was called out— mark four, mark six, etc. *Twain* was the word used for "two," and when "mark twain" was called out, it meant that the water level was two fathoms, or 12 feet (3.7 m). This was the shallowest water a steamboat could navigate in without danger. In the book *Life on the Mississippi,* Twain wrote about his years piloting the Mississippi.

Questions to Ponder

❑ Twain was born in Florida, Missouri. What is the capital of Missouri, and what two great rivers border or travel across Missouri? (*Jefferson City is the capital of Missouri. The Mississippi River forms the eastern border of Missouri, and the Missouri River flows west to east across the state, joining the Mississippi above St. Louis.*)

❑ Twain was born when Halley's comet was in view. He died the next time Halley's comet could be seen streaking across the galaxy. How many years passed between the sightings of the comet? (*75*) Do you know anyone who has seen Halley's comet?

❑ How did Missouri become part of the United States? (*In 1803, as part of the Louisiana Purchase, the land passed to the U.S. from France. Missouri became the 24th state on August 10, 1821.*)

❑ Is the bow of a ship the front or the back? (*bow = forward; stern = back.*)

❑ What are the capitals of California and Nevada? (*Sacramento and Carson City*)

Elisha Otis
(1811–1861)

Your family decides to go to the top of the Empire State Building. You go up 102 stories. Next, you visit the Sears Tower in Chicago. You go up 110 stories. How did you get there? Did you walk? If you are like most people, you took the elevator. Would there be skyscrapers if there were not any elevators? Would anyone work on the 110th floor if they had to walk up the stairs? Could a skyscraper even be built if there were not elevators to hoist up the materials and equipment?

In 1852, Elisha Otis invented an automatic safety device to prevent the fall of hoisting machinery. Otis had been hired as a master mechanic at a manufacturing business, and he had to build an elevator so that the heavy and bulky equipment could be hauled up to the second floor. Elevators at that time worked on a single cable. If the cable or rope broke, everyone and everything riding on the platform or elevator would crash to the ground.

Otis's automatic safety device used a simple wagon spring. Otis connected the spring so that if the cable broke, the spring would straighten out and its ends would catch in ratchets on the side rails of the elevator shaft. The platform would then remain there until a new cable was attached.

Otis made his safety elevators for several businesses, but elevators did not catch on with the general public. Too many accidents had happened, and no one wanted to trust their lives to a cable rope. In order to get the public to accept his idea, Otis set up a demonstration at the American Institute Fair in New York. Otis stepped onto an open elevator platform that he had built and rode up on the platform to the height of four floors. Then his assistant cut the cable! In front of all the spectators, the platform began to plummet to the ground. The gasps and screams of the onlookers turned to disbelief as the elevators halted in mid-fall. Otis's safety device worked.

Otis's dramatic demonstrations helped to change the public's way of thinking. In 1855 he installed 15 freight elevators; and in 1856 he installed 27. He installed his first passenger elevator in a store in New York City in 1857. Otis's safety elevator was truly a basic step in the development of the skyscraper.

Questions to Ponder

❑ Otis was born in Halifax, Vermont. Is Halifax the capital of Vermont, and can you find Vermont on the map? (*The capital of Vermont is Montpelier.*)

❑ Was Vermont one of the 13 original colonies? (*No, Vermont was the 14th state.*)

❑ What is the highest floor of an apartment building on which you would live if there were no elevators?

❑ Demonstrations are a way for a manufacturer to introduce his or her product to the public and convince them that it is safe or the best of its kind. What demonstrations that introduce a product have you seen? Have you ever been given free samples of food?

❑ Many elevators do not have a button for the 13th floor. Why is that? (*Many people have a superstitious fear about the number 13. For this reason, many hotels simply go from the 12th to the 14th floor.* Triskaidekaphobia *is a word that means "the fear of the number 13."*)

Roald Amundsen

(1872–1928)

It was a race! Who was going to go down in history as the first man to reach the South Pole? Amundsen, a Norwegian, or Scott, an Englishman? Amundsen was a master organizer, and he left as little as he could to chance. To prepare for his expedition, Amundsen learned all that he could from the Inuit, the people who were accustomed to living and thriving in Arctic conditions. Amundsen learned that dogs pulling sledges are much better at hauling supplies than ponies or men. Huskies, the type of dogs used, have thick, oily fur that keeps out the cold. Strong and built for endurance, a team of six or more huskies can pull heavy loads up to about 50 miles (80.5 km) a day. If the snow conditions are right, a husky team can occasionally reach speeds of over 18 miles per hour (29 kph) and can sometimes go for 18 hours a day!

Amundsen also learned about what to wear: two layers of furs—one with the fur turned toward the body, and the second layer with the fur turned out to the air. These two layers of fur trap air in between, and this air then becomes an effective form of insulation. When one has to carry all of one's food, one has to consider carefully what to bring. It takes energy to walk around in heavy clothing! Think about how much more difficult it would be to run around the track while wearing a backpack containing all of your books than it would be to run around the track without it. The Inuit's way of dressing (about 11 pounds) was half the weight of the European polar clothing. This made a difference when it came to how much the men had to eat in order to survive.

Amundsen planned his food very carefully. Pemmican, a form of dried meat prepared by the Inuit, was used. Amundsen added vegetables and oatmeal, and the portions were molded into blocks to last one man for one day. The pemmican could be eaten raw or cooked.

On December 14, 1911, Amundsen became the first person to reach the South Pole. The journey took 99 days, and his team returned on the exact day Amundsen had predicted that they would.

Amundsen's planning and foresight is what allowed him to succeed. Yet, unfortunately for Amundsen, he was never awarded the glory that most explorers receive. Remember that Amundsen was racing Scott. Though Scott did reach the Pole, it was a month after Amundsen; and Scott and his men died on the way back. As a result of the tragedy associated with Scott's exploration of the Pole, many view him as the more heroic figure.

Questions to Ponder

❏ Amundsen was born in Norway. At the time of Amundsen's birth, Norway was still part of Sweden. Can you name both these countries' capitals, and can you find the countries on the map? (*Oslo, Norway. Stockholm, Sweden.*)

❏ Are there polar bears at the South Pole? (*No, polar bears are at the North Pole.*)

❏ Which one sits on a continent: the North Pole or the South Pole? (*The Arctic is a frozen ocean, and the North Pole sits on a layer of ice over seawater. Antarctica, where the South Pole is found, is a continent with a land mass bigger than Australia. Antarctica is covered with a coating of ice that is, on the average, a mile thick.*)

❏ How long is a "polar night?" (*about 10 weeks*) How would you feel if you could not see the sun for 10 weeks? Would it be strange to go to school when it is dark?

Rosa Parks

(1913–)

Some people say that when Rosa Parks sat down, the whole world stood up. In 1955, Parks paid for her ticket and then went to sit down on the bus. She had worked as a seamstress all day long, and she was tired. A man got on the bus, paying the same amount for his ticket as Parks did. Parks was told to get up; she was told that she had to give up her seat for the man. It was the law in the city of Montgomery, Alabama, that all African-American people had to sit in the back of the bus and, if there were not enough seats, African Americans had to stand. Parks was arrested because she would not give up her seat for a white man.

Many people got together and decided that Parks needed to be supported. The bus company was not treating its customers equally. In protest, African Americans began boycotting bus companies. A boycott is when people refuse to have dealings with a store, company, organization, product, or person. The bus company was not worried, though. They knew many people lived far away from where they worked, and pretty soon everyone would get tired of walking. However, Rosa Parks' action gave many people courage.

The Montgomery Improvement Association, headed by Dr. Martin Luther King, Jr., was formed. This organization and many churches bought as many cars and station wagons as they could afford. People could phone in and ask for rides. People would get up very early in the morning so they could walk to work and still get there in time. Some people threw bottles at the walking workers, and some houses were bombed. Still, the buses were mostly empty. The newspapers around the country began to call Montgomery "the walking city." The bus companies lost thousands and thousands of dollars as months and months went by and African Americans still refused to ride the bus. Even in the rain and the cold, the buses remained empty.

The Supreme Court, our highest court, said that the bus company had not been obeying our Constitution. The bus company had to change its rules. The bus boycott had worked. The Civil Rights Movement was on its way!

Questions to Ponder

❑ When do you think someone should give up his or her seat?

❑ In Montgomery and in many other places at the time of the bus boycott, African Americans and white people could not use the same elevators or restrooms or drink out of the same water fountains. How did Rosa Parks's action help to change this?

❑ What body of water is to Alabama's south? (*the Gulf of Mexico*)

❑ What is the capital of Alabama? (*Montgomery*)

❑ Does the Mississippi River, which empties into the Gulf of Mexico, flow through Alabama? (*No, but the state of Mississippi borders Alabama.*)

Josef Gingold

(1909–1995)

During World War I, when Germany declared war on Russia, Josef Gingold was almost five. Gingold and his family were forced to leave their home. Gingold and his family joined a group of about 200 people who were taking refuge in the fields between Russian and German lines. One day Gingold was chasing a friend around, and Gingold's mother, wanting to separate the boys so that she could have some quiet, insisted that the family take a little walk away from everyone else. After they left, a shell struck the place where the refugees were staying. Gingold's mother would later say that it was Gingold who had saved the family.

Gingold's family was rounded up a few weeks later by the Germans. They had to sleep on the floor of a large armory, and the older members of the family did forced labor. They were slowly being starved to death. Then one day Gingold heard the sound of a fiddle outside in the yard. Gingold went to the German soldier and motioned that he could play the violin. The soldiers let him through the barbed wire and handed him the fiddle to play. Later that night, two soldiers appeared with bayonets. They demanded that the little boy who could play the violin come with them. Gingold played, and when he was finished, some of the soldiers began to put some money in a hat for him. Gingold shook his head and instead just pointed to his open mouth and rubbed his belly. The soldiers then sent four soldiers carrying bags of food back to the barracks with Gingold. Gingold's first fee was paid in food, and he never forgot it.

Gingold's family made it to the United States in 1920. They had to walk up five flights of stairs to their small apartment, and they did not have a bath. They shared the toilet with four other families. Yet Gingold said that it was free and wonderful: no longer did they have to be afraid that someone would kill them for being Jewish.

Gingold went on to become one of the world's finest violinists. He played all over the world. When Gingold was asked if he would teach at Indiana University, he accepted the position. With this job, he could share his love of music and the violin not just with his performances, but also with his teaching. Students came from all over to study with Gingold and to attend his classes.

Questions to Ponder

❑ Gingold was born in Russia. What is the capital of Russia, and does Russia share a border with India? (*Moscow; No, India shares a border with China and Pakistan.*)

❑ Gingold has taught hundreds of students. Many of them are now famous musicians playing around the world. When somebody once asked Gingold to name his favorite student, he replied, "The one I'm teaching at the moment." Do you think this answer helps explain why Gingold is ranked as one of the best music teachers in the world?

❑ Gingold was very strict about proper stage deportment. He said, "If, when you tune with the piano, you bend your derriere to the audience, that's insulting." He also said that many young musicians harmed their careers by being careless with their stage deportment. Does the same apply to job interviews? What would happen if you showed up at a job interview in your bathing suit (and the job you were interviewing for was not to be a lifeguard!)?

Anton van Leeuwenhoek

(1632–1723)

Anton van Leeuwenhoek used to carry worms in his pockets. He wasn't crazy! He was just trying to learn everything he could about certain insects. The worms were really larvae that he had seen hatch from the eggs of an insect he was studying. He knew the larvae had to stay warm to stay alive, and, in the cold Dutch winters, he figured his pockets were the best place!

Another time, van Leeuwenhoek wanted to learn how many young lice would appear in a certain amount of time. He put two female lice into a clean sock and wore it. He used a black sock because he wanted to be able to see the white lice well. He tied his sock shut at the knee so that the lice could not escape. After six days, he found about 100 eggs in the sock. This man was so eager to know everything he could about little creatures that he left the sock on for 10 more days! By that time, about 25 eggs had hatched into lice, and the rest were ready. Finally, he called an end to his observations! He wrote that he "threw the stocking into the street" and "rubbed his leg and foot very hard" to kill any lice still there.

Van Leeuwenhoek is actually most famous for his microscopes. He made over 247 of them, and some of them magnified objects up to 270 times. At first, many people did not believe that he could be seeing living creatures. At the time that van Leeuwenhoek was making his observations, many people did not ever brush their teeth. Van Leeuwenhoek compared what he found in his mouth to what was in the mouths of people who had never cleaned their teeth even once in their lives. When van Leeuwenhoek looked at plaque scraped from their mouths, there were always more creatures in the plaque from the people who had never brushed their teeth. van Leeuwenhoek guessed that it was these creatures that caused "stinking" breath.

When van Leeuwenhoek was alive, people did not know that germs could be spread through dirty water. Van Leeuwenhoek described some of the creatures he found in water, but many people did not believe him. Later, it was discovered that it is some of these little creatures that make us ill. If water is not pure, it needs to be boiled or treated so that all microorganisms, or little creatures, are dead.

Questions to Ponder

❏ van Leeuwenhoek was born in Holland. By what other name is Holland called? (*the Netherlands*) Can you find it on the map?

❏ What is the capital of the Netherlands? (*Amsterdam*)

❏ The geographical feature that the Netherlands is perhaps most famous for is its dikes. What are dikes? (*Much of the land in the Netherlands is below sea level. It has been drained, and dikes keep the sea at bay. Dikes can be artificial watercourses like ditches or walls made of earth or stone.*)

❏ Just because we cannot see something does not mean that it does not exist. What can't you see that you know exists?

❏ van Leeuwenhoek did not teach other people how to make microscopes, and he rarely let people look through his! For almost 100 years few tried to repeat or add to van Leeuwenhoek's work. Do you think we would have figured out sooner that the microorganisms in water were making us ill if van Leeuwenhoek had shared his microscopes?

Zora Neale Hurston

(1901–1960)

We hear and read folk tales all the time. Did you ever stop to think about how the folk tales were collected? Zora Neale Hurston, the leading authority of her time on African-American folklore, once said that folklore was not "as easy to collect as it sounds." She had to travel extensively around Florida and Louisiana, and she had to make people comfortable enough to talk to her. To gain the trust of one New Orleans conjurer, she had to lie facedown on a couch for 69 hours without food or water and with a snakeskin touching her!

Hurston certainly had the personality for traveling to remote places and getting people to talk! Born in Eatonville, Florida, an all-black town founded and governed by African Americans, she was intelligent, energetic, and possessed with an incredible sense of adventure. At the age of 16, she joined a traveling theatrical company and ended up in New York City. It is said that there, she once punched a man who tried to embrace her in an elevator—and as she exited she didn't even bother to look back at him lying on the floor!

Hurston studied anthropology at Columbia University. Anthropology is the study of man. Hurston was a cultural anthropologist, a scientist who studies culture, how people behave, and their beliefs. In addition to African-American folklore, Hurston studied voodoo. She traveled to remote areas of the Bahamas, Haiti, Jamaica, and all over the American South collecting data. She survived bedbugs and hurricanes, among other things!

Hurston also wrote novels. Hurston's book *Their Eyes Were Watching God* has been called "one of the main foundations of African-American literature." Many writers, including Toni Morrison and Ralph Ellison, were influenced by Hurston's work. In tribute, one writer, Alice Walker, placed a marker on Hurston's unmarked grave. Now, in that segregated cemetery, are the words "A Genius of the South," inscribed on granite.

Genius always doesn't mean money, and it certainly didn't with Hurston. Hurston was evicted from her apartment for non-payment of rent on the day that she found out that she had sold her first novel! Another time, when her stories appeared in a famous magazine, she was busy working as a maid to support herself! What kept Hurston going was her attitude. For example, when a white doctor hurried her into a laundry closet to examine her so that his other patients wouldn't have to see her, Hurston's response was "How can they deny themselves the pleasure of my company?"

Questions to Ponder

❑ Hurston was born in Florida. What is the capital of Florida, and was Florida one of the original 13 colonies? (*Tallahassee is the capital of Florida. Florida became a state on March 3, 1845, and was the 27th state.*)

❑ Hurston once became friends with a Jamaican medicine man who supposedly could quiet thousands of frogs. Where is Jamaica, and can you name its capital? (*Jamaica is a Caribbean island south of the island of Cuba, east of Central America. Kingston.*)

❑ Hurston has been described as flamboyant, always draping bangles and beads on herself and wearing a hat. What does "flamboyant" mean? (*Flamboyant means showy, resplendent, given to dashing display. Do you see the similarity between "flame" and "flamboyant"? A flamboyant person burns with colorful brilliance, like a flame.*)

Jim Lovell

(1928–)

Jim Lovell was 200,000 miles (321,869 km) away from Earth when he found out that he and his two crew members had only one hour and 52 minutes of oxygen left. Lovell was commander of the Apollo 13 lunar mission. The plan had been to land on the moon. Lovell had been on three previous space missions, including the one that had been the first manned flight to orbit the moon. Every mission had gone according to plan—until this one. A mysterious explosion rocked the ship. Oxygen and power began to drain away. Lovell said, "Houston, we've got a problem."

Lovell and his men were forced to abandon the main ship for the lunar module, the LEM. The LEM was the tiny craft that was supposed to land on the moon. It had been designed to keep two men alive for just two days. Now three men were in it, and they were four days away from home.

Whenever there is an enormous catastrophe, if one is not going to be overwhelmed, one must "work" the problem. Transferring the men to the LEM saved them from the most immediate part of the catastrophe or problem—suffocation. Now, NASA engineers worked on finding a way to filter air so that it would be breathable for the trip back home, while scientists worked on how to get the stranded astronauts back home—when they should fire up their rockets and what course they should take.

Because there were meticulous lists about exactly what was on the spacecraft, the engineers knew exactly what they had to work with. The cardboard pages of a LEM manual that gave instructions on how to lift off the moon became part of the filter, as did the duct tape that had been intended to tape refuse to the hull. Specially designed thermal underwear had been designed for the men: dozens of feet of slender tubing had been woven into the fabric of the underwear, through which water could have circulated to keep the men cool while they worked in the hot, lunar sun. This underwear was now useless. What was important was the plastic it was wrapped in! It was needed for the filter! How quickly what is valuable can change!

Questions to Ponder

❑ What is triskaidekaphobia? (*There are some people who fear the number 13 because they think it can bring bad luck. There are some hotels that choose to not even have a 13th floor. Instead, the floor above the 12th is referred to as the 14th. Triskaidekaphobia is fear of the number 13. NASA personnel must not have suffered from triskaidekaphobia: Apollo 13 lifted off at 13:13 hours.*)

❑ Lovell was born in Cleveland and attended the U.S. Naval Academy in Annapolis. In which states are these two cities? Which one is a capital? (*Cleveland is a large city in Ohio, and Annapolis is the capital of Maryland.*)

❑ Lovell was not accepted into the astronaut program the first time he applied. But when he read that 10 more astronauts were needed, he tried again. Even though he was much older, he figured he was more experienced. Does this show that attitude and determination are needed for success? What proverbs do we have that fit this? (*"If at first you don't succeed, try, try again" would be one example.*)

❑ Some feel that NASA's finest hour was not landing a man on the moon but bringing Lovell and his crew home safely. How do you feel about this?

Birute M.F. Galdikas

(1946–)

Galdikas had just clambered over an enormous log about four feet in diameter. To her dismay, once she got to the other side, she discovered another log, this one even thicker. Trapped between the two, she struggled to heave her whole body over the second log. She didn't think that it could get worse, but it did.

Galdikas was deep in the forests of Borneo, and she was studying orangutans. The orangutan above her, sitting high in the tree, had had enough of Galdikas following her about. Realizing that Galdikas was trapped, the orangutan began to push branches and other snags in the tree down on Galdikas. Galdikas thought of diving under the logs for protection, but there was not enough space beneath the logs to crawl into. Galdikas wrote later that she fully expected to die. Her body shook and her legs quivered. She survived only because the orangutan was not strong enough to manipulate the snag. Galdikas was lucky she was watching a female that day and not a grown male.

Little was known about orangutans because of their solitary nature and where they lived—deep in the tropical jungle. In 1971, Galdikas went to study them in their natural habitat. She has now spent over 25 years with them. Orangutans are the largest animals in the world that survive mainly on fruit. Most of their time, about eight hours a day, is spent in foraging for food.

While looking for orangutans in the trees above her, Galdikas often had to wade up to her armpits in acidic, tea-colored swamp water. Leeches were a common problem for Galdikas. Looking like harmless inchworms, the leeches in Borneo are heat sensitive. They lie frozen until someone passes by. Then, sensing heat, they then quickly crawl into action. Often Galdikas did not know she was bitten until the leech had dropped off and she felt the gush of her blood. One time at dinner, a leech crawled up the candle she was using for light. The leech would move up to the flame's heat, but then go back down when it got too hot. Over and over the leech went up and down the candle.

Questions to Ponder

❏ Galdikas studied orangutans in Borneo, part of the Malay Archipelago. What is an archipelago, and can you find Borneo on the map? (*An archipelago is a group of islands. Look above Australia, below China. Did you know that Borneo is the third largest island in the world?*)

❏ The island of Borneo is divided among several countries. Can you name at least one of them? (*Indonesia, where Galdikas studies, makes up about 70% of Borneo. Brunei and the Malaysian states of Sabah and Sarawak make up the rest.*)

❏ You come to a tree and there are three orangutans, of three different ages, all sitting at different heights in the tree. At what height would the youngest orangutan be sitting—bottom, middle, or top? (*The younger an orangutan is, the higher he is likely to swing and climb in the tree because they are lighter and more active. Older ones weigh more so they need sturdier branches.*)

❏ Orangutans are arboreal. What does *arboreal* mean? (*Arboreal animals inhabit or frequent trees. With arms longer than their legs, orangutans are suited for an arboreal life.*) Can you find other words in the dictionary that have *arbor* in them?

❏ What animal would you like to study in the wild? What do you think your living conditions would be like?

Jonas Salk

(1914–1995)

Polio is an infectious disease caused by a virus. Antibiotics (for example, penicillin) do not work on viruses: antibiotics work on illness caused by bacteria. The polio virus caused inflammation of certain nerve cells in the spinal cord. If one was lucky, one only had a mild reaction. For those who suffered a more severe reaction, there was the risk of paralysis (becoming paralyzed), permanent disability, and even death.

Many critically ill polio victims were unable to breathe on their own: nerve cells in the brain stem that ordinarily controlled breathing were damaged, and so they had to live in iron lungs. Iron lungs were cylindrical metal tubes. A person's head was the only part of their body that was outside of the tube. A snug rubber collar fit around the patient's neck to create a seal that kept the air inside the chamber. An electric motor could then pump air into the iron lung. The added pressure made the patient's chest compress so that air was forced out of the lungs through the nose and mouth. Next, air would be let out of the chamber, and the lungs could expand and fill with air. People would have to live in these 24 hours a day! The only time they were let out was when they were hooked onto portable breathing machines and bathed. The portable breathing machines were not as good as the iron lungs because the constant motion on the chest made the skin irritated and sore.

In your grandparent's (and some of your parent's) lifetimes, polio went from a major public health problem to a minor one. How did this happen? At first, no one knew how polio was spread. There were huge epidemics in which children, especially, seemed to get sick. Neighbors were afraid of neighbors, and public swimming pools were closed. People burned everything that someone who developed polio had touched.

Scientists and medical researchers worked hard to identify where polio came from and how to protect people from it. Dr. Jonas Salk is the man credited with developing the first vaccine. The United States government licensed Salk's vaccine in 1955. At first there were not enough vaccines, and so a plan was developed that provided 7,000,000 free vaccinations to first-, second-, and third-grade children. No adults, except pregnant women, were given the vaccine until all young people under the age of 20 had been immunized.

Questions to Ponder

❑ Salk was born in New York. What is the capital of New York? (*Albany*)

❑ One of our presidents suffered from polio. He hid the fact that he could not walk unaided from the public. Who was he and why? (*Franklin D. Roosevelt thought that if people knew he could not walk, they would think he was weak, and they would not vote for him.*)

❑ Does having a disability mean that someone is weak?

❑ The common cold is caused by a virus. Antibiotics do not stop the common cold. Yet doctors say that when people come to them when they are ill with a cold they want antibiotics. Why do you think this is so? (*Many people get better when given placebos (fake pills). The thought of treatment is often enough to make one better.*)

❑ When there was a limited amount of vaccine, children came first. Do you agree with this policy?

Elijah McCoy

(1844–1928)

"Grease monkeys" was the name given to the children, many of them orphans, who did the dangerous work of oiling locomotive engines by hand. The locomotives had to be lubricated to prevent them from breaking down and catching fire. What the oiling did was reduce the friction between the screws, gears, levers, and other moving parts that wore down. The children were paid just pennies a day, and they were often injured or killed. At night, it was common to find them sleeping on the dirty, oily floors where they worked.

Elijah McCoy invented something that made this job much less dangerous. McCoy was working for the railroads in Detroit, Michigan, but he had been born in Canada. His parents were escaped slaves, traveling the Underground Railroad from Kentucky to Canada. McCoy was born, as everybody should be, a free man. Realizing that McCoy had a special talent when it came to working with tools and machines, McCoy's parents saved their money and sent McCoy to study engineering in Edinburgh, Scotland. While he was studying, the Civil War broke out in the United States. The war was over by the time McCoy had finished his training as a master mechanic and engineer. He went to Michigan, hoping to find work as an engineer.

McCoy's degree and experience were not respected at that time in the United States because people did not want to accept that a black man could have more education and knowledge than they did. The best job McCoy could find on the railroad was working as a fireman, the person who shoveled the coal onto the burning fires inside the firebox at the back of the cab of the engine.

What McCoy invented to help lubricate the locomotives was a special type of oil drip cup that was attached to an engine or machine. He patented his device on July 2, 1872. Soon, railroads, shipping lines, and factories throughout the world were buying the McCoy lubricating cup. There were many imitations out there, but people learned the difference. McCoy's cup never broke or worked incorrectly. Engineers and train workers learned to ask, "Is it the real McCoy?" McCoy did much more than just invent his oil cup. Over the years, he received over 40 patents for his inventions—for example, special tires, a lawn sprinkler, and the first portable ironing table. The term "the real McCoy" is still used today to mean that the item is the real thing and not an imitation.

Questions to Ponder

❏ McCoy was born in Colchester, Ontario, Canada. What is the capital of the province of Ontario, and what is the capital of Canada? (*Toronto is the capital of Ontario, and Ottawa is the capital of Canada.*)

❏ Can you think of at least one other Canadian province? (*Canada's provinces are Alberta, Manitoba, Saskatchewan, New Brunswick, Nova Scotia, Prince Edward Island, Newfoundland, British Columbia, and Quebec.*)

Florence Nightingale

(1820–1910)

When one enters a hospital today, it is very clean. Nurses, doctors, and other staff work their hardest to disinfect everything and keep infections from spreading. Rubber gloves are worn and then changed after each patient is treated. Medical staff must wash thoroughly in a certain way before even entering operating areas. Patients are given their own drinking flasks, pillows, and other personal items, which they then take home or throw away when they leave. Patients even have a choice when it comes to what they can eat. It wasn't always this way.

Before Florence Nightingale, the founder of modern nursing, it was quite common to have two very ill people sharing the same bed. Sheets were not changed between patients, even when they were filthy and stained. Patients with infectious diseases were not separated from others. Everyone was housed together, and often people would enter the hospital for one reason, but would die of something completely different that they had caught after being exposed to it at the hospital! The stench was so horrible that people often sprayed the rooms with perfume before entering. Doctors would make their rounds with handkerchiefs over their noses. They would not wash their hands between patients, even when performing surgery. Many times the surgical instruments were not even washed.

Because the conditions were so atrocious, nursing was a profession that "decent" women were not allowed into. Defying her family, Nightingale said, "The first requirement of a hospital is that it should do the sick no harm." Nightingale worked relentlessly to improve conditions. With data she collected and then presented, she proved that during the Crimean War, for every one soldier who had died in battle, seven other soldiers died needlessly of infections and diseases that they contracted while in the hospital and under medical care! Her statistics showed that if the hospital was clean, ventilated, and served nutritious food, these deaths would not have occurred. Nightingale also showed that the death rate for British soldiers in peacetime was double that of Britain's civilian population. Hygienic barracks and decent food made a difference! Nightingale started the first nursing school in England, and in 1907 she became the first woman to be given the British Order of Merit.

Questions to Ponder

- ❏ Though Nightingale was English, she was born in Florence, Italy. Can you name the capitals of England and Italy; and, before you find them on the map, can you name a country between them? (*London is the capital of England, and Rome is the capital of Italy. There are many countries between them, including France, Germany, Switzerland, and Belgium.*)

- ❏ In 1855, Nightingale took over Barrack Hospital. Built over a decaying sewer, waste had soaked in everywhere. Within her first two weeks there, Nightingale had removed 556 handcarts and large baskets of garbage and had buried 26 assorted animals, including two horses. How does our government make sure that conditions like this do not exist in our hospitals today?

- ❏ In the past, nurses were thought of as drunks who did not have any morals. What do we think of nurses today?

- ❏ How often do you wash your hands per day?

John Harrison

(1693–1776)

Though they were returning victorious from battle against the French Mediterranean forces, Admiral Sir Clowdisley Shovell was afraid. It was 1707, and for twelve days he and his naval troops had been completely shrouded in fog—and no one, not even the Admiral, knew exactly where they were. Shovell summoned all of his navigators and ordered them to figure out their position on the dark ocean. Were there dangerous shores nearby? The navigators said no. However, there was one sailor who disagreed, but this sailor was a mere crew member and "such subversive navigation by an inferior was forbidden in the Royal Navy." The sailor knew this, but he figured that the danger was so great that he needed to speak up. The admiral had the sailor hanged for mutiny on the spot. It is wondered whether the admiral thought of this sailor after his ships crashed onto the rocky shores that the sailor had said were close by. Two thousand men died. The admiral was one of only two survivors.

At that time, it was not that rare or unusual for ship captains to not know where they were. This was because of "the longitude problem." Lacking the ability to determine longitude, sailors had no way of knowing where they were once they lost sight of land. They were literally lost at sea. Horrible crashes of ships running aground on rocky shores were common. Sea journeys often turned into battles against time. Not sure of where they were, captains had to criss-cross and go extra miles, all of which added precious days and weeks to their journeys. It became a race against diminishing food supplies and scurvy. If captains did follow the safe, well-known routes, they were easy prey for pirates. The known shipping routes became crowded and dangerous.

In 1714, England's Parliament offered a prize of 20,000 pounds for the solution to the longitude problem. In today's currency, this would be equivalent to several million dollars. John Harrison, an unknown clockmaker, found the solution: he built a clock that kept steady time on the ocean—despite the weather, the cold, the change in temperature, and the up and down and rocking motions of a ship. Without any formal education or apprenticeship to a clockmaker, Harrison constructed clocks without pendulums. Essentially friction-free, his time-keepers did not rust or require lubrication or cleaning; and because of the combination of the different metals he used (if one expanded due to a temperature change, another contracted), they kept a constant rate. Because of jealousy and disbelief that a simple clockmaker could solve the problem, it took over 40 years for Harrison to be awarded the prize. Harrison's five clocks can still be seen today—keeping time!

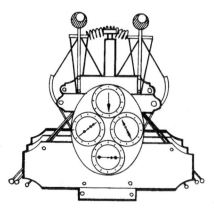

Harrison's Invention

Questions to Ponder

❑ Harrison was born in England. What is the capital of England, and what is the capital's longitude and latitude? (*London is the capital of England. The longitude is zero degrees and the latitude is 51 degrees, approximately.*)

❑ Longitude is calculated from Greenwich, England. It is from this place, zero degrees longitude, where east meets west, by which the world sets its watch. What is another name for this longitude from which all other longitudes are measured? (*the prime meridian*)

❑ Can you give the approximate longitude and latitude of your school?

Carl Friedrich Gauss

(1777–1855)

Carl Friedrich Gauss's father was once adding up the payroll. Gauss heard him and corrected him. What is amazing about this is that Gauss was only three years old and he was merely listening to his father as his father said out loud the numbers that he was adding together. Gauss himself once remarked that he could add and subtract before he could talk.

Another story about Gauss goes like this: His teacher at school gave this assignment to the students: Add up all the numbers from 1 to 100. The teacher thought that this would take a while, for the teacher thought that everyone would solve it in the conventional or usual manner of $1 + 2 + 3 + 4 + 5$, etc. Gauss's teacher was angry when Gauss stopped working on the problem in a couple of minutes. He told Gauss that there was no possible way he could be even halfway finished. Then Gauss gave his solution.

Gauss did not add up the numbers in order. Instead, he saw that $1 + 100 = 101$, $2 + 99 = 101$, $3 + 98 = 101$, $4 + 97 = 101$. He saw that there would be fifty pairs (the last pair being $50 + 51 = 101$), so all he had to do was multiply 50×101—which equals 5050—and he was done.

Gauss came from a poor family. Fortunately for Gauss and the world, he found a mentor in the Duke of Brunswick. (A mentor is someone who helps guide another person.) The Duke paid for all of Gauss's school fees. Gauss was the first man to prove the fundamental theorem of algebra. He also did great work as an astronomer, and once, from just a few observations, he was able to predict the orbit of the asteroid Ceres when it was discovered by the Italian astronomer Piazzi. Sure enough, one year later, it was exactly where Gauss had said it would be.

Questions to Ponder

❑ Gauss was born in Germany. Can you name Germany's capital, at least two countries that border Germany, and then find them all on the map? (*Berlin is the capital of Germany. Several countries, including France, Switzerland, Austria, and Poland, border Germany.*)

❑ Gauss found a way to construct a regular polygon of 17 sides using only a ruler and a compass. When a polygon is said to be regular, it means that all the sides and angles have the same measurement. Can you do it?

❑ Gauss invented the heliotrope. What does a heliotrope do? (*A heliotrope is a device that measures distances by means of reflected sunlight.*)

❑ Gauss refused to publish much of his work until he had complete proof. Because of this, many discoveries were not credited to him and were remade by others later. Should Gauss have published his work earlier?

❑ Our Food and Drug Administration (the FDA) decides when our new drugs are no longer experimental and can be sold to the public. Some people think the FDA moves too slowly, while others believe it is not rigorous enough. The FDA is supposed to make sure that the drugs are safe and that there are not harmful side effects. Many times, drugs can be sold in other countries before they can be sold in the U.S. Do you think Gauss would be a good candidate to work for the FDA?

Yoshiko Uchida

(1921–1992)

Yoshika Uchida had no choice: she had to get rid of Laddie, her beloved dog. She gave him to the first boy who responded to her ad in the paper because he seemed kind and caring. When he came, Uchida gave him Laddie's doghouse, leash, brushes, and favorite toy. Years later, Uchida wrote how she could still hear Laddie's plaintive barking even after the car turned the corner and she could no longer see it.

Uchida was an American. As a child, every morning she went to school and recited the Pledge of Allegiance. She loved her country as much as any other American. Yet often, just because of her features, she was considered a foreigner. Uchida was once introduced to a woman who had never met a Japanese American. The woman said, "My, but you speak English so beautifully." Uchida knew that this was meant as a compliment, but it hurt to know that this woman had seen only Uchida's outer self.

In 1942, despite having seen a state-department report testifying to the "extraordinary degree of loyalty" among West Coast Japanese, President Roosevelt signed an Executive Order that resulted in the forcible eviction of all Japanese "aliens and non-aliens." The Fifth and Fourteenth Amendments were ignored. These amendments guaranteed "due process of law'" and "equal protection under the law for all citizens," but Japanese Americans were forced into internment camps. They had to leave behind all of their possessions. Many people lost their homes and businesses. However, Americans of German or Italian descent—countries with which the U.S. was also at war—were not imprisoned.

First, Uchida's father was taken away by the FBI. Then, Uchida and her mother and sister were ordered to report in 10 days to a processing center. They were allowed to keep only what they could carry in two suitcases. Surrounded by armed guards, they were sent to a camp, where they lived in a small, dark horse stall, which was 10 x 20 feet (3 x 6.1 m). Manure lay right underneath the filthy linoleum that had been hastily laid down. After five months, the Uchidas were sent to another camp—this one in a desert, where they suffered through frequent dust storms, rain squalls, and severe snowstorms.

Uchida eventually became a teacher and published many books. Throughout her life, she never lost respect for her Japanese heritage or her love of her homeland—the U.S. In 1988, Congress passed a bill that partly compensated Japanese Americans for their huge financial losses. The U.S. had finally acknowledged its mistake.

═══════════════════ **Questions to Ponder** ═══════════════════

❏ Uchida was born in California. What is the capital of California, is it east or west of the Rocky Mountains, and what ocean does California border? (*California's capital is Sacramento. The state borders the Pacific Ocean and is west of the Rocky Mountains.*)

❏ The Uchida family spent much of their interment in a cluster of tar-paper barracks on the edge of the Sevier Desert. In what state is this desert, and what is the capital of that state? (*The state is Utah, and its capital is Salt Lake City.*)

❏ The Uchidas were given numbered tags for all their belongings. They were Family 13453. How would you feel if you were stripped of your name?

❏ Uchida's mother said, "Don't ever be indifferent. That is the worst fault of all." What did she mean? (*When one is indifferent, one does not care either way. One has no interest or concern. Uchida's mother wanted Uchida to be kind and caring.*)

Thomas Hopkins Gallaudet
(1787–1851)

Thomas Gallaudet was so smart that he entered Yale University as a sophomore and graduated when he was 17 years old. Yet, despite his fine record at Yale, Gallaudet was not allowed to give the valedictory speech at commencement. Being a top student and debater was not enough. Gallaudet was only five-and-a-half feet tall, too short to be seen in the back rows of the auditorium, and so a classmate who was four inches taller was chosen.

Gallaudet knew what it was like to be left out. As a child, Gallaudet seldom joined in the games, races, and adventures that his friends did because he was not able to keep up. Since his birth on December 10, 1787, Gallaudet had always been smaller and weaker than other children his age. Gallaudet didn't like being different, but he kept his complaints to himself.

Gallaudet was America's pioneer when it came to educating deaf people. He felt that people, whatever physical characteristics they had, should always be treated with kindness and should not be made to feel even more alone.

Gallaudet started the first free school for the deaf in America. He helped develop the American Manual Alphabet, and he taught deaf students to communicate using signs. Gallaudet married one of his students, and their children continued working in the field of deaf education. They started schools in New York and Washington, D.C. Gallaudet College in Washington, D.C., is now a world-famous institution of higher education for the deaf. People come from all over the world to study there.

The American Manual Alphabet

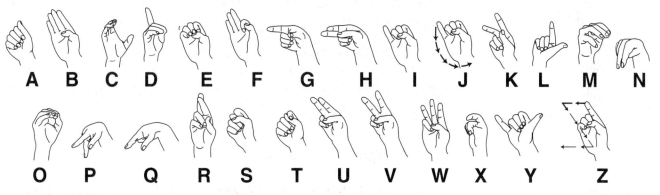

Questions to Ponder

❑ Can you sign your name using the American Manual Alphabet?

❑ Gallaudet was born in Philadelphia. In what state is Philadelphia, and is it the capital of that state? (*It is in Pennsylvania. No, the capital is Harrisburg.*)

❑ Is Harrisburg east or west of the Mississippi? (It's *east of the Mississippi.*)

❑ Do you think it would be harder to learn how to read if you could not hear?

❑ How could you let your mother know that you were going to spend a night at a friend's house if you both could not hear and you made the decision after you left for school?

Cesar Chavez

(1927–1993)

What if your year was not measured in days or months, but rather by crops? What if you measured time by melon picking, broccoli harvesting, cherry picking, and beet topping?

Many of our crops are picked by migrant workers. Migrant workers are workers who travel from field to field. As each crop ripens, they travel to those fields so that they can harvest the crops.

It is often very hot while the workers pick, and one's back begins to hurt with all the bending and carrying. It is very hard labor. What if one has to use the bathroom while they are in the middle of a large field? What if someone gets sick while they are working? What if pesticides are on the crops that the migrant workers have been asked to pick?

Cesar Chavez became a migrant farm worker when his family lost their home during the Great Depression. He remembered once picking peas for three hours with his family: Chavez's entire family (both his parents, Chavez, his sisters and brothers) received only 20 cents!

Because the migrant workers were always traveling, they had very little rights. They did not vote, and most did not speak English. They were afraid that if they complained about not being compensated fairly, they would never get a chance to work again. No matter how unfairly they were treated, they had to provide food for their families. Chavez knew that an empty stomach made it hard to fight, even when one knew that he or she was right.

Chavez helped to create the United Farm Workers Association. If the farm workers stuck together as a group, wages could not be decreased after they had already been hired, workers could not be fired and forced to leave before they were paid, children could be sent to school, the workers could be treated fairly, and health insurance could be provided.

Despite death threats and hate mail, Chavez said that change had to come without violence. He organized peaceful demonstrations and boycotts of produce that had been harvested using non-union labor. Chavez made a difference in many people's lives. When Chavez died, over 25,000 people followed his coffin to say their good-byes.

Questions to Ponder

❑ Chavez was born in Yuma, Arizona. What country is directly south of Arizona? (*Mexico*)

❑ What is Arizona's capital? (*Phoenix is the capital of Arizona.*)

❑ As new strains of vegetables and fruits are being developed and new machines are being invented, more and more crops are being harvested by machine. Is this good?

❑ If you followed your family as your parents harvested different crops, would it be hard to keep up in school? Would each new school be doing what the old school was doing?

❑ Cesar Chavez was only five-feet six-inches tall. Yet, many would say that he was a big man. Why do you think people would say that?

Duke Ellington
(1899–1974)

Jazz is a distinctly American form of music. It grew out of African-American musical traditions at the beginning of the twentieth century. Jazz's roots lie in several types of music, including blues, ragtime, spirituals, marches, and folk music; and jazz relies heavily on improvisation. When something is improvised, it is composed or invented right at the moment.

Duke Ellington was an African American who is one of the most respected figures in the history of American music. Ellington's talents—as a pianist, a bandleader, and a composer—are credited in helping jazz to be considered a serious art form. Throughout his lifetime, Ellington composed over 2,000 jazz compositions. Many of these pieces, like "Take the 'A' Train," and "Mood Indigo," are still performed in jazz bands all over the world today.

Many people today say that Ellington's greatest accomplishment was in his leadership. As a bandleader, he was able to bring different musicians together and blend their talents. Ellington allowed his musicians, with all their very different styles, to express their personalities within the music. In his unique way, Ellington had different sections of his orchestra—the saxophones, clarinets, trumpets, and trombones—play passages that were in contrast with each other or that were accompaniments to a soloist. Ellington's musical innovation showed his genius, and the world took notice.

After playing in New York's Cotton Club in Harlem, Ellington and his band made nationwide radio broadcasts. Ellington and his band became the first African-American musicians to be featured at New York's Carnegie Hall. Ellington also helped to spread his form of jazz by touring the world. Ellington went on tours of Europe and Japan, as well as the Middle East and Africa. For many of the people who heard Ellington and his band play, it was the first time they had ever heard jazz.

Questions to Ponder

❏ Ellington was born in Washington, D.C. Is Washington, D.C., a state? (*Washington, D.C., is not a state. It is a district, and it is our nation's capital.*)

❏ Can you name at least three famous buildings or memorials that can be found in Washington, D.C.? (*the White House; the Capitol Building; the Washington, Jefferson, Lincoln, and Vietnam Memorials; etc.*)

❏ Ellington was awarded many honors and awards throughout his life. One special award was the Medal of Freedom. What is the Medal of Freedom? (*The Medal of Freedom is the highest award that the federal government can give to a civilian.*)

❏ Do you think sharing music is a good way of promoting international relations? What other American things could we share? (*traveling art exhibits, animals lent to zoos, etc.*)

❏ You are in a musical or play, and the singer or actor opposite you has forgotten the words. How could you improvise and help?

Theobald Smith

(1859–1934)

Think of white-coated scientists today studying microbes in air-conditioned labs. Gloves are worn, and everything is sterile. Now envision Theobald Smith standing in the over 100-degree sun, clouds of dust so thick around him that it is sticking to his sweaty forehead, picking off by hand (from three cows that are constantly swishing their tails and kicking) hundreds and hundreds of ticks. Think of those parasitic ticks—the blood engorged ones that mash into a disgusting mess when pulled, and the little ones that seem to have the knack of crawling quickly under hair to escape the cramped fingers trying to pluck them.

Theobald Smith was there by choice. He had come to figure out everything he could about Texas Fever. Texas Fever was an epidemic disease that cattle were contracting and dying from in Texas. Entire herds were decimated.

The cattlemen said, "No ticks—no Texas Fever!" But many scientists thought that this theory was ridiculous. What did farmers know? While scientists were busy arguing about whether the disease was spread by bacteria in manure or in saliva, cattle continued to die by the hundreds, even while on trains being shipped to the east.

Smith went to Texas and set up a laboratory—six dusty, fenced-off fields. He first experimented by seeing if cows that were clean of ticks became ill. Then he began to take ticks from cows that were ill and place them on cows that seemed healthy. He also studied the ticks' lifecycles. He raised thousands of ticks.

Through his careful experiments under the hot sun, Smith found that it was the baby ticks that carried the disease. The disease took a certain time to contract because the mother tick had to drop off the cow and lay her 2,000 or more eggs. After 20 days, the eggs had to hatch, and, the baby ticks had to wait until a leg came near that they could scamper up. Smith also discovered why cattle that were not moved from the northern or southern part of the state did not get ill. These cows had been bitten by the ticks at a very young age and injected then with the microbes that caused the disease. By the time the cows were full-grown, they were immune. Smith showed the world that, if the carrier can be wiped out, a disease can be wiped out. Cattle today are sprayed for ticks when needed. Our herds are healthy.

Questions to Ponder

❏ Smith lived in Texas while studying Texas Fever. What is the capital of Texas, and what body of water touches Texas's southeastern border? (*Austin; the Gulf of Mexico*)

❏ Texas Fever was considered an epidemic. What is an epidemic? (*An epidemic is when there is an outbreak of a particular illness that affects many individuals within a population at the same time. Antibiotics have helped tremendously in stopping medical epidemics.*)

❏ Now, knowing what an epidemic is, what do you think an epidemiologist does? (*Epidemiology is the branch of medical science that deals with the incidence, distribution, and control of disease in a population. An epidemiologist tries to trace diseases from start to finish. When and where did they first show up? How are they spread? Are they perhaps due to environmental factors or bacteria? How can the disease be stopped from spreading and how can it be eradicated? Epidemiologists today are working on understanding the AIDS and Ebola viruses, among other things.*)

Geronimo

(1820s–1909)

When Geronimo surrendered to General Miles in 1886, General Miles wrote, "He was one of the brightest, most resolute, determined looking men that I have ever encountered. . . . Every movement indicated power . . . and determination." Even though General Miles was on a different side than Geronimo, he could only look at Geronimo with respect. Geronimo had fought long and hard for his territory and his family.

Geronimo was an Apache leader who was one of the last Native Americans to fight against the new settlers intruding on and taking his land. For at least 1,000 years, the Apaches had roamed the mountains and plains of the American southwest—what we now call Arizona and New Mexico. The Apaches were a fierce group—they had to be. For hundreds of years Spanish conquerors of Mexico, and then later Mexicans, would sweep into Apache villages to murder men and then rope the survivors together, including women and children, and force them to live out the rest of their lives as slaves. Geronimo's real name was Goyathlay. This means "Yawning One." It was the Mexican soldiers who gave Goyathlay his nickname of Geronimo. Geronimo's first wife and three small children were massacred by Mexican soldiers. Geronimo led many raids against the Mexicans because of what had happened to his family.

Conditions did not improve for Geronimo when, after winning the Mexican War in 1848, the United States took control of Arizona and New Mexico territories. Settlers and gold miners felt that the land was wasted on the Native Americans, and they wanted it all to themselves. The government agents running the reservations (land on which the government forced the Native Americans to live) often did not care about the Native Americans at all. Sometimes the agents did not give out the blankets they were supposed to, and people froze to death. Other times, the only food they passed out was rotten meat.

Geronimo reacted by engaging in guerrilla warfare. Guerilla warfare is when one engages in quick and sudden attacks, then retreats until the next surprise attack. Geronimo became known because he escaped several times when he was captured. As a result, people and newspapers began to exaggerate greatly when it came to stories about Geronimo. It was claimed once that Geronimo led over 150 warriors on a rampage. In reality, Geronimo was traveling with only 20 other men and another 20 women and children.

Questions to Ponder

❑ During World War II, when U.S. paratroopers jumped from planes over enemy territory, they shouted, "Geronimo!" What did "Geronimo" mean to them? (*Shouting "Geronimo" helped the paratroopers feel brave. Geronimo fought fearlessly to protect his home and keep his family safe. The paratroopers wanted to fight as bravely and as fiercely as Geronimo did.*)

❑ Geronimo traveled throughout Arizona and New Mexico. What are these states' capitals, and what country do these states border? (*Phoenix, Arizona; Santa Fe, New Mexico; Mexico*)

❑ When Geronimo was a young boy, part of his education dealt with how to survive in their hot lands. One of his tasks was to take a mouthful of water and then run up a hill and down it, all without swallowing the water in his mouth. Can you do that?

William T.G. Morton

(1819–1868)

When you have your teeth pulled, stitches, or any type of surgery, you are usually given an anesthetic. An *anesthetic* is something that relieves or dulls the pain. Before anesthetics, people were strapped down. William T.G. Morton was haunted by an operation he witnessed while he was in medical school in which a man's leg needed to be amputated. Even though the surgeon was skillful, the poor patient screamed in agony. The patient finally fainted from pain, but not until his face had turned purple and tears and sweat had streamed down his face.

Morton felt that he had to find a way to stop this painful suffering. Initially, Morton trained as a dentist. Through experimentation, he figured out a way to make dentures that were much better than the other dentures being made. Yet Morton could not stand the pain his patients suffered when he pulled their old teeth from their sockets. Morton found that when he offered whisky, wine, or laudanum (an opium-based drug), his patients did not feel the pain as much; but this was not enough.

While at medical school, Morton started to experiment with ether. Morton must have been a true believer in what he was doing, because he initially tried out the ether on himself. He would record how long he remained unconscious by checking the clock before and after he woke up.

In 1846, Gilbert Abbott was the first person to be operated on while anesthetized. With a crowd of medical doctors and students watching, a surgeon removed a three-inch tumor that was imbedded in Abbott's neck while Morton held the inhaler filled with pure ether. When the operation was over, the surgeon said to the amazed observers, "Gentlemen, this is no humbug."

Morton was never rewarded financially for his discovery, though doctors everywhere were soon using ether. Some people took a collection and handed Morton their donation in a box with the words, "He has become poor in a cause which has made the world his debtor."

Surgery under aneshesia is commonplace today. We can even schedule some procedures, like having one's tonsils removed or remolding body parts, ahead of time. Surgeons can take their time and perform the surgeries properly because we have been anesthetized and cannot feel pain. Yet before Morton's work with anesthesia, surgery was a last resort. No one would agree to being cut open while they were awake unless it was a life and death situation.

Questions to Ponder

❑ Morton was born in Charlton, Massachusetts, but Morton's great-great-great-grandfather was born in Scotland. He had come to the U.S. in 1700. What are the capitals of Massachusetts and Scotland? (*Boston, Massachusetts; Edinburgh, Scotland*)

❑ What is an anesthesiologist? (*An anesthesiologist is a physician who specializes in anesthesiology. An anesthesiologist is the one who would put you to sleep before another doctor, the surgeon, operates. An anesthesiologist must be present during the entire operation, for he or she has to continually monitor your vital signs and whether you need more or less anesthetic. The anesthesiologist even looks at how much you weigh because he or she does not want to give you too little or too much.*)

❑ Do we still use ether? (*No, doctors use much safer and better anesthetics today.*)

Sally Ride

(1951–)

Ride, Sally, ride! On June 18, 1983, Sally Ride became the first American woman in space. Ride was a crew member on the space shuttle *Challenger*. Ride had prepared and trained for this position for many years. Ride was studying for her Ph.D. degree at Stanford University when she saw the advertisement in a campus newspaper that changed her life. Ride was chosen for NASA's astronaut training program because she had studied science extensively, was in excellent physical shape, had good eyesight, and was a team player. Sally knew how to work hard and get along with others.

Sally did special training for her space ride. She practiced hanging from a parachute for long periods of time; was ejected out of jets; and once, while wearing the parachute, was dropped from a moving boat. She had to learn how to release the parachute while the boat dragged her along. The parachute weighed 45 pounds (20.4 kg), so Ride ran and lifted weights every day to make herself stronger. Ride also rode the "vomit comet." The "vomit comet" is a training plane. The inside of the plane has been emptied, and the walls are padded. When the plane flies in a parabola (a curved path) at high speeds, one can experience weightlessness for a short time. If one has ever ridden free-fall rides or roller coasters with steep drops at amusement parks, one can get a feel for what one experiences on the "vomit comet."

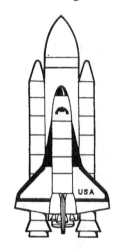

Despite all the technical work Ride performed, she always kept her sense of humor. NASA's tradition is to wake the astronauts up from their first night's sleep with some music. On Ride's second flight into space, she and her fellow crew mates played back a prerecorded message to Houston after they were woken up by the traditional music. The message said, "The crew is temporarily out. Please leave your name and address so that we may return your call later on."

Questions to Ponder

❏ Ride was born in Los Angeles, California. Is Los Angeles the capital of California? (*No, Sacramento is.*)

❏ What do the initials NASA stand for? (*National Aeronautics and Space Administration*)

❏ Once in orbit (about 200 miles above the surface of the earth), the Challenger orbited the earth every ninety minutes, traveling at a speed of five miles per second. How far can you travel in one second?

❏ While orbiting at the aforementioned speed, Sally and her fellow astronauts would see 16 sunrises and 16 sunsets every 24 hours. How did Sally know when to sleep? (*Sleep schedules were arranged according to the clock, not to the sun!*)

❏ Why do many astronauts prefer to tuck their arms into the sleeping bag rather than leave them out when they sleep? (*If not held down, the arms float out in front of the body at shoulder height.*)

❏ What is the only man-made object that can be seen from outer space? (*The Great Wall of China is the only man-made object that is visible from space.*)

Dr. Seuss

(1904–1991)

Dr. Seuss, the famous writer of such children's books as *Green Eggs and Ham, The Cat in the Hat,* and *The 500 Hats of Bartholomew Cubbins,* was not born with the name Dr. Seuss. When he was born, he was given the name Theodore Seuss Geisel. While attending Dartmouth College, he made the first change. He was editor-in-chief of the college humor magazine, but he was at risk of losing his post because of some minor infraction of the rules. He started signing his works with his middle name Seuss.

After graduating from Dartmouth, Seuss went on to study in England. When a student pointed out to him after looking at his notebook, which was more filled with drawings than notes, that, "You're not very interested in the lectures," he realized that she was right and dropped out. He knew that his father would be disappointed with him for not returning home with a doctorate, so he simply added Dr. to his middle name!

Dr. Seuss has had only one drawing lesson. While in class, he turned his paper upside down so that he could study the composition. His teacher walked by and said, "Ted, real artists don't turn their paper upside down." Dr. Seuss never returned to class!

The first children's book that Dr. Seuss published was *And to Think That I Saw It on Mulberry Street.* Dr. Seuss sent this book to 28 different publishing houses, and the book was rejected by every single one! Dr. Seuss then met an old Dartmouth friend on the street who had very fortunately become a children's book publisher just that morning! *And to Think That I Saw It on Mulberry Street* was finally published.

In the 1950s, an article was published that blamed the fact that America's children were having difficulty learning to read was because the books they were being taught out of were about "abnormally courteous, unnaturally clean boys and girls." Dr. Seuss's answer was *The Cat in the Hat.*

Questions to Ponder

❑ On March 2, 1904, Dr. Seuss was born in Springfield, Massachusetts. Springfield is not the capital of Massachusetts, but a different Springfield is the capital of another state. What is that state, and what is the capital of Massachusetts? (*Springfield is the capital of Illinois. Boston is the capital of Massachusetts. Despite what many people believe, Chicago is not the capital of Illinois.*)

❑ Dr. Seuss had a cat named Thing One. In which book did Dr. Seuss have the creature named Thing One? (*In* The Cat in the Hat, *the cat brought in the box with the creatures Thing One and Thing Two.*)

❑ What is your favorite Dr. Seuss book?

❑ Many people become known as great artists although they have never received formal training. One does not need a license to be an artist. Medical doctors and dentists, on the other hand, cannot legally practice without a license. Is this fair? Why or why not?

Robert Scott

(1868–1912)

Robert Scott was an English man who died, along with his men, while returning from the South Pole. He had hoped to be the first man to reach the South Pole, but he reached the Pole only to find a tent and letter that Amundsen had left there for him about a month before. Scott's tragic death and his journal writings have forever placed Scott in polar history.

On January 17, 1912, after reaching the Pole, Scott wrote, "Great God! This is an awful place and terrible enough for us to have laboured to it without the reward of priority." Scott made his last journal entry while badly frostbitten, weak with hunger, and knowing that he could not go on. "We shall stick it out to the end but we are getting weaker of course and the end cannot be far. It seems a pity but I do not think I can write more—R. Scott. Last Entry—For God's sake look after our people."

The bodies of Scott and two of his men were found eight months later, along with their journals, frozen in their tent and sleeping bags. Scott had actually reached the Pole with five men. One of them had died from frostbite and exhaustion about a month before, and the other, overcome with exhaustion and frostbite, had walked out of his tent on his birthday saying that he would be gone for some time. He did not want his slow progress to keep the others from making it home.

Though there is no denying that Scott pushed himself well beyond what most humans could ever endure, the question remains whether or not he brought upon himself his early death. Successful Arctic explorers learned what they could from the Inuit, the native people of the Arctic regions. These explorers knew that dogs were the best means of transporting supplies, and they adapted the clothing of these experienced inhabitants. They also carefully prepared food supplies. Nothing was left to chance.

Scott tried to use ponies, and the ponies only floundered in the snow and starved. Scott then pushed his sledges with man-power, a process that is slow and expends more energy than if one had traveled with dogs and skis. Scott also decided at the last minute to take a party of five, rather than the four he had originally planned for, to the Pole. If there had been only four men, there is a good chance that they would not have run out of food. In Scott's possessions was a dramatic photograph of the men toiling and straining under harnesses pulling the heavy sledge while one is pushing on the heavy sledge with all his strength. Snow and ice surrounds them.

Questions to Ponder

- ❏ Scott was born in England. What is the capital of England, and can you find it on the map? (*London*)
- ❏ Are there penguins at both the South and North Poles? (*Penguins are found at the South Pole only.*)
- ❏ Some English men claimed bitterly that Amundsen cheated because he used dogs. Do you agree or disagree?
- ❏ How would you feel if you thought you were going to be the first person on Mars, but when you landed you found a letter saying you had missed being first by a month?

Harriet Tubman

(1820–1913)

When Harriet Tubman was 28 years old, she knew was going to be sold. She might never see her family again. Tubman, with only a scrap of bread and salt herring, ran away the night she found out. Traveling along on the Underground Railroad, Tubman finally made it to Philadephia, a city where no person could be a slave.

The Underground Railroad was not a railroad with tracks: it was a network of safe houses (stations) where runaway slaves (passengers) were helped while they traveled to freedom. The people that led the runaway slaves from station to station were conductors. Being part of the Underground Railroad was very dangerous. People were beaten and sent to prison. If runaway slaves were caught, they were often tortured and then sold away from their families to the Deep South, where escape was almost impossible.

Tubman became a conductor on the Underground Railroad. She led over 300 slaves to freedom, and she never lost a passenger. Tubman's courage was legendary. Once, she had to travel through a village where someone who had owned her lived. She bought some chickens and hobbled through town, walking as if she were very old. When she saw her "owner," she dropped the chickens and put on a great show of trying to catch them. Everyone laughed to see the clumsy old lady so upset. If only Tubman's previous owner knew at whom he was laughing!

A $12,000 award was offered for Tubman's capture; at that time, $12,000 dollars was an incredibly huge amount of money. It made Tubman's conducting even more dangerous for her. Despite the price on her head, Tubman never considered curtailing (stopping) her conducting.

During the Civil War, Tubman worked for the Union forces. This brave and strong woman worked as a laundress, a nurse, and a spy. Tubman's own words when she talked about her original escape best describe her: "There was one of two things I had a right to, liberty or death; if I could not have one, I would have the other; for no man should take me alive. . . ."

Questions to Ponder

- ❏ Harriet Tubman first took the Underground Railroad from Dorchester County, Maryland, to Philadelphia, Pennsylvania. Can you find these places on the map?
- ❏ The second Fugitive Slave Act was passed in 1850. This allowed slave hunters the right to snatch runaway slaves back, even those slaves who had escaped to free states in the north. This act made it so that Tubman had to conduct slaves all the way to Canada. How much farther is this on the map?
- ❏ It was against the law for one to teach slaves how to read and write. How does not having an education keep people down?
- ❏ Slaves often communicated through songs. One song advised listeners to "follow the drinking gourd." What was the "drinking gourd"? (*It was the Big Dipper, a constellation that points to the North Star.*)
- ❏ If an Underground Conductor was given the message, "by Thursday you should receive a shipment of six and one half kegs of molasses," what might that be a code for? (*To prepare for the arrival of six adults and one child.*)

Charles Goodyear

(1800–1860)

Charles Goodyear said, "The advantages of a career in life should not be estimated exclusively by the standard of dollars and cents." Goodyear would be the man to understand fully what these words meant—he worked and died in poverty, but his invention of vulcanized rubber changed the world.

Goodyear's financial problems were always precarious. In fact, he was in debtor's prison so often that he referred to it as his "hotel." Once, when Napolean III awarded him the prestigious cross of the Legion of Honor for an exhibition in Paris, the medal had to be delivered to the prison where Goodyear was locked up for his latest debts! Yet even being in prison could not stop Goodyear's determination to improve rubber. Goodyear wanted to develop a rubber that would not melt into a foul-smelling, sticky mess in the hot sun or become brittle and crack in the winter's cold.

Goodyear actually started his experiments with rubber while in prison. Goodyear had absolutely no background in chemistry, but he did have use of a tiny kitchen in a small cottage on the prison grounds. Goodyear's method was to test everything in the world he could. Something that he mixed into the rubber was bound to make it more elastic and stronger! The cream cheese, ink, soup, and castor oil that Goodyear tried did not prove successful!

Goodyear made his breakthrough by chance. He accidentally dropped a lump of rubber mixed with sulfur on a hot stove. Goodyear thought the lump would melt, but it didn't. Instead, it charred like leather. Goodyear took the rubber and then nailed it outside in the cold. It did not become brittle but instead remained flexible. Goodyear had discovered vulcanization. *Vulcanization* is the process of treating crude (or synthesized) rubber chemically to give it such useful properties as elasticity, strength, and stability. With more experiments, Goodyear had it down: apply steam at 270 degrees Fahrenheit (132°C) for four to six hours. Varying amounts of sulfur determine the rubber's degree of softness. Goodyear did not make lots of money off his patent. In fact, the lawyer who successfully defended him in court against patent pirates charged Goodyear $15,000 dollars for two days of work in court. This sum was more than Goodyear had earned in half a century!

Questions to Ponder

❑ Goodyear was born in Connecticut. What is the capital of Connecticut, and was Connecticut one of the thirteen original colonies? (*Hartford. Connecticut became a state in 1788, and it was fifth of the original thirteen states to ratify the Constitution.*)

❑ Can you name five things that make use of Goodyear's improved rubber? (*Things made of rubber are tires, inflatable lifeboats, rubber balls, shoe soles, rubber bands, etc.*)

❑ Goodyear once wrote, "Man has just cause for regret only when he sows and no one reaps." What did Goodyear mean by this? (*When something is sowed, it is planted or set in motion. When something is reaped, it is harvested or obtained. By this choice of words, Goodyear was saying that the only time one should regret one's work is if no one else benefits from one's work. Do you agree?*)

❑ Someone once wrote that Goodyear's career had taken more bounces than a rubber check. What did they mean? (*A rubber check is one that has bounced, meaning there was insufficient funds in the bank account for the money to be drawn.*)

Galileo

(1564–1642)

How would you feel if you were under house arrest for the rest of your life? House arrest is when you cannot leave your house or yard. Even if you needed to see a doctor, you could not leave your property to visit one.

Galileo Galilei was an Italian astronomer and physicist who was sentenced to life in prison. After six months, he was allowed to go home, but he was placed under house arrest. This was in 1633, and all because Galileo had written the book *Dialogue Concerning the Two Chief World Systems*. After Galileo's sentence, this book was banned, and the copies of the book that were found were ordered burned. What was so horrible about this book?

The accepted view of the universe had been that Earth was the center of it. The sun and the other planets traveled around Earth. A man named Copernicus disagreed with this view. In Copernicus's view, the sun was the center of the universe, and Earth turned (rotated) each day. Galileo agreed with Copernicus. Galileo secretly wrote to another astronomer, Johannes Kepler, and told him that he agreed with Copernicus's view. Galileo was afraid to say this openly because it went against the traditional teachings and religious views of that time. The religious teachings said that Earth was the center of all things.

Galileo had observed planetary motion for a long time with his telescope. He had performed mathematical calculations, and he had come up with a theory about the rise and fall of the tides. He felt that the tides on Earth were linked to the movements of both the moon and the sun.

In his book, Galileo challenged the teachings that there were two sets of natural laws, one for heaven and one for Earth. Galileo put forth the view that Earth is a planet that is part of a solar system, and that solar system is part of an even bigger universe. He said that humans and all things on Earth are subject to natural laws. Galileo also described all the advances that had been made in physics.

At his trial in 1633, Galileo defended himself strongly in front of the Church Inquisition. Galileo said that scientific observations and facts could not be ignored. Despite the fact that Galileo was right, Galileo was forced to renounce all of his beliefs and writings that supported the Copernican theory.

Questions to Ponder

❏ Galileo was born in Italy. What seas border this country, and what is the country's capital? (*Italy borders the Ionian Sea, the Adriatic Sea, the Tyrrhenian Sea; and its islands, Sicily and Sardinia, lie in the Mediaterranean Sea. The capital of Italy is Rome.*)

❏ If you did not have a telescope or know mathematics, would you be able to tell that the sun did not move around Earth?

❏ While Galileo was under house arrest, he wrote the famous book *Discourses and Mathematical Demonstrations Relating to Two New Sciences Concerning Mechanics*. This book was smuggled out of Italy and printed in the Netherlands in 1638. How do you think it was smuggled out?

❏ Galileo was under house arrest from 1633 until his death in 1642. How many years was he imprisoned at home? (*approximately nine years*)

❏ Should books be banned?

Eleanor Roosevelt

(1884–1962)

In 1939 when Eleanor Roosevelt attended a meeting of the Southern Conference for Human Welfare in Birmingham, Alabama, she was told that black and white Americans could not sit together: it was the law. Roosevelt had a chair placed in the center aisle, in the middle of the separated sides, and sat there. Eleanor Roosevelt, the First Lady, wife of President Franklin Roosevelt, was a woman of action and dignity who believed strongly that all Americans were equal, and that it was the responsibility of the government to work to alleviate poverty and injustice.

From a very early age, Roosevelt knew that her mother was disappointed in her. "My mother was troubled by my lack of beauty. . . . She tried hard to bring me up well so that my manners would compensate for my looks, but her efforts made me more keenly conscious of my shortcomings," Roosevelt wrote in her autobiography. Shy about her height and protruding teeth, Roosevelt never expected to lead a public life. Her life became very public and open to daily scrutiny, though, after her marriage to Franklin Roosevelt.

Franklin Roosevelt became physically disabled after contracting polio, but he did not let his infirmity stop his political career. For all the years that he was in office, Eleanor became his information source. She did things and went places that no other First Lady had ever done or been. She took a two-and-a-half mile trip down an Ohio coal mine to report on the safety conditions of the miners, how they lived, and what their pay was. She toured slums in Puerto Rico, inspected factories, visited with tenant farmers in their tarpaper shacks in cotton fields; and during World War II, she visited wounded men and refugees in war-ravaged countries. The first First Lady to fly in an airplane, her energy was boundless, and her determination to provide for the welfare of the common man was fierce.

Many people were uncomfortable with her outspokenness. Cartoons depicted her as crazy, and the Secretary of the Interior said, "I wish that Mrs. Roosevelt would stick to her knitting." The world is lucky that she didn't.

Questions to Ponder

❑ Roosevelt was born in New York. What is the capital of New York, and can you name a state that touches New York? (*Albany is the capital. Vermont, Massachusetts, Connecticut, New Jersey, and Pennsylvania each border New York.*)

❑ Eleanor was a niece of Teddy Roosevelt, her father's older brother. Why should you know who Teddy Roosevelt is? (*Teddy Roosevelt was the 26th president of the U.S. The stuffed animal the Teddy Bear was named after him.*)

❑ Roosevelt was sent to an exclusive finishing school on the outskirts of London, England. Is London the capital of England? What is a finishing school? (*London is the capital. A finishing school is school where young women, usually wealthy, go to learn social graces. A language might be taught, as well as music, literature, and etiquette.*)

❑ How many years was Eleanor First Lady? (*Excellent guess if you answered eight, but sorry! Roosevelt won reelection four times, but he died in his office during his fourth term. Eleanor was a First Lady then for a little over 12 years. After Roosevelt, a law was passed that allows a president to serve no more than two terms.*)

Garrett Augustus Morgan

(1877–1963)

You are coming to an intersection. There are hundreds of cars coming down every street. The potential for disaster is great. Yet no car runs into the other. Only cars going in one direction at a time enter the intersection. How does this happen? How do people know when it is their turn? Simple: they are obeying the traffic lights. Red for stop, yellow for caution, green for go.

Garrett Augustus Morgan was once witness to a tragic accident. Cars, people, and horse-drawn wagons had competed for space at a typical intersection in the busy city. Police officers often helped to direct traffic, and signals were sometimes set up that would flash "stop" and "go," but this was not enough to prevent or stop frequent collisions and accidents. Morgan decided that a better way of controlling traffic had to be developed. In 1923, he was granted a patent for his traffic light. Morgan later sold the rights to his patent, but every traffic light we see today evolved from Morgan's original design.

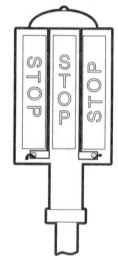

On July 24, 1916, an explosion erupted in a tunnel about 250 feet (76 m) below Lake Erie. Firefighters and police could not rescue the workers trapped in the tunnel. Several firefighters had already died in the rescue efforts. Morgan and his brother saved 32 workers who had been overcome by the smoke, poisonous gases, and dust. How did they do it? Morgan and his brother used Morgan's Safety Hood invention. On Morgan's patent application, which he was granted in 1914, Morgan wrote that his Safety Hood would enable "a fireman to enter a house filled with thick, suffocating gases and smoke and to breathe freely for some time." Morgan's Safety Hood, which is what we know as a gas mask, is now standard equipment for soldiers, firefighters, and police officers.

Morgan was an amazing man. The son of a former slave who gained her freedom in 1863, Morgan barely finished elementary school. But nothing could stop his inquiring mind; and his inventions, many of which are still in use today, have helped to save a countless number of lives.

Questions to Ponder

❑ Morgan was born in Paris, Kentucky. Of which country is a different Paris the capital, and what is the capital of Kentucky? (*Paris, France. Frankfort, Kentucky.*)

❑ Morgan later moved to the cities of Cincinnati and Cleveland. In which state are these cities, and are either of these two cities the capital? (*Ohio. The capital is Columbus.*)

❑ Does the saying "When life gives you lemons, make lemonade" apply to Morgan?

❑ If one is in a smoke-filled room and one does not have a gas mask, should one stand up and walk out? (*No! One should crawl. Hot air rises, and so there will be less smoke down by the floor.*)

❑ In many countries, like England and Australia, traffic circles are used to control traffic instead of traffic lights. What is a traffic circle? (*One does not stop, but instead immediately enters into the flow of one-way traffic going around the circle. One simply turns off when they come to the street at which they want to exit.*) Would you prefer a stop sign, traffic light, or traffic circle when traffic is light, fair, or heavy?

Wolfgang Amadeus Mozart

(1756–1791)

Wolfgang Amadeus Mozart was born in Salzburg, Austria. He was a musical prodigy. A prodigy is a highly talented child. When Mozart was just three years old, he listened to his sister take clavier lessons from their father, a composer and musician himself. A clavier is an early keyboard instrument from which the piano developed. Even though Mozart was playing with his toys while his sister had her lesson, afterwards he could play everything from memory that she had been taught. By the age of five, Mozart had composed two minuets of such quality that his father wrote them down. Mozart also played the violin. His father gave him lessons after Mozart played perfectly some difficult music that he had simply listened to.

Mozart's father took Mozart and his sister throughout Europe so that they could play for kings, queens, and wealthy aristocrats. Mozart and his sister got a lot of attention because they were so talented at such a young age. By the time Mozart was seven, he had composed two pairs of sonatas for violin and piano. At age 13, Mozart had written concertos, sonatas, symphonies, and operettas.

The following story exemplifies the amazing ability Mozart had when it came to remembering every musical note he ever heard. Mozart visited the Sistine Chapel and listened to a concert that consisted of an organ and an entire choir. There was a rule at that time that no one but the musicians of the chapel could have copies of the music performed there. No one had been able to write it down from memory: the task was too difficult. When Mozart left the concert, he went home and wrote down every single note.

Another time, the emperor in Vienna asked Mozart to compose some pieces for a concert. When the time came to play, Mozart had not yet written his piece for the piano, though he had written the parts for the rest of the instruments. The emperor saw the blank sheets Mozart had placed on the piano. When he asked Mozart where his part was, Mozart pointed to his head and replied that it was in there. At the end of the performance, the emperor stood up and yelled, "Bravo! Bravo!"

One would think that with all of his talent, Mozart would have died rich and famous. Mozart died a pauper at the age of 35, and he was buried in a pauper's grave, without a funeral or a marker. (A pauper is someone who is very poor.) Yet, Mozart has left us some of the greatest classical music in the world. His music has kept his name alive, and his work has enriched our lives.

Questions to Ponder

❑ Some of Mozart's most famous operas are *The Marriage of Figaro* and *Don Giovanni*. What is an opera? (*An opera is a drama set to music and made up of vocal pieces with orchestral accompaniment. Operettas, which Mozart also composed, are light operas, usually humorous, that contain some spoken dialogue and dance.*)

❑ Is Salzburg the capital of Austria? Can you find the capital of Austria on the map? (*Vienna is the capital of Austria.*)

❑ What is a sonata, and how does a sonata compare to a symphony? (*A sonata is an instrumental composition of three or four independent movements that vary in mood, character, and tempo. A symphony is a sonata for an entire orchestra, usually in four contrasting movements.*)

❑ Does being a musical prodigy guarantee success and a prosperous life?

Jane Goodall

(1934–)

How do we learn about animals in the wild? How do we learn what their social structure is and how they eat, sleep, and care for their young? Information like this does not come easily. Scientists today are still learning about many animals.

When Jane Goodall was asked by Dr. Leakey to try to find out some of the answers to these questions about chimpanzees, she did not hesitate. Working with animals in Africa was what this young English woman had always dreamed of doing.

In 1960, Goodall went to Tanzania. Living in just a tent, she spent years in the wild watching the same chimpanzees. During the first months, she was lucky to observe anything at all. When she did get close to a chimpanzee, she was threatened. Over time, though, the chimpanzees began to see Goodall as just part of the landscape. Soon Goodall could identify every chimpanzee in the area. She was able to identify family relationships and watch mothers interact with their infants. Years later, Goodall then observed how those infants—now adults—raised their own infants. She could study how brothers and sisters treated each other and each other's children.

Before Goodall saw otherwise, one of the things that had defined humankind was that we made tools. A baboon might pick up a stick and throw it at another creature, but that was not the same as making a tool. The baboon threw the stick simply because it was there.

Termites live in mounds of earth. During the rainy season, when the termites mature to the stage where they can leave the nest, they rise to just under the surface of the mound. Goodall saw several chimpanzees gather pieces of vine, stems, and twigs. On some of the twigs, they carefully stripped off the leaves. Using these items as simple tools, the chimpanzees then scratched open passages into the termite mounds. Next, they poked the long grass into the mound. When they pulled out the stems, they would eat the insects that were clinging to it. If the stem or twig they were using became bent, they would make another one. These skills of making the "fishing" tools had to be taught to each generation of chimpanzees: it was not instinctual behavior.

Goodall was also the first to observe chimpanzees hunting and killing other mammals for food. Before, scientists thought that chimpanzees were mainly vegetarians. Today, Goodall works hard to protect all chimpanzees, those still in the wild and those that are being used for research.

Questions to Ponder

❏ What ocean does Tanzania border? (*Tanzania borders the Indian Ocean.*)

❏ When did Tanzania gain its independence? (*Tazania gained independence in 1961.*)

❏ Dr. Leakey, the man who gave Jane her job, was both an anthropologist and a paleontologist. What is the difference? (*An anthropologist studies the origins of humans. This includes physical, social, and cultural development as well as human behavior. A paleontologist studies fossils from prehistoric times. The fossils they study may be bones, stone tools, leaf imprints, or even footprints.*)

❏ Dr. Goodall has a Ph.D. in ethology. What is a Ph.D., and what is ethology? (*A Ph.D. is a Doctorate of Philosophy. Ethology is the study of animal behavior.*)

❏ If you studied an animal in the wild, what animal would you choose? How would you habituate the animal to your presence? What if it were nocturnal? How would you live?

Joseph Lister

(1827–1912)

Before surgeons operate, they have to "scrub-up." After changing into sterile clothing that is used only for a single operation, they go into a special room where they scrub their hands and arms with an antiseptic soap under running water for at least five minutes. The soap penetrates the pores of the skin and forms a protective film. They then powder their hands with an antiseptic powder and put on sterilized gloves. Down to the tiled surfaces, the masks, and the surgical instruments that have been sterilized by high-pressure steam machines, everything is set up so that no germs can enter the open wound of the surgical patient and cause an infection.

Believe it or not, these pre-operation procedures became standard only recently. Before the middle of the twentieth century, anyone undergoing an operation was often in greater danger from losing his life due to lack of hygiene than from the operation! Surgeons seldom bothered to wash their hands, and they wore black mourning coats, congealed with blood and dirt. When done with their instruments, the doctors would simply toss them into a drawer until the next operation! The operating tables were wooden, and a bucket of sawdust was used to soak up the mess.

Joseph Lister was an English surgeon who introduced to surgery the principle of antisepsis. Lister read a paper by Pasteur that discussed germs. Before Pasteur, no one knew about the existence of tiny microbes that could carry disease. Lister immediately set out to see if Pasteur's theory applied to surgery. He first tried wiping everything with carbolic acid. On his first patient, the patient remained infection free and survived—but the acid burned the patient's skin quite badly and caused him great pain. With laboratory tests, Lister found equally destructive antiseptics that were gentler on the patient.

Lister had one notable failure. He decided that perhaps the best way to insure that no germs got into the wound was to kill them in the air. Ready to operate, he set up a machine that would spray the operating room with a fluid that created a dense fog. The problem was that the doctors and nurses could only cough and sputter, and their eyes watered to the point where they could not see what they were doing.

Over the years, Lister showed how the risk of infection could be reduced with heat sterilization of dressings and instruments as well as the clothes worn by the medical staff. Thanks to Lister, post-operative fatalities have decreased dramatically.

Questions to Ponder

❑ Lister was born in England. What is the capital of England, and what channel separates England from France? (*London; the English Channel*)

❑ How does Lister's work apply to why cooks should always wash their hands before preparing food? (*Cooks can spread their germs to the food they are preparing, and then those who eat it become infected.*)

❑ First and foremost, physicians are supposed to do no harm. Was that harder to do before antiseptics? (*Yes. Many people survived the operation, but died from infection later. Before, a physician would want to operate only as a last resort.*)

❑ In surgery today, a total count of every sponge and instrument is taken before and after the operation. Why? (*It insures that nothing gets accidentally left inside.*)

An Wang

(1920–1990)

In 1965, An Wang was awarded a patent for a desktop calculator that could add, subtract, multiply, divide, compute square roots, and do some other types of calculations that scientists and engineers needed for their work. The price of this calculator was $6,500 dollars. Think for a moment about that: in 1965, $6,500 dollars was worth a lot more then what it is now. Less than a year later, Wang started selling yet another calculator that he developed. This one sold for only $1,695. At this cheap price, sales went wild! Today, we can find cheap pocket calculators everywhere. Some of them are less than 10 dollars!

In 1971, Wang introduced to the world the first word-processing typewriter. A person could type a letter and correct mistakes line by line. Then, in 1976, Wang presented something even more revolutionary. People were so excited about what they were seeing that at the show where it was being exhibited for the first time, people stood almost 10 deep. Invitations had to be given out so that the crowd could be kept under control. What was it?

Wang was demonstrating his new word-processing system in which an entire document could be viewed on a screen. Words or sentences could be moved or corrected from any part of the document. There were also "menus," which were directions in simple language that guided one while using the word-processing system.

Wang started his company with only $600 dollars in savings. He did not have any contracts or orders for work. He was the only employee, and he did not even own any office furniture! Wang's company became highly successful, and he earned great wealth—yet he never owned more than two suits at a time! Instead, he generously donated to the world, funding scholarships, helping restore Boston's performing arts theater, giving to the Massachusetts General Hospital outpatient clinic, and providing a computer network system to New York City's center for the homeless.

Questions to Ponder

❏ Wang was born in Shanghai, China. People in China speak many dialects. What dialect is the basis for China's national language—Cantonese or Mandarin? (*Mandarin*)

❏ The Mediterranean Sea, the Yellow Sea, and the East China Sea—which one does not border China? (*The Mediterranean Sea does not border China.*)

❏ As well as in the U.S., Wang Labs had offices in Belgium, Taiwan, and the United Kingdom. Can you match these countries to these capitals: London, Brussels, Taipei? (*Brussels, Belgium; Taipei, Taiwan; London, the United Kingdom*)

❏ An Wang's name means "Peaceful King." If you could choose a two-word name, the first word being an adjective and the second a noun, what would you name yourself?

❏ At the time that Wang wanted to attend junior high, there were not enough public junior high schools to serve the great number of children who wanted to attend. Less than 200 students were admitted each year, and being admitted depended on how one performed on a single examination. How would that policy affect your school?

❏ How have the calculator and word-processing advances changed our schools and ways of doing things?

Rachel Carson

(1907–1964)

A friend wrote Rachel Carson that 14 robins had died a horrible death after DDT, a poison that kills mosquitoes and other bugs, was sprayed over her yard. Could Carson do something about it?

Carson was already known for her two books *The Sea Around Us* and *The Edge of the Sea*. These books were beautifully written and had made the bestsellers lists. Carson's books introduced the notion of ecology to many people. Ecology is the branch of science that deals with the interrelationship of all organisms and their environment. Carson's books showed us how Earth is a balanced planet, where nothing is ever wasted.

Now Carson began to research pesticides (chemicals that are used to kill pests). She wrote an article, but no one would print it. The magazine editors did not think that Carson's facts were right. Carson did not give up. She started the book *Silent Spring* in secret. It took her four years to write it. She double-checked every fact. She asked other scientists to read what she wrote, again wanting to make sure that she was correct. In 1962, *Silent Spring* was finished.

Silent Spring was first published in *The New Yorker* magazine. People were shocked about what they read. Did pesticides really affect the animals, the air, the ecological balance, and themselves? The chemical companies that made the pesticides were very angry. One company said, "Her book is even more poisonous than the pesticides." But President Kennedy, who asked for a special report from top scientists after *Silent Spring* was published, agreed with Carson. Our government began to establish laws that would control chemical pollution in the United States.

Perhaps we should remember Carson with her words to a man from a chemical company who tried to prove that she was wrong: "Man is a part of nature, and his war against nature is . . . a war against himself."

Questions to Ponder

❏ Before Carson had ever seen the sea, she used to put a conch shell against her ear to listen to the ocean. What was she really hearing? (*She was hearing echoes of the pulse in her own ear.*)

❏ Carson was born in Springdale, Pennsylvania. What is Pennsylvania's capital, and can you name a state that borders Pennsylvania? (*Pennsylvania's capital is Harrisburg. Its bordering states are New Jersey, Delaware, Maryland, West Virginia, Ohio, and New York.*)

❏ In the book *The Sea Around Us,* Carson used more than 1,000 sources. What does that mean? (*Carson took information from more than 1,000 places. Those places were scientific papers, books, encyclopedias, and interviews with people who were at the top of their fields. This way she knew that she was describing the entire picture of the ocean and had not left out important pieces of information. Her information had been checked and cross-checked.*)

❏ Many people say that today we are now seeing the effects of not using so many pesticides. There are more mosquitoes, and they are transmitting dangerous diseases. Should we go back to using banned pesticides like DDT?

Solomon A. Andree

(deceased 1897)

Solomon A. Andree once said, "The thing is so difficult that it is not worth attempting it. The thing is so difficult I cannot help attempting it." What was he talking about?

Back in the 1890s, before man had ever reached the North Pole, Andree wanted to balloon over it. He died in the attempt, but a story was told by the photographs and diary he left behind.

When Andree set out, his balloon stood about 100 feet (30.5 m) high and was able to lift five tons. Supplies included three sleds, marker buoys, a boat, enough canned goods to feed the three men for four months, scientific instruments, gourmet foods for immediate consumption, and even a cozy bedroom for one flier at a time. The silken gasbag enclosed 176,582 cubic feet (5,000 cubic meters) of hydrogen gas.

When the balloon took off on July 11, 1897, two-thirds of Andree's draglines were left behind after they had caught on the rocks fringing the beach outside the balloon house. Andree had not planned to fly above 800 feet (244 m), but without the draglines the balloon quickly rose to about 1,800 feet (548.6 m). Today we can keep in contact by radio, but at that time, radio was not yet in regular use. The only means Andree had of communicating was with passenger pigeons! Andree carried 36 of them, but because of the distances and polar magnetism, not much success was expected from the pigeons. Andree was just hoping that by chance some of the pigeons might just blunder around until someone spotted them.

One pigeon was found by a Norwegian sailing vessel, proof that the balloon had flown at least 46 hours. Three of the 12 marker buoys were found, two with messages written earlier than the pigeon post, and one without anything. Then there was nothing for 33 years.

A whaling ship, gone ashore for walrus, spotted a tin can. From there, they found the bodies, but also cameras and diaries. The diaries showed that the balloon started leaking almost immediately. On July 14th, just three days after lift off, they were 480 miles (772.5 km) short of the North Pole, and 376 miles from where they had lifted off. The men survived for three months on the ice floes, eating their supplies and polar bears, seals, and birds that they shot. They lived in a large igloo that they built. Then their floe split in two, and they had to scramble to save what they could. They were close to tiny White Island, and they somehow made it there. The final dated entry in a diary was October 17th. It is not known how the men died. Some feel that it is quite probable that the stove they were having problems with leaked carbon monoxide, and that the men drifted off into an endless sleep.

Questions to Ponder

❏ Andree was Swedish. What is the capital of Sweden, and can you name a country that borders Sweden? (*Stockholm is the capital of Sweden. Norway and Finland border Sweden.*)

❏ Andree took off from the Arctic islands of Spitsbergen (now Svalbard). Can you find these islands on the map?

❏ Do you think radio contact would have changed the outcome?

❏ Think about Andree's words at the beginning. Have you ever felt that way?

Neil Armstrong

(1930–)

"The Eagle has landed." Millions of people all over the world heard the words transmitted to Earth by Neil Armstrong when the lunar module he was piloting set down on the moon. The moon is about 240,000 miles (386,243 km) from Earth. It took Armstrong three days to get there. There is not any air or water on the moon. Temperatures range from burning hot—250 degrees F (121 degrees C)—to incredibly cold—minus 250 degrees F (minus 121 degrees C).

Armstrong exited from the lunar module on July 20, 1969, to become the first man on the moon. Armstrong's memorable words were, "That's one small step for man, one giant leap for mankind."

The first thing that Armstrong did was to scoop up about two pounds of lunar soil, bag it, and put it in a special pocket on the thigh of his space suit made for this exact purpose. If for some reason, the mission had to be aborted or abruptly stopped, then at least they would not go back to Earth empty-handed.

When Armstrong left the moon, more than his footprints remained. Armstrong left a plaque that said, "Here men from the planet Earth first set foot upon the moon, July 1969 A.D. We came in peace for all mankind." An American flag was also planted. Because there is no wind on the moon, a thin wire was sewn on the flag to make it look as if it were flying. In addition, a one-and-a-half-inch silicone disk that had goodwill messages from the leaders of 72 other countries besides greetings from our president and former presidents was left. Three astronauts on the Apollo 1 mission had died in a fire, and these men were honored by a patch that was left. Two Soviet cosmonauts who had died were also honored. Their medals were left on the moon with the other items.

Questions to Ponder

- ❑ Armstrong was born in Ohio. What is the capital of Ohio? (*Columbus*)
- ❑ The mission could not have been possible if it were not for Mike Collins orbiting the command module while Armstrong and "Buzz" Aldrin piloted the lunar module *Eagle* onto the surface of the moon. How do you think Collins felt about all the attention Armstrong received? How do you think Aldrin felt being the second man on the moon?
- ❑ After Armstrong splashed down, he and the others were quarantined. A special lunar receiving laboratory was designed for their quarantine. During quarantine, this lab housed three doctors, technicians, a cook, a public-relations man, and the astronauts. The astronauts could not leave this lab or touch their family until quarantine was over. How come? (*It was not known if they brought back from the moon any new diseases or minute organisms that human beings had not developed any natural resistance to.*)
- ❑ Armstrong's landing on the moon was part of the Apollo program. What was the Apollo program, and who was it named after? (*The Apollo program was a series of space flights with the ultimate goal of getting man on the moon. The program was named after the Greek and Roman god Apollo. Apollo was the only God common to both Greek and Roman religion. Apollo was the god of medicine, music, and prophecy.*)
- ❑ If you landed on the moon, what would you think of the things you found that were left by the astronauts? What would you leave?
- ❑ How would you feel if you thought you were first, but then you found something that some other creature (perhaps not even human!) had left?

Ben Carson

(1951–)

Two boys, conjoined twins, were born in Germany in 1987. They were joined together at the back of the head. They shared a section of the skull as well as a major vein responsible for draining blood from the brain and returning it to the heart. Though they were definitely two separate people, with different personalities and sleeping habits, they would never be able to walk, play, or even get up out of their bed on their own. Dr. Ben Carson, a neurosurgeon, changed this.

Carson prepared for the operation to carefully separate the twins. Seventy people, including surgeons, nurses, and technicians would be involved. For five months, the team, led by Carson, trained and studied intensely. They planned where every person would stand, and they went through all the possible incidents that could happen during the operation. Life-sized dolls attached at the head by Velcro were used during five three-hour dress rehearsals. Months before the actual surgery, Carson arranged for one team member to insert inflatable balloons under the twins' scalps. Carson knew that he would need extra skin to cover the huge wounds after separation, and the inflatable balloons gradually stretched the skin until there was enough.

On September 5, 1987, at 7:15 A.M., Carson started operating. The operation was much more difficult than anyone had expected, but Carson never gave up. At one point, when the hospital ran out of its entire blood supply, people on the surgical team began to offer theirs. Fortunately, the Red Cross came up with the additional blood needed. Twenty-two hours after it had begun, the operation ended. The seven-month-old boys had entered the operating room on one bed; they left on two.

Though Carson is now an eminent physician, in elementary school he once thought he was stupid. One year he was happy that he got a "D" in math—he had gone up an entire grade. Carson also had to deal with poverty and racism. Carson was threatened on his way to school and warned off of teams just because he was African American. Carson also had to learn how to control his temper. Once, just because a friend made a comment about music that he did not like, he tried to stab his friend. Fortunately, his friend was wearing a big, heavy belt buckle, and when the knife made contact, the blade broke in half and dropped to the ground. This particular incident made Carson determined to change. Once Carson used a knife to threaten someone; now he uses one to change lives and make them better.

Questions to Ponder

❑ Carson was born in Detroit. In what state is Detroit, and is Detroit that state's capital? (*Detroit is in Michigan. The capital of Michigan is Lansing.*)

❑ After completing his residency, Carson worked in Perth, Australia. All but a few of the world's marsupials are found in Australia. What is a marsupial? (*Marsupials are pouched mammals. The young are born in an underdeveloped state and crawl to the mother's nipples that are in a pouch, or marsupium, formed by a fold of abdominal skin. Kangaroos, koalas, Tasmanian devils, and wombats are all marsupials.*)

❑ When Carson first started his internship at Johns Hopkins Hospital, patients and nurses often mistook him for an orderly. Because of the color of his skin, they assumed that he was not the doctor. Should we jump to conclusions about anyone just because of their skin color, race, religion, or language?

Jane Addams

(1860–1935)

If this were 100 years ago, you might not be in school. Instead, you could be working 14 hours a day. You could have started work at the age of five, and you might work six days a week. If you were very small, your job might be to scramble in between dangerous machinery. Some of you would even have to climb onto the dangerous machines to adjust them while they were running! Many of you would be severely injured; and, for most of you, by the time you reached the age of a teenager, you would have already experienced a harsh, adult life. For millions of children this was a terrible reality: many children were once exploited horribly in the U.S.

Jane Addams, a social worker from Illinois, knew that conditions had to change. Addams opened a settlement house, called Hull House, in one of the poorest sections of Chicago. Hull House was a house where new immigrants could come for help, whether it be food, housing, medical, childcare, or just for company. Many of the new immigrants could not speak English, but at Hull House they found people who would treat them respectfully and help them. Immigrants were taught skills to help them survive in their new country, while at the same time there were encouraged to take pride in their heritage. Addams lived at Hull House, and she worked alongside everyone. Once she found a burglar in the house. She calmly asked him what he was doing and found out his story: he was an unemployed laborer, and his family was starving. Addams invited him to come back the next day. He returned nervously only to discover that Addams had found him a job.

There were no public playgrounds in Chicago, and Addams started the first one in 1882. She convinced a wealthy businessman to donate the land, clear it, and pay for the equipment.

Garbage was everywhere in the poor sections of the city. Piles of it spewed into the streets, making it hazardous to walk. Alleys smelled like sewers, and many sewers were unconnected to the houses. Rats, mice, and flies carrying disease were everywhere. Addams started a public campaign. She followed garbage trucks that would pick up the garbage and then just dump it a few blocks away. She made sure that city officials had to do something rather than just pocket money from dishonest garbage collectors. The death rate dropped once the streets were cleaned.

Addams wrote about her work and spoke to others about what they could do. She worked hard for the passage of the first child-labor laws ever enacted in this country. She protected children from unsafe factories and dangerous jobs. More settlement houses were opened in other places in the United States. Addams started a worldwide peace group, called The Women's International League for Peace and Freedom, which is still working today to improve living conditions for every person. In 1932 Addams was the first American woman to win the Nobel Peace Prize.

Questions to Ponder

❏ Hull House still exists and is operating in Chicago, Illinois. Is Chicago the capital of Illinois? (*No, Springfield is the capital of Illinois.*)

❏ We have laws today that make it mandatory that children attend school. Is this fair?

❏ In 1905 the average child received 40 cents for a 12-hour day. What is today's minimum wage?

Willem Einthoven

(1860–1927)

You are a doctor. You are standing with several other doctors around the bed of a patient. You are all trying to figure out what is wrong with him. Before you can even come up with a diagnosis, a doctor who is not even in the same room with you, a doctor who is actually about a mile away, sends you the correct diagnosis. How do you feel?

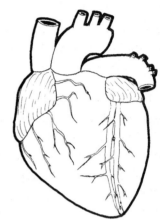

Willem Einthoven was the doctor a mile away. What made his diagnosis possible was the machine he invented: the electrocardiograph. You might know this machine as an EKG. Whenever you see a television show or movie where there is monitor showing the patient's heartbeat, that machine is an EKG. A normal heart shows a pattern of regularly occurring spikes and dips, and doctors and nurses are trained how to "read" what the monitor is showing. They can recognize a normal heart beat, and they can detect when something is not right. Today, just from looking at a record of your heartbeat, many doctors can, like Einthoven could, diagnose what the problem is and prescribe treatment.

You may be wondering why Einthoven was a mile away. Why wasn't he at the patient's bed? Einthoven's first machine was so huge that it could not be moved from his laboratory. It weighed 600 pounds, and five people were needed to operate it. Metal sensors were stuck on the patient's skin, and these sensors then sent electrical signals to the machine. The signals were sent through telegraph wires. Even with this first machine, the details of the recorded graph were incredible. Over the years Einthoven continued to improve and refine his machine. He also conducted research on how to interpret the machine's readings. In 1924 Einthoven was awarded the Nobel Prize in medicine and physiology. Einthoven, lecturing in the U.S. at the time, found this out by picking up a newspaper and reading an article where it reported that he had won the prize!

Questions to Ponder

❏ Einthoven was born on the island of Java. His mother moved the family back to the Netherlands when he was 10. To what country did Java belong, and what country is it part of now? (*Under Dutch rule from 1619 to 1946, Java used to be part of the Dutch West Indies. Java is now part of Indonesia.*)

❏ Why is having a printed record of one's heartbeat helpful to doctors? (*Your heartbeat record can be compared to other times in your life: while performing physical exercise or resting, before certain types of medicine, or after surgery. What is equally important is that a doctor can take your record and show it to other doctors. The doctors can confer and work together on finding out what is wrong with you. This way, even doctors who are working at research hospitals and are unable to visit you at your bed can help in identifying what is wrong with you and aid in your recovery.*)

❏ Einthoven rode a bike to the university where he worked, and once there, he changed into comfortable slippers. Do you study better when you are comfortable?

Samuel Morse

(1791–1872)

Samuel Morse is known as the father of the telegraph. The telegraph was the first machine that allowed us to transmit messages across wires. On May 24th, 1844, Samuel Morse transmitted his first telegraphic message while he sat in the Supreme Court chamber in Washington, D.C. He sent the words, "What hath God wrought?" to Baltimore, Maryland.

We have the telephone and e-mail now for instant news, but at the time, Morse's invention revolutionized the way people lived. Mail took weeks and sometimes months, but with this machine, news could be sent immediately.

Samuel was born in Charlestown, Massachusetts. Do you know the story of the tortoise and the hare? The two animals have a race. One would think that the hare would win because it is a much faster animal. Instead, the tortoise wins because it is steady and never stops. The hare loses because even though he is ahead at first, he stops doing what he is supposed to be doing and takes a nap. When Samuel was little, his father compared him to a hare. His father said that Samuel was always running off and asking too many questions and never concentrating on what he was supposed to do. His father was also not pleased that Samuel was interested in drawing. As Samuel got older, he divided his interests between drawing and electricity.

This chart shows what each letter and number is when translated into Morse code. A dot represents a short tap. A dash lasts as long as three dots.

Letter	Morse	Letter	Morse	Number	Morse
A	• —	N	— •	0	— — — — —
B	— • • •	O	— — —	1	• — — — —
C	— • — •	P	• — — •	2	• • — — —
D	— • •	Q	— — • —	3	• • • — —
E	•	R	• — •	4	• • • • —
F	• • — •	S	• • •	5	• • • • •
G	— — •	T	—	6	— • • • •
H	• • • •	U	• • —	7	— — • • •
I	• •	V	• • • —	8	— — — • •
J	• — — —	W	• — —	9	— — — — •
K	— • —	X	— • • —	Period	• — • — • —
L	• — • •	Y	— • — —	Comma	— • • —
M	— —	Z	— — • •		

Questions to Ponder

❏ Can you "knock" to the student sitting next to you what your favorite color or food is?

❏ What do you think Morse meant by his message, "What hath God wrought?"

Susan LaFlesche Picotte

(1865–1915)

Susan LaFlesche Picotte had 1,244 patients. Some of Picotte's patients lived in tipis, some in earth lodges, and some in frame houses. The problem was that Picotte's patients were spread all over the Omaha Indian Reservation. Every patient had to be reached by horseback; and if there was a road, it was usually so rugged that it was as if it was not a road at all. Picotte would ride to her patients, with her supplies packed into saddle bags, even in the coldest prairie winters. Despite all the layers of clothing that she wore, often by the time she reached patient's homes she was half frozen. Thawing herself by the patient's tiny cookstoves was extremely painful, but there was never a blizzard that kept Picotte from attending to the ill. Picotte was the only doctor for her people, and she was determined to do all that she could for them.

For all of us, the world changes greatly during our lives. New inventions change how we do things. Think of how often today we use a computer and the Internet, whereas just a few years ago this was not possible! But for Picotte and her people, the Omaha Native Americans, the changes in their lives that were being forced upon them were much more sudden and with wider impact than ones caused by new inventions. Before, the Omaha's society and economy focused on the buffalo. There were millions of buffalo on the Great Plains, and the buffalo provided the Omaha with food and skins to make shelter and clothes. However, with the slaughtering of the buffalo by men greedy for the quick profit and with settlers wanting land to farm, the Omahas were unable to live as they used to. Forced onto reservations, the Omaha's lives could never be the same.

Picotte's father was an Omaha chief. He knew that if his people were going to survive, they would have to learn new ways. He encouraged Susan and all of his children to go to school and learn everything that they could. He wanted them to be a bridge between the old and new ways.

Picotte won a scholarship to medical school at a time when few women went to medical school. She was the only Native American in her class. She would not allow herself to give up, for she kept remembering how the non-Native American doctor who was supposed to take care of her people did not seem to care about them. When Picotte became a doctor, she tried to help all sick people, regardless of race or color. Picotte had many non-Native American patients. Indeed, her doctoring skills were so great that people came from all over to be helped by her.

Picotte worked hard for many years to raise enough money for a hospital. Finally, in 1913, with the support of both Native Americans and non-Native Americans, enough money was raised so that a hospital that would serve all people, regardless of ethnicity, could be built. Today, the Dr. Susan Picotte Memorial Hospital is on the National Register of Historic Places.

Questions to Ponder

❏ Picotte was born on the Omaha Reservation in Nebraska. What is Nebraska's capital? Can you name a state that borders Nebraska? (*Lincoln is the capital. Nebraska is bordered by Iowa, Missouri, Wyoming, South Dakota, Colorado, and Kansas.*)

❏ How are some things different for you now than they were for your parents when they were your age? How about changes in the medical field?

❏ Have you ever been so cold that it hurts when you begin to warm up?

Archimedes
(287 B.C.–212 B.C.)

The Case of the Dishonest Goldsmith: King Hieron once gave a certain amount of gold to a goldsmith with the instructions that he was to make it into a crown. But when the goldsmith brought the crown to him, King Hieron suspected that the man had kept some of the gold for himself and had substituted silver in its place! The king weighed the crown, but its weight equaled that of the gold. How could the king make sure that he was not cheated?

The king asked Archimedes for help. The story goes that Archimedes pondered the problem for a while and then took a bath. As he stepped into the bathtub, he noticed that the water level rose and his body felt lighter. He realized that the density of an object can be measured by determining how much water it displaces. In other words, if Archimedes took equal weights of gold and silver and weighed them in water, they would no longer appear equal: the silver has a greater density, and so it displaces more water. All the king had to do was see if his gold crown displaced as much water as the amount of gold he gave to the goldsmith should. Leaping out of the bathtub, Archimedes ran to the palace shouting, "Eureka! Eureka!"

Archimedes was an amazing mathematician and inventor. Without the use of a calculator or a computer, Archimedes proved that pi (the ratio of the circumference of a circle to its diameter) was between 3 1/7 and 3 10/71. Archimedes even helped protect his home from being conquered by the Romans with his invention of the "scorpion," small catapults which kept the Roman army under a stinging shower of rock. Some historians claim that Archimedes designed a giant mirror. The mirror was in the form a hexagon, and it was surrounded by polygons. The mirror reflected the sun's rays so that they would focus on the invading ships and set them on fire!

Archimedes was also an engineer. He figured out how to move things with levers and fulcrums. Fulcrums are the support about which a lever turns. It has been said that when Archimedes realized what his giant levers could do, even when operated by one man, he cried, "Give me the place to stand and a lever long enough, and I will move the Earth!"

Questions to Ponder

❏ Archimedes was born in Syracuse, a Greek Colony. Can you find the country of Greece on the map?

❏ What is the capital of Greece? (*Athens is the capital of Greece.*)

❏ Eureka means, "I have found it!" When have you had cause to yell, "Eureka!"?

❏ Archimedes was born in 287 B.C. How old would he be if he were alive today? (*To get the answer, add 287 to the present year.*)

❏ The powerful mirror that Archimedes designed was in the form of a hexagon. How many sides does a hexagon have? How about a polygon? (*A hexagon has six sides. A hexagon is a polygon. A polygon is an object with many sides. Poly means "many," and gon means "side."*)

Eugenie Clark

(1922–)

Eugenie Clark was working at her marine laboratory when she happened to look out the window. To her shock and horror, she saw a little boy about four years old sitting on the wooden feeding platform of the shark pen and dangling his feet in the water! Sharks, by the way, are attracted to thrashing movements! Clark ran out of her lab as fast as she could to the shark pool and pulled the child to safety. She found the parents outside wandering around, paying no attention to all of the signs that clearly stated "DANGER—SHARKS." When confronted, the parents told Clark that, yes, they had seen the signs, but the pool looked empty to them. The boy was incredibly lucky, because swimming in the pool right then was an enormous shark.

Clark had wanted to be an ichthyologist ever since her mother dropped her off at an aquarium when she was only nine years old. (An ichthyologist studies fish.) Clark's mother had to work, and Clark's grandmother was too ill to take care of her.

When Clark was in college, she had to dissect animals. She had to learn all their body parts and how they were put together. When a friendly pet-shop owner offered Clark a monkey that had died, Clark could not say no. Extra practice, Clark figured. She took it home and put it in the refrigerator. When her unsuspecting grandmother opened up the refrigerator and found a dead monkey staring at her, she ran out of the kitchen screaming! Another time, Clark was offered a big rat that the grocer had killed. The grocer wrapped it up for her, and she skinned it at home and then put it in one of her grandmother's cooking pots: she needed to boil it down so that she could get its skeleton. Her grandmother came home and then said, "Genie, darling, what are you cooking?" as she lifted up the lid.

Even though Clark was never again allowed to cook in her grandmother's kitchen, she did earn a doctorate in ichthyology. She studied fish and sharks all over the world and has worked on the mystery of the "sleeping sharks." Scientists thought that sharks had to keep moving to keep water—which holds the oxygen that the sharks needed—flowing over their gills to stay alive. Yet, Clark has swum in hidden caves among colossal, streamlined giants that, even when poked, would just settle back to their sleeplike state again. When the sharks were in this state, Clark saw tiny remora fish going in and out of the gill openings of the sharks. The remora were nibbling off the parasites that clung to the sharks' bodies.

Questions to Ponder

❑ Clark had her own lab in western Florida. What is the capital of Florida, and what body of water touches western Florida? (*Tallahassee; the Gulf of Mexico*)

❑ When Clark was invited to visit the crown prince of Japan, she gave him a trained shark. What is the capital of Japan? Does the Pacific, Indian, or Atlantic Ocean border Japan? (*Tokyo is the capital of Japan. The Pacific Ocean borders Japan.*)

❑ Clark discovered a fish that emits a milky fluid that makes sharks avoid it. Why do you think businesses (as well as scientists) are interested in this fish? (*Think of the profit one can make off of a shark repellant!*)

❑ What is the largest organ in a shark's body? (*The liver—it can be 25% of a shark's weight. The liver of a basking shark can weigh over 1800 pounds and contain 600 gallons of oil! Shark liver oil is a good source of vitamin A.*)

Diego Rivera

(1886–1957)

Someone tells you to paint a picture. "All right," you think, "No problem. I can fill the canvas pretty easily." But what if the picture you are asked to paint is three stories high, two city blocks long, and one block wide? In other words, a total of 17,000 square feet (1,579 square meters)! Enough to fill the entire courtyard of the Ministry of Public Education in Mexico City!

When Diego Rivera, one of modern Mexico's foremost painters, was asked, he did not waver for a minute. Incorporating Mexican life, history, and social problems into his pictures, Rivera planned 124 frescoes. A fresco is a painting that is painted on freshly spread plaster. Special watercolors are used. Thus, Rivera did not only have to plan ahead and sketch what he was going to paint, but he also had to plan ahead for his plaster and watercolors.

The plaster Rivera used had to have a certain amount of lime. It was heated up over a wood fire, processed for three months, and then shipped in rubber bags that would keep out any moisture to where Rivera was painting his mural. Rivera's aides would apply all but the final layer of plaster. Then, with a sharp tool, they would dig the outlines of Rivera's full-size sketches into the plaster. Next, late at night, a final thin coat of lime mixed with marble dust would be spread over the outline. As soon as this layer was firm—but not dry—Rivera would start to paint.

Every morning, his paints had to be freshly mixed, the pigments ground by hand and mixed on a slab of marble. Only when Rivera deemed them perfect would he climb on a ladder and start brushing them on the wall. Rivera would paint as long as there was daylight. He could not paint under artificial light because it would alter the appearance of the colors. There were some days when, after climbing down from the scaffolds where he had perched all day long, Rivera would say that what he had painted that day was not good enough, and he would insist that all the plaster be scraped off so that he could start again! It took Rivera years to finish, but this particular mural is considered one of the greatest in the world today.

Throughout his life, Rivera painted many murals and smaller paintings. He also created controversy with many of his paintings. For example, in one mural, painted for John. D. Rockefeller in his RCA building in New York City, he painted V. I. Lenin, a communist leader of Russia. Despite protests from artists, this mural was destroyed.

Questions to Ponder

❏ Rivera was born in Guanajuato, Mexico. What is the capital of Mexico? (*Mexico City*)

❏ Mexico is in Central America. There are eight countries that make up Central America. Can you name four of them, not including Mexico? (*The other seven countries are Guatemala, Belize, El Salvador, Honduras, Nicaragua, Costa Rica, and Panama.*)

❏ Can you answer at least two out of three: what gulf, what sea, and what ocean border Central America? (*Gulf of Mexico, Pacific Ocean, and Caribbean Sea*)

❏ Rivera spent time studying and painting in France and Spain, but he wanted to go to the country that in all the world had the richest fresco treasures. What country is that? (*Italy. Raphael's and Michelangelo's frescoes were there, as were frescoes that decorated the burial vaults in the ancient catacombs.*)

❏ How many of your classroom walls would it take to total 17,000 square feet?

Thomas Alva Edison

(1847–1931)

Listen to this list of inventions: telegraph repeater, printer for stock ticker and telegraph, perforator for automatic telegraph, mimeograph, electric pen, loudspeaking telephone, phonograph, carbon-button telephone transmitter, tasimeter, incandescent lamp, electric generator, electric locomotive, ore separator, cement works, electric distributing system, kinetoscope (motion picture camera), microphone, and alkaline storage battery.

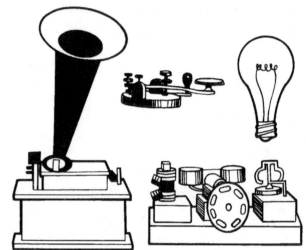

Can you tie these inventions to a boy who was not a good student? Edison's teacher called him "addled." Edison said years later, "My father thought I was stupid, and I almost decided I must be a dunce."

Edison did get in trouble a lot. When he was six, he set fire to his father's barn just "to see what it would do." (His father whipped him publicly in the village square as punishment.) He once wired together the tails of two cats and rubbed their fur in an experiment he thought up about static electricity. Needless to say, the result was angry cats, a scratched-up Edison, and science not advanced! He got fired from a telegraph job because in the middle of taking messages, he would tell the operator on the other end to wait while he then jotted down some notes about an invention he was working on!

Yet, once Edison focused on his interests, he could not be stopped. His workshops, large buildings with equipment and many men to help, became the forerunners of the modern industrial research laboratory. Rather than a lone inventor, teams of workers systematically investigated a problem. Today, many companies have research labs, but Edison was the first.

Questions to Ponder

❑ Edison was born in Ohio. Can you name the capital of Ohio, and can you name the Great Lake that borders Ohio? (*Columbus; Lake Erie*) Did you need to use a map?

❑ How many silent movies have you seen in your life?

❑ What is the longest you have gone without using an electric light?

❑ Edison originated the proverb, "Genius is one percent inspiration and ninety-nine percent perspiration." What did he mean?

❑ In cartoons and in comic books, if someone thinks up a great idea, a light bulb is often shown above his or her head. Why?

❑ Should someone's intelligence be judged solely on his or her school grades?

❑ Edison's teacher called him addled. What does *addled* mean? (*When one is addled, one is confused and his or her thinking is muddled.*)

Amelia Earhart

(1897–1937)

Amelia Earhart was the first woman to pilot an airplane across the Atlantic Ocean. The flight took her 15 hours and 18 minutes. During this flight, the altimeter (the instrument that records height above the ground) broke. There wasn't any moonlight by which she could see because the moon was behind clouds. Because of the fog, Amelia could not tell how far away she was from the ocean. She nosed her plane upwards until it began to lose speed. Ice was forming on her plane's wings! She put the plane into a spin, knowing that she had to reach warmer air. She dropped 3,000 feet (914 m) straight down until she saw the waves breaking on the surface of the water beneath her. She pulled up just in time.

As if not enough had already happened, Amelia saw flames coming through a broken weld in the engine's exhaust outlet. She knew that if the section separated, the plane would fall apart and Amelia would drown. Amelia figured that if she turned around though, trying to land with her heavy load of fuel would be incredibly dangerous: the plane would probably explode on impact. She decided, "I'd much rather prefer drowning to burning up."

Amelia landed in the middle of a cow pasture, "frightening all the cows in the country." When she climbed stiffly out of the plane, she saw a farmer who was gaping at her in disbelief.

"Hi. I've just come from America," she said.

"Have you now?" the farmer replied skeptically.

Amelia was a woman of firsts. She was the first woman to fly across the Atlantic (1928), the first woman to fly it alone (1932), and the first person to fly from Hawaii to California (1935). In 1937 Amelia set out with Frederick J. Noonan to fly around the world. The plane disappeared mysteriously between New Guinea and Howland Island. People have looked for Amelia's plane for years, and some people believe the parts of the wreckage have been found. Other people say that Amelia was a spy for the United States and that she was captured by the Japanese. Another rumor claims that Amelia lived in disguise on a South Pacific island.

What is most probably true is that Amelia ran out of fuel and crashed. One of her last messages, at 6:45 was, "Please take a bearing on us and report in half an hour. I will make a noise in microphone. About 100 miles out. Position doubtful." At 7:42 this message was transmitted: "We must be on you but cannot see you. But gas is running low. Have been unable to reach you by radio. We are flying at 1,000 feet." Her last message, at 8:43 on July 3, 1937, said, "We are on the line of position 157–337. We are running north and south."

Questions to Ponder

❑ Amelia was born in Kansas in 1897. Can you name the capital of Kansas? (*Topeka*)

❑ Is Nebraska to the north, east, south, or west of Kansas? (*Nebraska is to the north.*)

❑ Can you find New Guinea and Howland Island on the map?

❑ When people get covered in snow or are in a white out (a blizzard), they lose their bearings, too, as did Amelia when she crossed the Atlantic solo. Did you ever think about how important the horizon is to you? Have you ever not been able to tell up from down?

John James Audubon

(1785–1851)

John James Audubon loved practical jokes. One time Audubon was out riding with a visitor from Europe who was not yet familiar with the United States. Audubon wrote how they "spied a beautiful black and pale yellow animal with a bushy tail." The visitor commented that it was "a beautiful squirrel." Audubon agreed that it was and also told the visitor that it was the type that would let one approach it and hold it. The visitor then went close and hit the squirrel with a stick. The squirrel, as Audubon knew full well, was a skunk. The visitor got what he deserved: a smell that he could not rid himself of for days.

Audubon had been sent to the United States by his father to learn how to run a farm. Audubon was not good at running a farm or the store he managed later, but he did become America's finest painter of birds. He wanted his pictures to look like real birds, not like stuffed, stiff ones in unnatural poses. In order to make his paintings realistic, Audubon studied the anatomy of birds. He knew how they were put together and exactly how their feathers were attached. When he was finally ready to paint a particular bird, he would shoot it and then quickly clean it. Next, he would wire it into a position he had chosen. Pinning it against a sheet of graph paper, he would get everything in scale. His measurements were accurate because he used compasses and calipers. He was meticulous about getting the colors exactly right. The results were extraordinary. Today, his paintings are in museums and books all over the world.

Audubon loved his frontier adventures. Once Audubon was out riding his horse when the great earthquake of 1811–12 struck the Midwest. For months the earth shook in a series of tremors and aftershocks. The Mississippi even ran backwards for a short while as riverbanks caved in and islands disappeared. Audubon wrote in his journal that he expected "the ground to open up and reveal an abyss to engulf me." He wasn't swallowed, but his horse did run off without him!

Questions to Ponder

❏ Audubon was born in Haiti. In what ocean does Haiti rest, and what is Haiti's capital? (*Both Haiti and the Dominican Republic share the island of Hispaniola, which is bordered by the Atlantic Ocean and the Caribbean Sea. Its capital is Port-au-Prince.*)

❏ After his mother died, Audubon was brought by his father to France. What is the capital of France, and does France border the Caribbean Sea or the Atlantic? (*Paris is the capital of France. The Atlantic Ocean borders France.*)

❏ Audubon was ambidextrous. What does ambidextrous mean? (*When one is ambidextrous, one can use both hands equally well. Part of the reason Audubon could draw so fast and efficiently was that he could draw with both hands at once. Try it!*)

❏ Audubon was witness to the migratory flight of the passenger pigeon. For three days, the birds passed overhead in almost-solid flocks. Audubon wrote, "The air was literally filled with pigeons; the light of the noon-day was obstructed as by an eclipse." Why haven't you seen the passenger pigeons? (*They are extinct. They were slaughtered by the million yearly and sold in city markets. The last one died on Septmeber 1, 1914, in the Cincinnati Zoo. Just think, there were so many, they used to darken the sky!*)

Ray Charles

(1930–)

At the age of 14, Ray Charles learned how to ride a motorcycle. Once, while he was racing up and down streets and hills, some strangers reported Charles to the authorities. They reported Charles, not because of his age or his lack of a license, but because they did not believe that he was blind! If he couldn't see, why wasn't he crashing? Since Charles received state money to attend a school for the blind, he had to undergo an eye exam to prove that he was unable to see. After it was confirmed that Charles was indeed blind, he immediately climbed right back on his motorcycle and raced away. How did Charles do it? He would ride directly behind a friend or close beside a friend on another motorcycle. Just the sound of the other motorcycle's exhaust was enough to guide Charles.

Charles had lost his sight at the age of six due to glaucoma, a disease of the eye that, if detected early enough today, can be treated with drugs. From the very beginning, Charles' mother knew that she had to raise her son to take care of himself. Once, when she told him that he needed to chop wood, two neighbors scolded her. They asked his mother how she could be so cruel to a blind boy. She replied, "He's blind, but he ain't stupid. He's lost his sight, but he ain't lost his mind."

Charles's mother sent him to the state school for the blind. Charles thought it particularly strange that he and other African-American students stayed in one part of the school while white children stayed in another. After all, they could not see each other!

Despite being on his own from the age of 15 after his mother died, Charles always knew that he wanted music to be part of his life. His mother taught him determination and not to be afraid. He wasn't. Wanting to leave Florida to strike off on his own, he had a friend read off names of big cities on a map. He chose Seattle because Seattle was eight inches away, while New York City was only five and Los Angeles was seven. After his long bus ride, Charles found a job singing and playing music—before he even ate his first meal! Charles had talked his way into a club even though he was underage. He entered a singing contest. The applause was loud, and over the years it has continued to be. Charles has received countless awards, performed all over the world, acted in movies and commercials, and was also one of the original inductees into the Rock 'n' Roll Hall of Fame.

Questions to Ponder

❏ Charles was born Florida. What is the capital of Florida, and can you name Florida's two neighboring states? (*Tallahassee; Georgia and Alabama*)

❏ When Charles first attended school at the age of seven, he was horribly homesick. Yet when the time came, Charles was the only child to remain at the school. His mother did not have any money, and no one had told Charles that families had to provide travel costs. How would you feel if you were expecting to go home and then couldn't?

❏ Charles once said, "Most people take their ears for granted. I can't. My eyes are my handicap, but my ears are my opportunity." What did he mean by this? Do you take your ears for granted?

❏ After one audition, Charles was told that he was not good enough. After hearing this, he went back to room and cried all day. Then he continued to sing. Why do some people quit before others? Is the road to success always easy?

Vincent van Gogh

(1853–1890)

Vincent van Gogh is considered today to be one of the greatest artists of all time. His paintings are auctioned off for millions, and museums have to guard heavily against theft. Yet, van Gogh's life was a troubled one. Throughout his entire life, he sold only one painting (and that was purchased by his brother). At one point, in a fit of mental imbalance and depression after threatening his friend Gauguin, another painter, van Gogh went home and cut off part of his own ear.

Van Gogh knew that there was something wrong with him. He was stricken by epileptoid seizures, suffered from hallucinations, and would hear strange voices. Van Gogh had himself admitted to an asylum in the hope of gaining back his mental stability. The asylum was in Arles, and it provided a studio. Van Gogh was also able to go outdoors and paint the orchards and wheat fields surrounding the asylum.

The majority of van Gogh's work was produced in just 29 months of frenzied activity. Van Gogh worked with such intensity and speed that he often produced one painting a day. Sometimes he even put the paint directly on the canvas from the tube. Van Gogh wrote to his brother, "I am working like mad and feel a blind rage to work more than ever. And I believe that this will contribute to my recovery."

Unfortunately, van Gogh never did recover. He shot himself while in the hayfields he was painting. Some of the most poignant or touching words that van Gogh every wrote were, "I have walked this earth for thirty years and out of gratitude I want to leave a token of remembrance in the form of drawings or paintings—not made to please a certain taste in art, but to express a genuine human emotion."

There is no doubt today that van Gogh succeeded in expressing human emotion in his paintings. How sad that he did not realize while he was alive that he had accomplished what he had set out to do.

Questions to Ponder

❑ Vincent van Gogh was born in the Netherlands. For what flower is the Netherlands known? (*The tulip—the Netherlands exports a large number of bulbs.*)

❑ Two of van Gogh's most famous paintings are *Starry Night* and *Sunflowers*. Have you ever seen a copy of either of them?

❑ What can we do today to help people who are mentally ill? (*First, we recognize the symptoms. We know that people are not acting crazy simply for attention. Doctors and social workers then work hard to find the correct medicine and placement for treatment and therapy. Even today, scientists are finding more and more how chemical imbalances in the brain affect our mental state. Drug companies are working hard to develop drugs for controlling depression, seizures, and hallucinations.*)

❑ Van Gogh studied art in Brussels for awhile. Is Brussels the capital of Italy or Belguim? (*Brussels is the capital of Belgium. Rome is the capital of Italy.*)

❑ Van Gogh was at times so poor that he would go hungry so that he could buy paint supplies. Is there anything you are so passionate about that you would trade food for it?

Polly Bemis (Lalu Nathoy)

(1853–1933)

When Lalu Nathoy was a young girl in China, if a girl wanted to be attractive and have a good chance at getting married, her feet had to be bound. Strips of cloth would be wound so tightly around a child's foot that the bones would crush. Some grown women had feet no longer than three inches (7.6 cm).

Rather than being bound, Lalu begged her parents to let her help in the fields. Lalu worked hard in the fields for five years. Still, the famine continued. Marauding bandits started stealing whatever they could, and Lalu's father was told that unless he traded Lalu, he and the rest of his family would be killed. Lalu was stolen from her home for two bags of soybeans. Lalu never saw or communicated with her family again.

The bandits sold Lalu some years later to a man in Shanghai. This man then resold her to a special buyer in America. At the age of 19, Lalu was sent to San Francisco, California. To reach there, she had spent weeks in the sweltering heat of a hold of a cargo ship. It was filthy and filled with human vomit and waste.

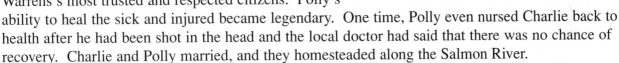

At the Chinatown marketplace in San Francisco, Lalu was auctioned off to the highest bidder. She was sold to a man who lived in the mining town of Warrens, Idaho. This man changed Lalu's name to Polly. The man cheated and abused Polly, but when this man lost Polly in a poker game to Charlie Bemis, Polly's life took a new turn. Polly opened up a boarding home, and she became one of Warrens's most trusted and respected citizens. Polly's ability to heal the sick and injured became legendary. One time, Polly even nursed Charlie back to health after he had been shot in the head and the local doctor had said that there was no chance of recovery. Charlie and Polly married, and they homesteaded along the Salmon River.

Polly suffered horribly throughout most of her life. She was abused and taken from her family. Though her name could be taken and changed, nothing could take away Polly's spirit or her kindness. When Polly died in 1933, the entire town of Warrens turned out to honor her. They remembered her as the woman who had the rare power of making them all feel happy.

Questions to Ponder

❏ Polly lived the last years of her life in Idaho. What is the capital of Idaho? (*Boise is the capital of Idaho.*)

❏ Does Idaho border a foreign country? If so, which one? (*Yes, the northern part of Idaho borders Canada.*)

❏ What do both girls and boys do to their bodies today to make themselves more attractive? Should some of these things, like feet binding, be stopped?

❏ Marauding bandits rode into Lalu's village and stole her. What does *marauding* mean? (*Maraud means "to roam about and raid in search of plunder."*)

Isaac Newton

(1642–1727)

Isaac Newton once figured out a way to build a kite with an enclosed lantern. He mischievously flew it in secret at night over the village fields. He laughed when he heard people talking of ghosts hovering in the sky. Newton also invented a small mill that mechanically ground wheat into flour. The mill was run by a mouse that Newton harnessed to it! This same man, it has been said, cut two holes into his door, one for his cat and the other for her kitten. It has also been said that Newton was once leading his horse up a steep hill, and it wasn't until he reached the top that he realized that the animal had wandered off and that he had been dragging up an empty bridle!

There are lots of fun stories about what Newton was like and what he did, but what is undisputed is that Isaac Newton was a mathematical genius and an amazing scientist. He invented calculus, discovered that white light is composed of every light in the spectrum, and showed how his principle of universal gravitation explained both the motions of heavenly bodies and the falling bodies on Earth. Every time an apple falls to the earth, think gravity! Newton's book *Mathematical Principles of Natural Philosophy* is a masterpiece. He also wrote *The Universal Arithmetic*. Newton built the first reflecting telescope.

Questions to Ponder

❏ Newton was born in England. What is the capital of England, and is England on the continent of Europe? (*London is the capital of England. England is an island off the continent of Europe.*)

❏ Newton once said, "If I have seen a little farther than others, it is because I have stood on the shoulders of giants." What did Newton mean? Was Newton being modest or conceited?

❏ Newton formulated three laws of motion. The third law is, "To every action there is an equal and opposite reaction." This law is essential to the understanding of rocket power and jet propulsion. Can you apply it to your own life?

❏ In 1664, the Great Plague struck England. As the disease swept the country, the university closed down. Newton was sent home for two years. Newton used this time to study and invent. Some of his greatest work was done during this time. If you were forced to go back home and spend two years without school, what would you do?

❏ The Great Plague spread due to appalling sanitary conditions. Why? (*Appalling sanitary conditions means that everything was disgustingly filthy. The disease responsible for the Great Plague was spread by fleas that had bitten infected rats. We have hot running water in our schools and in our homes. How does that keep rats and fleas away? What else do we do to stop infections from spreading?*)

Martin Luther King Jr.

(1929–1969)

In 1963, at a large rally in Washington, D.C., Martin Luther King Jr. gave a powerful speech about a dream he had. Part of the speech goes like this:

> *I have a dream that one day on the red hills of Georgia, the sons of former slaves and the sons of former slaveowners will be able to sit down together at the table of brotherhood. I have a dream that my four little children will one day live in a nation where they will not be judged by the color of their skin, but by the content of their character.*

King was born in Atlanta, Georgia, at a time when white children and black children had to go to separate schools. Black people were forced to use separate drinking fountains, bathrooms, and could not sit at the front of the bus. The color of one's skin determined where one could eat, if one could use a library, and where one could find lodging.

King went to Morehouse College in Atlanta. Morehouse College is an all black college known for its high academic standards. King decided to become a minister, and he read many books and studied very hard. King learned about a man named Gandhi who had led his country of India to independence with a method of protest he called passive resistance. Passive resistance is standing up for rights without using violence.

When Rosa Parks was arrested for refusing to give up her seat to a white man on the bus, King was contacted. He organized a successful bus boycott. For over a year, people walked or shared rides. The buses remained nearly empty; the bus companies lost a lot of money; and finally, a change occurred. The right to ride the buses and sit anywhere, regardless of color, was won using non-violent means.

Many people were angry and frightened by King's organizing the bus boycott. They were afraid of how the world might become more equal. One night an explosion tore through King's house. Fortunately, no one was hurt, and King was not deterred in the slightest. He said, "Remember that, if anything happens to me, there will be others to take my place."

King continued to work for the betterment of all people. He worked hard to make it so that every American, regardless of color, could register to vote. King was awarded the Nobel Peace Prize in 1964. Then tragedy struck. While King was in Memphis, Tennessee, planning a march for anti-poverty legislation, he was shot and killed. Yet, dreams, and especially good dreams, cannot be killed that easily. Today people are working hard to make sure that King's dream comes true.

Questions to Ponder

- ❏ What national holiday is celebrated on January 15th? (*Martin Luther King Jr. Day*)
- ❏ King was born in Atlanta, Georgia. Is Atlanta the capital of Georgia? (*Yes*)
- ❏ Was Georgia one of the original 13 colonies? (*Yes, Georgia was the 4th of the original 13 states to ratify the Constitution.*)
- ❏ Which American president was born in Georgia? (*Jimmy Carter*)
- ❏ Does it make sense to call King a peaceful warrior? Can you think of other oxymorons? (*bittersweet, jumbo shrimp, good grief, taped live, etc.*)

Marie Curie

(1867–1934)

Marie Curie's hands were stiff, cracked, and covered with ulcers. Suffering from ill health, she always looked tired, and her entire body ached. Yet, she never stopped working. It was only during her last years that she realized that her work was what made her ill.

Marie Curie is one of the most famous scientists of all times. She was the first person to win a second Nobel Prize. Once a year, Nobel Prizes are awarded in several categories. In 1903, Marie shared the Nobel Prize in Physics with her husband, Pierre, and with another scientist (Antoine Henri Becquerel) for their work on radioactivity. Radioactivity is the property of spontaneously emitting particles or rays found in some elements (for example, uranium). It is caused by the disintegration of the nuclei of atoms. In 1911, she received the Nobel Prize in Chemistry for her discovery of polonium and radium.

Polonium and radium are radioactive! Today, we know the dangers of radioactive materials, and there are international laws about the use of radioactive materials and how to dispose of them. People working with these materials today have to have special clearance and permission. They wear suits that cover their bodies completely, and they breathe through special filters or tanks. If there is a radioactive spill, the spill is monitored carefully, and humans are not allowed to live where the readings are high or consume any food produced in the area, animal or plant. An international warning symbol has been created that is used worldwide.

Yet, when Curie was working to isolate these elements, she used her bare hands! She and her husband kept some radioactive substances that glowed with unearthly light in glass bottles to show to people. Her husband even carried some of this material in a small glass tube in his pocket so that at social gatherings he could pull it out as a party trick! Is it any wonder that when the Curies were awarded the Nobel Prize in Physics that they did not feel well enough to attend the awards ceremony in Sweden?

For many years after Curie's death, her notebooks and the chair that she sat in while she worked in the lab were highly radioactive.

Questions to Ponder

❏ Curie was born in Warsaw, Poland. What is the capital of Poland, and does Poland border the Baltic Sea or the Mediterranean Sea? (*Warsaw is the capital of Poland. Poland borders the Baltic Sea.*)

❏ Curie worked as a governess for several years to help with family finances. What is a governess? (*A governess is a woman who moves in with another family and takes care of their children, like nannies today—but a governess is also responsible for teaching the children.*)

❏ Curie went to study at the University of Paris because it allowed women. In what country is Paris? (*Paris is the capital of France.*)

❏ There is an old saying: "Ignorance is bliss." How does this saying relate to Curie and her work? Was the end result really bliss?

Frederick Banting

(1891–1941)

Thirteen-year-old Leonard Thomson was bedridden and weighed a mere 65 pounds (29.5 kg). Despite his weight, doctors were keeping Thomson to a daily diet of only 450 calories. Why? Thomson had diabetes. Diabetes is not a contagious disease, but before the discovery of insulin, doctors had no way to control it except through starvation.

Diabetes occurs when something goes wrong with the pancreas, one of our body's organs. The pancreas makes insulin, a substance our bodies need in order to change the food we eat into energy. When the pancreas does not make insulin, our bodies cannot burn the sugar contained in the foods we eat and change it into energy. Consequently, large amounts of sugar build up in our blood. When the sugar levels get too high, death occurs.

When Banting was only 14, he was devastated when he witnessed a good friend die from diabetes. His friend went from being able to outdistance him in a swimming race to becoming so weak that she could not go to school. After she died, Banting decided that he was going to find a cure for diabetes.

The first practice Banting tried to start was not a success, but Banting did have some ideas about the cure for diabetes that he wanted to try out. Banting went to see Dr. Macleod, an expert on diabetes research. Though skeptical of Banting, Macleod granted him the use of his lab while he was on vacation and provided him with a lab assistant named Best, one of Macleod's best students. Banting was not paid, but Macleod allowed Banting to continue using his lab because of Banting's progress.

On January 11, 1922, Banting was ready to try out his insulin on people. Leonard Thompson, the thirteen-year-old child too weak to do anything except lie in bed, was the first person in the world to receive insulin injections. After just a few weeks, Leonard left the hospital! Having to receive daily injections of insulin was a small price to pay for a normal life!

When Banting tried out his insulin on diabetics at the Veterans Hospital in Toronto, men who had been too ill to move were suddenly restored to health. A public announcement was made in November 1921, and diabetics from all around the world began to arrive at Banting's doorstep. Although they could have made a fortune, Banting and Best turned over all the profits to the University of Toronto for medical research. They felt that medical discoveries belonged to the whole world.

Questions to Ponder

❑ Banting was born in Alliston, Ontario, Canada. What is the capital of the province of Ontario? Is it the same as Canada's capital? (*Ontario's provincial capital is Ontario. The national capital is Ottawa.*)

❑ Banting, along with Macleod, was awarded the Nobel Prize in Medicine for the discovery of insulin. Banting was upset: he felt that Best, his lab assistant, had been crucial to his success. Banting was not going to accept the prize, but he was told, "The honor is for Canada. If you turn it down, you will hurt your country." Banting publicly announced that he would be dividing his prize money with Best. Are prizes sometimes unfair? How would you make them fair?

❑ Do you think medical discoveries belong to the entire world? What if the research was funded by private companies? Do you think private companies would research the problem if they could not make a profit? (These are difficult questions.)

Ludwig van Beethoven

(1770–1827)

If you were deaf, would you be able to compose music? Ludwig van Beethoven is considered to be one of the greatest composers who ever lived. But Beethoven began to go deaf in 1801, and by 1817 he was completely deaf. When one of Beethoven's last compositions, the Ninth Choral Symphony, was performed (with solo singers, a large chorus, and a large orchestra), Beethoven went and followed along with written pages of music. When the performance ended, one of the singers had to tug on his sleeve to get him to stand up. It was only when he turned to the audience that he "saw" the thunderous applause.

Beethoven, it seemed, had always been able to hear music in his head. Once, when he was eight years old, Beethoven brought in a piece that he had composed for the organ. His teacher told him, "You cannot play that piece. Your feet cannot reach the pedals and your hands cannot stretch to play all those notes."

Beethoven simply answered, "But, I will play it when I am bigger."

Losing his hearing was agony for Beethoven. He was embarrassed and depressed. He wrote to a brother about how humiliating it was to stand next to someone who could hear a flute while he heard nothing. He wrote, "Such incidents drove me almost to despair; a little more of that and I would have ended my life—it was only my art that held me back. Ah, it seemed to me impossible to leave the world until I had brought forth all that I felt was within me." Beethoven's father started teaching him when Ludwig was only five years old. There is documentation that Beethoven's father was not an easy teacher. One person remembered Beethoven as "standing in front of the clavier and weeping." Another person wrote, "Beethoven's father used violence when it came to making him start his musical studies." "He treated him harshly," said another, "and sometimes shut him up in the cellar." Beethoven's father used him, even at the age of six, to earn money: he would charge people to hear his son play.

For those of you who have difficulty with mathematics, take heart! Mathematics was Beethoven's most difficult subject at school, and he never learned to do arithmetic other than simple addition and subtraction. When Beethoven was in his 50s, his nephew tried to teach Beethoven his multiplication tables, but he did not succeed. Also, Beethoven was not a good writer. He misspelled words, and his handwriting was almost illegible. Beethoven said, "I often compose the answer in my mind, but when I wish to write it down, I usually throw the pen away because I cannot write as I feel." Yet Beethoven could speak Latin, French, and Italian, besides his native German. Beethoven had a passion for reading, too, and he could understand poetry.

Questions to Ponder

❏ Beethoven was born in Bonn. In what country is the city of Bonn? (*Germany*)

❏ Beethoven went to Vienna and studied briefly with Mozart. In what country is Vienna, and can you find it on the map? (*Vienna is the capital of Austria.*)

❏ Beethoven also studied for a short time with Haydn. Haydn wanted Beethoven to write "pupil of Haydn" on the title page of all of Beethoven's compositions. Beethoven refused. Should Beethoven have written "pupil of Haydn" on all of his compositions?

❏ How many of you have heard Beethoven's *Ode to Joy*?

Bessie Coleman

(1892–1926)

Bessie Coleman learned to fly in a plane that did not have a steering wheel or brakes. Made of wood, wire, aluminum, cloth, and pressed cardboard, it was 27 feet (8.2 m) long and had wings that spanned 40 feet. The plane was controlled by a stick in front of the pilot and a rudder bar under the pilot's feet. The braking system was nothing but a metal tail on the back of that plane, which dug into the earth after the tail was lowered.

Could you learn your lessons as well if you could not hear your teacher? Coleman learned in a biplane, meaning that there was room for two pilots, one behind the other, and each pilot had his or her own stick and rudder. The controls for each pilot could not be used together, though either one of them could be used to steer the plane. The pilots flew in open cockpits. There was little protection from the elements. Because of the propellers making so much noise and the wind howling so ferociously, Coleman often could not hear a word of what her instructor, sitting in the front seat, was saying. Coleman would simply hold her steering mechanisms and feel what the teacher was doing with them. Whenever she did this, she was always careful not to hold them so tightly that she interfered with her instructor's actions. Coleman knew too well what happened to students who had "frozen" at the controls, and she had even witnessed the death of a fellow student during her training.

When Coleman received her license on June 15, 1921, she was the first woman of African American and Native American descent to do so. She had taught herself French and had crossed an ocean for her lessons. She had not allowed her dreams to die when people in the United States refused to teach her. Though she had little education, her school attendance cut short by her hours in the cotton fields and laboring at home, she refused to let it hold her back.

When Coleman flew in air shows, people came from all over to watch. At one air show, when Coleman found out that African Americans would not be admitted, she refused to fly until they were allowed in.

Coleman died performing. The plane in which she was riding as a passenger went into a tailspin and flipped over at 500 feet (152.4 m). Coleman was not wearing her seatbelt (it would have prevented her from leaning over to study the ground) and she fell out. Investigation of the plane showed that a wrench that had been left on the floor of the plane had slid into the gears and jammed them. A newer plane would have had protective covering for its gears. Thousands of people came to pay their respects to the woman who had refused to say no to her dreams.

Questions to Ponder

❑ Coleman was born in Atlanta, Texas. Of which state is Atlanta the capital? What is the capital of Texas? (*Atlanta is the capital of Georgia. Austin is the capital of Texas.*)

❑ When Coleman applied for her passport, she lied about her age. She said that she was 24, not 28. Coleman frequently lied about her age. At that time, women were supposed to be married by the age of 20 and considered middle-aged at 30. Coleman was late getting started with her career because of the obstacles she had to overcome. She did not want to be further hindered by her age. What does *hindered* mean, and should one's age or color hinder one? (*When one is hindered, one is held back.*)

Louis Braille

(1809–1852)

Louis Braille could see as well as anyone until he was three years old. Then, an accident changed his life. Braille's father made saddles and harnesses in a village about 25 miles (40.2 km) east of Paris, France. One day, Braille hoisted himself up onto his father's workbench and tried to punch a hole in the leather with an awl—the same way he had seen his father do many times before. An awl is a pointed tool that is used for marking surfaces or piercing small holes in wood or leather.

Somehow, the awl slipped, and Braille damaged his eye. The infection spread to the other eye. Because the antibiotics we use today did not yet exist, there was no known way to control the infection. Braille lost his sight in both eyes. What a daunting and difficult thing it would be to have to relearn the world, now as one who is blind. Braille still attended school with the other children, but he could learn only when the lessons were spoken. He could not read or write.

awl

Braille won a scholarship to a school for the blind in Paris. There the only books he could read were embossed books. Embossed books were made when large letters of the alphabet were pressed into waxed paper. Then, on the other side of the paper, the raised impressions could be read by tracing the outlines of the letters. Embossed books were not only hard to find, but they were very expensive and too big to be carried around—or even held comfortably on one's lap. Each page contained only a few sentences!

While Braille was a student, an Army captain named Barbier had invented a code that used raised dots. This way, even at night, the commanders in the field could read their orders. The problem was that this code was based on sounds. There was not a way to show punctuation or numbers, and many dots were needed to represent a single word. Many of the symbols were too big to be read with a single finger.

Braille took this system and invented what is now known as Braille—the universal system of writing and printing for the blind. Braille used a cluster of six dots, two across and three down. The cluster (or Braille cell, as it is known today) is just the right size to fit within the tip of a finger. Each letter of the alphabet is represented by a set pattern of raised and lowered dots (see page 81).

At first, no one wanted to use Braille's system. People who could see felt that it would be too difficult to learn another alphabet, and a large amount of money had already been spent on the embossed books. One director of the school banned the use of Braille, but all the students used it in secret.

When Braille's system was demonstrated to the government, a seeing person read from a book. A blind person copied down what was being said. Then a blind person who had left the room during the reading came back and read what had been taken down. When she read the text correctly, several of the ministers thought that it had been staged! They made the girl leave the room again, and this time one of the ministers had a ticket stub he had in his pocket read. When the girl came back into the room, she again read what had been printed in Braille correctly.

Louis Braille *(cont.)*
Louis Braille's Alphabet for the Blind

Each unit below is called a braille cell. Depending on how the arranged dots are raised in each cell determines the letter, number, punctuation symbols, and even some word endings. Below are the Braille cells for the letters A-Z and the number 0-9.

When these cells are actually imprinted, the size of the cell fits easily within the width of a fingertip. Notice how the first 10 cells represent both letters of the alphabet and Arabic numerals.

Questions to Ponder

❑ What would your name look like in Braille?

❑ Is Paris the capital of France? (*Yes, Paris is the capital of France.*)

❑ Could you study well if your books had only a few sentences per page?

Gail Borden

(1801–1874)

Gail Borden's wife and son died of yellow fever in Galveston, Texas. This was 60 years before Walter Reed discovered that mosquitoes carried the fever. Bereft and devastated, Borden could not stop thinking about the disease. He realized that it struck in summer, and that after the first frost, it abated. Borden decided that if he had a giant refrigerator, he could chill the deadly disease out of existence. Planning on using ether as a cooling agent, Borden wrote, "I mean to keep you for a week as if under a white frost. If we had the refrigerators ready, I could lock up every soul in a temporary winter." No one volunteered.

As crazy as Borden's solution was, it shows how Borden identified problems and tried to remedy them. The invention for which Borden is most famous is the process he developed for condensing milk. Borden used a vacuum pan with a heating coil inside that warmed the milk slowly and evenly. This allowed for gradual evaporation, and thus the milk was not burned or scalded. Burned milk tastes revolting!

Before there was condensed milk, if one wanted milk, one had to have a cow. (Remember, there were no refrigerators like there are today.) Borden got the idea for the condensed milk when he was returning from a trip to England in 1851. On that trip, he saw children die because there was not enough milk from the shipboard cows.

Borden also pioneered sanitary handling of milk. If farmers wanted to sell him milk, they had to wash the cow's udders before milking, sweep the barns clean, spread manure away from the milking stalls, and scald and dry their wire-cloth strainers morning and night.

Condensed milk was even used during the Civil War! It was a field ration, and soldiers valued the milk that stayed fresh. During the Civil War, Borden also produced some concentrated blackberry juice. General Sherman then wrote to Borden saying that Borden's free gift did more than all the Army surgeons to overcome an epidemic of dysentery.

Borden is not as well known for his machine that was supposed to work well on both water and land. It was a wagon, pulled by a horse, and it had a mast and a square sail in front rigged with pulleys. The wheels were supposed to make the wheels serve as makeshift paddle wheels. When he took it on its maiden voyage, all of his dinner guests were dumped screaming into the water!

Questions to Ponder

❏ Gavelston, Texas, borders part of the same body of water that Louisiana and Mississippi does. What is the body of water? (*the Gulf of Mexico*)

❏ How does Texas rank in size compared to the other states, and what is its capital? (*Texas is the largest of the contiguous, or continental, United States; and it is the second largest—behind Alaska—of all the states. Its capital is Austin.*)

❏ Is our food safer today than it was when Borden was alive?

❏ Scurvy was a dreaded illness that used to strike sailors. Would Borden's evaporated milk stop scurvy? (*No, scurvy is caused by lack of vitamin C. Vitamin C is found in citrus fruits, tomatoes, peppers, cabbage, potatoes, and berries. Sailors with scurvy would suffer from bleeding gums, anemia, internal hemorrhaging, and ultimately die. Early sea captains worried greatly about scurvy. Borden's concentrated blackberry juice would help stop scurvy.*)

Babe Didrikson

(1911–1956)

The AAU (Amateur Athletic Union) Nationals for track and field were also serving as the Olympic trials in 1932. If a woman placed first, second, or third in any event, she would automatically go on to compete in that event at the Olympics.

Traveling from Texas to Illinois to compete, Babe was almost late to the Nationals. Up all night with a stomach ache, Babe overslept and had to jump into a taxi and change into her track suit in the back seat. She arrived just in time for the opening ceremonies.

All the teams were introduced to the crowd. Some teams had as many as 15 athletes. Babe stood alone among the over 200 women on the field: she was the team. There was no one else representing the Golden Cyclones. As if this was not amazing enough in itself, Babe was participating in every event. This meant that for the next three hours, Babe would be competing against women who would be better rested. Despite Babe's hustling from event to event, there were still a few times when the officials could not start the next event until Babe reached the starting line.

The result was that Babe won the long jump, the 80-meter hurdles (setting a world record with 11.9 seconds), the javelin (breaking her own previous world record with a distance of 139 feet 3 inches), the baseball throw (breaking her own previous U.S. record), the shot put, and the high jump. Too bad she was only fourth on the discus! At the Olympics, Babe set new world records and won gold medals in both the javelin throw and the 80-meter hurdles. Babe also won a silver medal in the high jump.

Throughout her life, Babe was very interested in athletic events. Today she is considered to be perhaps the greatest woman athlete of all time. Yet, when Babe was a child, she was called a freak for her behavior, which included jumping over the neighbor's hedges and racing streetcars to see if she (with the family groceries in tow) could beat them to the end of the street. Babe responded to the negative reactions of others by choosing not to conform to how people thought she should behave. Instead, she would boast loudly, "I am going to win."

Babe excelled in basketball, baseball, and track. After taking up golf, she won the U.S. and British amateur titles once each and the U.S. Open four times. One golfer who often competed against Babe said, "Our sport grew because of Babe, because she had so much flair and color. With Babe, there was never a dull moment."

Questions to Ponder

- Babe was the first American woman to win the British Women's Amateur golf tournament when it was held in Scotland. It was her 16th win in a row. What is the capital of Scotland, and can you find Scotland on a map? (*Edinburgh*)
- Babe's parents moved from the country of Norway to the state of Texas. What are the capitals of Norway and Texas, and can you find both on the map? (*Oslo is the capital of Norway. Austin is the capital of Texas.*)
- If you stood at the free-throw line on a basketball court and shot the ball 65 times, do you think you could make 57 shots like Babe could?
- If you threw a baseball as far as you could, would you be able to throw it 272 feet and two inches (83 m)—almost the distance of a football field—as Babe could?
- Are women athletes considered freaks today?

Santorio Santorio

(1561–1636)

If you feel ill, you take your temperature. If it is only slightly above normal, you go to school. But what if it is three, four, or five degrees above normal? You have just been operated on, and your doctor wants to make sure that an infection does not set in. How does he monitor your progress? Your temperature is taken at regular intervals. If a fever develops, it is often a sign of infection.

Physicians have long known that high temperatures mean illness, but the only way they had of diagnosing a fever was by resting their hand against a patient's forehead. What felt hot to one doctor may feel only warm to another. Following the course of a fever was also another difficulty. When exactly did your fever spike? Did your fever go up and down, or was it just a steady, low-grade fever? Different diseases and infections can sometimes be diagnosed by what type of fever one has. When doctors go to medical school, they must memorize what type of fever goes with what illnesses. This helps them when they are trying to figure out what is wrong.

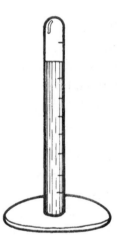

In 1612 Santorio Santorio (in Santorio's time, it was a common practice to give a child the same first and last name) took a thermoscope that Galileo had invented and turned it into the world's first thermometer. Galileo thought of his thermoscope as nothing but a "little joke," but Santorio realized what it could mean to doctors when it came to diagnosing illnesses. Galileo's thermoscope measured the change in air temperature by the movement of water in a tube. Santorio made it so that one had to breathe into the tube. Hot air takes up more space than cold air. The hotter one's breathe, the warmer the air, and the more water that is displaced. Santorio colored the water in the tube so that the doctors could more easily see it move. Most importantly, he added regularly spaced marks. Now a patient's temperature could be monitored to see if it was it higher or lower than just a few hours before. A patient's reading could also be compared to other people's—both healthy and sick.

Questions to Ponder

❑ Santorio was born on a tiny island in the Adriatic Sea. Where is the Adriatic Sea? (*The Adriatic Sea is an arm of the Mediterranean Sea. Venice is the chief port.*)

❑ What is considered to be a normal temperature for a human being? (*98.6 degrees F is normal. Recent research has shown that some people's normal temperature may vary slightly, but 98.6 is still used as a very important reference marker.*)

❑ Even in the Middle Ages, doctors knew that a high temperature was a sure sign of illness. When were the Middle Ages, and by what other name is this period of history known? (*The Middle Ages, also known as the Dark Ages, was a period in Western European history roughly from the fall of the Roman Empire in the 5th century to the 15th century.*)

❑ Feel your forehead with your hand, and then feel a few other classmates' foreheads. Do you all agree on whose head is the hottest?

❑ Santorio also invented a device that measures one's pulse rate. What is a pulse? (*A pulse is the rhythmical throbbing of arteries caused by the pumping of the heart. Different animals have different regular heart rates, as do animals of different ages.*)

Sacagawea

(1784–1884?)

When Sacagawea was about 12 years old, she was captured. She had run into an icy river, trying to hide, but her captor rode his horse into the water and plucked her out. Sacagawea was a Shoshone Native American. The man who captured Sacagawea was named Red Arrow. He belonged to the Hidasta tribe, and he brought Sacagawea to his village, where she had to work in the fields. Now, instead of living in a tipi, Sacagawea lived in a round, earth-covered lodge. These thick-walled huts were built so that the floor lay a foot or more below ground level. This made the huts cool in the summer and warm in the winter.

Sacagawea's life was turned around once again when Red Arrow gambled her away. Red Arrow lost a bet to the French Canadian trapper Charbonneau. Sacagawea had no choice but to become Charbonneau's third wife. Though Sacagawea had the title of Charbonneau's third wife, she was, essentially, his slave.

Charbonneau was hired by Lewis and Clark as a guide when they were making their expedition in 1805. President Thomas Jefferson had just purchased the Louisiana Territory from France, and he had sent Lewis and Clark to explore the land. He wanted Lewis and Clark to see if there was an easy route through the mountains to the Pacific Ocean. Lewis and Clark agreed to take Sacagawea, too; and it is a good thing that they did, for she proved vital to the success of their journey.

Despite carrying her young baby on her back for the entire journey, Sacagawea often walked along the riverbanks while the men rode in their boats. She gathered edible plants and roots and to supplement the men's diet of meat, meat, and more meat. Because of Sacagawea, the men did not grow sick from scurvy, the disease that is caused by lack of vitamin C. Sacagawea also acted as an interpreter and guide through Shoshone land. Many times, Sacagawea's presence alone stopped hostile attacks. The sight of a woman and a baby made people less afraid of the strange intruders. Both Lewis and Clark wrote in their journals about how important Sacagawea was to the success of their expedition. They wrote about one time when their boat was tipped on its side by a large gust of wind. Though the boat righted itself, much of its cargo spilled out. In the bedlam and chaos, no one but Sacagawea had the presence of mind to save the important journals, scientific instruments, and medicines that were floating away.

Questions to Ponder

❑ Can you name the largest mountain range that Sacagawea would have had to cross on the expedition to reach the Pacific Ocean? (*the Rocky Mountains*)

❑ When Sacagawea was first captured, she was taken to the Hidatsa village on the Knife River. The capital of North Dakota was built on this village site. What is the capital of North Dakota, and does North Dakota border another country? (*Bismarck. Yes, North Dakota borders the country of Canada.*)

❑ There are more monuments dedicated to Sacagawea than to any other American woman. In Washington state, there is a Sacagawea State Park and a Lake Sacagawea. What is the capital of Washington, and what is the large river that runs through it that Sacagawea went to the mouth of with Lewis and Clark? (*Olympia, the Columbia*)

❑ Lewis and Clarks's expedition crossed the Great Divide in knee-deep snow. What happens at the Great Divide? (*River water flows west instead of east.*)

Alfred Nobel

(1833–1896)

One of the workers in Alfred Nobel's nitroglycerine factory had to sit on a one-legged stool. Why? Nitroglycerine is an incredibly dangerous explosive. It must be treated very gently. The one-legged stool made sure that the worker could not nod off and fall asleep. If he did, the stool would tip over. By forcing him to stay awake and be alert, there were no errors made in the processing.

Alfred Nobel was a Swedish chemist and inventor. Along with his family, he was involved in the development and manufacturing of explosives. They owned several factories that made explosives, and they sent their product around the world. In an attempt to make their explosives safer, Nobel invented dynamite—a mixture of nitroglycerine and an inert filler of porous clay, which greatly improved the safety of explosives.

Nobel hated social gatherings; and if he could decline a public honor without giving offense, he would. Once, when asked for a picture for an anniversary publication of one of his works, Nobel replied that he would provide the picture only if every single workman were asked to do the same. He even said that the reason he was awarded the Swedish Order of the North Star was because his cook once pleased an influential stomach!

When Nobel died, he left most of his money for prizes that would be given annually to people whose work most benefits humanity. These prizes are awarded once a year in the fields of chemistry, physics, physiology or medicine, literature, and peace to the person or individuals who had "conferred the greatest benefit on mankind." With the honor and fame that comes from these distinguished prizes is a large sum of money.

Nobel's relatives fought the terms of his will. In their attempt to have it declared invalid, they even attempted to establish that a loyal Swede such as Nobel would not have dissipated (spread out) his fortune by giving prizes to foreigners. The courts decided that the will was indeed valid; and since 1901 the Nobel Prizes have been awarded every year in Stockholm, Sweden. The discoverers of penicillin and X-rays were awarded Nobel Prizes, as well as the Swiss philanthropist who inspired the foundation of the International Red Cross.

Questions to Ponder

❏ Nobel was born in Sweden. What is the capital of Sweden, and is Sweden north or south of Mali? (*Stockholm is the capital. Mali, a country in Northern Africa, is south of Sweden.*)

❏ Should your school exchange its four-legged chairs for one-legged stools?

❏ At Nobel's factory in Scotland, the female workers were searched for hairpins, safety pins, and metal buttons before they could enter the danger zone. Why? (*Any metallic object might give rise to sparks. Around any explosive, sparks are not a happy thing!*)

❏ Take a guess at when the first explosives were used. (*Historians are certain that highly inflammable materials were used as early as 500 B.C. by the military.*)

Nelson Mandela

(1918–)

Nelson Mandela was imprisoned for over 27 years. Many of his years in jail were spent on a small area of limestone rock called Robben Island. Mandela worked on a labor crew, on which he had to pound boulders into gravel. He was not permitted to receive mail, and when he was allowed a rare visit, it took place in a crude, wooden shack at the edge of the island where the warden stood close enough to hear every word. Because the prison was over 900 miles (1448.4 km) from where his family lived, and because his family did not have enough money to take time off of work or pay the travel fees, it was hard for Mandela to keep the family ties that he felt were so important.

Why was Mandela imprisoned? Mandela was a South African. He was the son of a tribal chief, and he was protesting apartheid, the forced separation of races. At that time, South Africa was ruled by a white, minority government. Millions of native Africans were not allowed to vote, go to the same schools, and live in the same areas as the white population. Separation was extensive—down to what beaches native South Africans could use, which hospitals they could go to, which teams they could play on, and seating in public-transportation vehicles.

For the entire time that Mandela was imprisoned, he never lost his dignity or his courage. He knew that all people should have equal rights, regardless of color. To control political activity, South Africa used to "ban" people. When a person was banned, he or she could not be in the presence of more that three people, no matter who they were—even family—and no matter what they were doing—even cooking! A banned person could not be published or even quoted in a newspaper or on television. For the entire 27 years that Mandela was in prison, he was banned. Mandela was even banned before he was sent to prison. This made it incredibly difficult for him to practice law, but he never gave up. He did not stop going to his law office, but he had to go at night. Despite Mandela being banned before and during his prison time, he became a symbol for what South Africa could become.

The South African government knew that it had no choice: it would have to change. The cry for freedom and equality could not be silenced. In February 1990, Mandela was freed. People of all colors rejoiced. It was further proof that democracy had prevailed and the human spirit had triumphed when Mandela, the greatly respected elder statesman of the anti-apartheid movement, was elected president of South Africa.

Questions to Ponder

❑ Which two of these four oceans border South Africa: Atlantic, Pacific, Indian, or Arctic? (*The Indian and Atlantic Oceans border South Africa.*)

❑ Warning: this is a more difficult question that you think! What is the capital of South Africa? (*Pretoria is the administrative capital, Cape Town is the legislative capital, and Bloemfontein is the judicial capital.*)

❑ Mandela was jailed for 27 years. What number cubed is 27? (*When a number is cubed, it is multiplied by itself three times. 3 x 3 x 3 = 27. Thus, 3 is your answer.*)

❑ How would you feel if you lived in a country with apartheid?

Martha Graham

(1894–1991)

Too old, too short, too heavy, and too homely—that was what was thought of Martha Graham when she decided to become a dancer. Graham did not pay attention to the naysayers. Dancing was Graham's reason for living, and nothing was going to stop her. Dedicating herself to her passion totally and without ever holding anything back, Graham went on to dance, choreograph, and teach for over 70 years. Graham even founded a school where her distinctive system of training was taught to others, and her dance company, The Martha Graham Dance Company, is the world's oldest continuously performing modern dance troupe.

Graham felt that dance could be used to reveal joy, passion, and grief. She felt that movements could be connected to emotions. Graham did not care that she was only 5'2", and she was not deterred by the fact that most future dance performers start serious study by the age of nine or ten. At the "old" age of 22, Graham enrolled in the dance school Denishawn, one of the first professional schools of dance in America. Graham did not impress anyone when she first arrived, but Graham was determined to learn everything. Graham would sit in advanced classes and listen and watch. Graham would then go into the studio alone, after classes were over, and she would practice by herself, dancing late into the night. After the first year, she was asked to help to show the younger students certain steps, but still no one thought that she could ever perform. Then, one day when she was sitting and quietly watching an advanced class, she got her chance.

The instructor said that it was too bad Graham did not know a particular dance, for Graham would look perfect for the part, with her straight black hair and high cheekbones. When Graham told him that she did know the dance, the instructor would not believe her because she had never danced the dance before. When Graham rose to her feet and danced the dance perfectly, her astounded instructor promoted her to one of his leading dancers.

After several years, Graham decided to go out on her own. She was poor, but she didn't mind because she was doing exactly what she always wanted to do. Over the years, she built up her own company and performed all over the world. Many of her new dances made other people angry, but other people felt they were finally seeing their emotions expressed in movement.

Questions to Ponder

❑ Graham was born in Allegheny, Pennsylvania. What is the capital of Pennsylvania, and does Pennsylvania border an ocean? (*Harrisburg. Though Pennsylvania is considered to be a mid-Atlantic state, it does not border the Atlantic Ocean.*)

❑ A choreographer is the person who creates the steps, movements, and patterns of a dance. Graham was both a dancer and a choreographer. Can you excel at being a dancer and not at being a choreographer? Can you excel at being a choreographer and not a dancer? Which job would you like the best: that of being a dancer or that of being a choreographer?

❑ Warning: do not try this! Graham could kick a leg straight upward in a split of 180 degrees. What does a 180-degree angle look like? (*a straight line*)

❑ Graham was a pioneer of modern dance. Do you know any other types of dancing? (*Ballet, folk, square, country, line, ballroom, disco, tap, and break are types of dance.*)

Robert Louis Stevenson

(1850–1894)

Do you know about the strange case of Dr. Jekyll and Mr. Hyde? Have you ever heard someone say, "You never know who my teacher is going to be today—Jekyll or Hyde"? Robert Louis Stevenson wrote the book *The Strange Case of Dr. Jekyll and Mr. Hyde*. In the story, the main character has a split personality: Dr. Jekyll is the kind side, and Mr. Hyde is the evil side. When Stevenson finished his first version of the book, his wife criticized it. She said that Stevenson should change it so that Dr. Jekyll represented the two-sided nature of Victorian society. On the outside, everyone was prim and proper, but underneath, people were lewd and unrestrained. Stevenson was so angry with his wife that he screamed at her. Then later, he said that she was right—and much to everyone's dismay burned the entire manuscript! He rewrote the version we know today in just six days! 64,000 words! Remember, this is at a time when there were no computers or word processing programs!

Have you ever heard of or read *Kidnapped* or *Treasure Island*? Stevenson wrote those adventure books, as well as *A Child's Garden of Verses*, a famous collection of poems that includes a poem about a shadow that "goes in and out with me, and what can be the use of him is more than I can see."

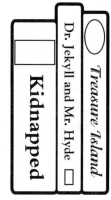

Though Stevenson suffered from tuberculosis, a lung disease for which there were no antibiotics at the time, he led an adventurous life. As a young man, he took a canoe trip from Belgium to France. He traveled to the United States, and he even chartered a 90-foot (27.4 m) schooner to take him and his family throughout the South Pacific. He visited Tahiti, the Marquesas Islands, the Sandwich Islands, and the Gilbert Islands.

Stevenson eventually settled on one of the Somoaan Islands, where he bought some land. On his property were huge banyan trees that were home to large, fruit-eating bats, or what many people know as flying foxes. Stevenson learned not to ask the Somoans their names, for that was considered rude. He also did not discuss pay with his workers; and, also following the Somoan way, if he liked what his cook prepared for him, instead of telling the cook that it was delicious, Stevenson would praise the cook by saying, "Great is your wisdom." Stevenson supported himself in Samoa by his writing.

Questions to Ponder

❏ Stevenson was born in Scotland. Does the Pacific, Atlantic, or Indian Ocean border Scotland? (*The Atlantic Ocean borders Scotland.*)

❏ What is the capital of Scotland? (*Edinburgh is the capital of Scotland.*)

❏ In 1889, Stevenson settled on the island of Upolu, an island that makes up part of Western Samoa. Can you find Western Samoa on the map? (*Hint: look at the island groups in the South Pacific Ocean.*)

❏ Is Western Samoa part of the United States? (*No, but American Samoa, the eastern half of the Samoa island chain, is a territory of the United States.*)

❏ Can you find Tahiti and the Marquesas and Gilbert Islands on the map?

Alice Hamilton

(1869–1970)

Dr. Alice Hamilton had painters and lead-factory workers as patients who showed an alarming pattern. They were all pale, thin, and prematurely wrinkled. They suffered from indigestion and often had difficulty in moving their wrists and hands properly. Dr. Hamilton suspected lead poisoning. She had other patients who suffered from an unusually high rate of pneumonia and rheumatism. Dr. Hamilton suspected that it was due to the conditions of the stockyards where they worked. Other patients told Dr. Hamilton about the carbon monoxide they breathed as they worked in the steel mills.

When Hamilton was a child, her mother had once told her, "There are two kinds of people: the ones who say, 'Somebody ought to do something about it, but why should it be I?' and those who say, 'Somebody must do something about it, then why not I?'" Hamilton wanted to be the type of person who does something. She had gone to medical school at a time when it was rare and difficult for a woman to gain admittance.

After medical school, Hamilton even went to Germany to further her studies in pathology. Pathology is the study of diseases, especially the structural and functional changes produced by them. Much to her dismay, Hamilton did not learn much more than she already knew because women in class were officially "invisible"! Once, when Hamilton wanted to attend one special lecture, she had to be taken to a chair in a corner of the room by an elderly doctor before any of the other doctors entered the lecture hall! It was when Hamilton was living and working at Hull House, a settlement house started by the social worker Jane Addams in Chicago, that she began to suspect that her patients were suffering horrible disabilities because of their jobs. Because of doing their jobs, her patients were dying!

Hamilton went to factories, stockyards, and even into mines to investigate what could be making workers ill. She was a medical detective, and over and over she showed how working conditions were poisoning her patients. She became an authority on industrial disease and hygiene. Hired as a faculty member of the Harvard Medical School, Hamilton was able to teach new doctors industrial medicine. Hamilton became a highly sought-after authority for many political and governmental groups, including the state of Illinois, the Labor Department, and the League of Nations health committee.

Questions to Ponder

❏ Hamilton was born in Fort Wayne, Indiana. What is the capital of Indiana, and what are Indiana's two main crops? (*Indianapolis. Corn and soybeans are Indiana's two main crops.*)

❏ It is now against the law to use lead-based paints inside of homes or to make water pipes that contain lead. Would Hamilton be pleased? (*Yes, Hamilton worked very hard for the passage of occupational labor laws. The first occupational labor law was passed in 1911 by the Illinois legislature due to the more than 500 cases of lead poisoning documented by Hamilton. In this same report, Hamilton also recorded her discovery of 77 lead-related trades.*)

❏ When Hamilton went into one mine so that she could figure out why the miners were getting ill (she discovered it was the dust), Hamilton had to ride on an elevator without walls that descended 800 feet (244 m) below the surface. Then she climbed down an 80-foot (24.4 m) ladder into a pit. Would you do what she did?

Johannes Gutenberg

(1397–1468)

There are many things that have changed our lives dramatically. On the top 10 of any list is the invention of mechanical printing. Think for a moment what your day would be like without the advent of mechanical printing. Even the book your teacher is reading from would not exist, and your teacher might not have any books at all!

Before the printing press, books had to be painstakingly copied by hand. Quill pens were used, and the scribes who copied the books had to be very careful about ink smears and transcription errors: there were no erasers or white-out. Copying a book was slow and laborious, and it could take up to several years to copy just one book! Books were so precious and rare that only very rich scholars or priests had copies. If books were for public use, perhaps in a cathedral library, they were chained to the shelves to prevent people from stealing them!

Johannes Gutenberg invented a press with moveable type. The letters of the alphabet were cast individually and then assembled to frame words. Gutenberg's training as a gold- and metal-worker had well prepared him, as well as the years at the mint (a building where money is made) watching gold coins being stamped with metal punches. But alas, a common problem—no money! Gutenberg formed a partnership with three men who agreed to give him money. Gutenburg started assembling his machine and was making great progress until one of the men died. That man had two brothers who demanded to be let in on the partnership—they saw what a printing press would be worth. Rather than let them steal his invention, Gutenberg dismantled it and looked for a better source of money.

He had to wait 10 years! As it was, he should have waited longer. The man who lent him money did so with interest, and then, when Gutenberg needed more, talked Gutenberg into a forming a partnership. When Gutenberg was finally ready to start printing, the man demanded the money back from his original loan, plus the interest. Gutenberg was unable to pay, so his partner seized the press and took over the business.

Gutenberg died penniless and destitute in 1468. Gutenberg may have died forgotten, but he changed the world. With his press, a printer could print in one day what a scribe would write in one year. Books were printed using Gutenberg's methods for nearly 500 years.

Questions to Ponder

- ❏ Gutenberg was born in Mainz, Germany. What is the capital of Germany, and does Turkey border Germany? (*Berlin. Turkey does not border Germany.*)
- ❏ What would your school day be like if the teacher were the only one with a book?
- ❏ What would you list in your top 10 inventions of all time?
- ❏ Gutenberg was right to worry that his invention would be stolen from him. *Purloin* is another word for steal. When something is purloined, it is stolen. How can inventors today protect their invention from being purloined? (*Patents help. They give the right of a particular invention to the person that applies for them. Of course, someone can steal the patented idea, but then one can try and prove his or her case to the patent office.*)
- ❏ Was Gutenberg the first to print a book? (*No, but he was the first European to do so. The Chinese had also invented a method of print with moveable type, but it was impractical because of their thousands of characters. The oldest surviving printed book is from China, dated 868 A.D.*)

Daniel K. Inouye

(1924–)

During World War II, the 442nd Combat Team was made up of Nisei, men who were born in America to parents who moved here from Japan. Daniel K. Inouye was on the team. The nickname of this team was "Go for Broke," and this was because the men gave everything that they had. During the battle to set free "the Lost Battalion," the 442nd Combat Team rescued almost 1,000 soldiers of the 141st Infantry unit who were surrounded by Germans and just about out of ammunition and supplies.

Inouye never gave up "going for broke." In April of 1954 Inouye led his men up a heavily guarded hill. Though Inouye was struck by several bullets, he refused to give up. He continued to advance until his men were able to take the hill. Even after his right arm was shattered by a German rifle grenade, he did not stop fighting. Inouye lost his arm, but with his spirit of "go for broke," he taught himself to write, tie his shoelaces, drive a car, use a knife and fork, and even play the piano with his left hand.

What had to change, though, was his dream of becoming a surgeon. Inouye had to forget about all the pre-medical classes he had taken or first aid classes he had taught before the war. Instead, he went to law school. When Hawaii became a state, Inouye was elected by an overwhelming majority to hold Hawaii's first seat in the United States House of Representatives. Inouye was the first Japanese American to serve in the United States Congress. After serving in the House of Representatives, Inouye was elected to the Senate. He has since been re-elected as a senator every time he has run.

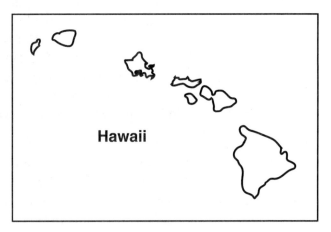

Hawaii

Questions to Ponder

❑ Inouye was born in September 7, 1924. Can you calculate his age today, to the month and day?

❑ Inouye was born in Honolulu, Hawaii. Is Honolulu the capital of Hawaii? (*Yes*)

❑ Was Hawaii the 27th, 31st, 37th, 49th, or 50th state? (*Hawaii was the 50th state. It became a state on August 21, 1959.*)

❑ Is Hawaii in the Pacific or Atlantic Ocean? (*Pacific*)

❑ Inouye's grandparents came to Hawaii to work on the sugar plantations. Inouye's grandfather worked 12-hour days, and he earned just 10 dollars a month. Inouye's grandparents came from Japan. What is the capital of Japan, and can you find it on the map? (*Tokyo is the capital of Japan.*)

❑ Is Japan in the Pacific or Atlantic Ocean? (*Japan is in the Pacific Ocean.*)

❑ Are both Japan and Hawaii archipelagos? What is an archipelago? (Yes, *Japan and Hawaii are both archipelagos. An archipelago is a group of islands.*)

❑ What plant is grown in Hawaii to produce sugar? (*sugar cane*)

❑ Can you tie your shoe with only one hand?

Henry Ford

(1863–1947)

Think of the time difference: one person decides to make a car. The different parts are all over the factory. He walks to the area of the factory where the part is, brings it back, puts it on, and then goes and gets the next part. In the other case, 10 people get together. They decide that they will all work together to make their 10 cars. They put all the parts in a line, and then as the car rolls down the line, they each do one particular job on each car. They become very good at the particular job that they are doing, and consequently, they can work much more quickly than someone else. Even though they all helped to make 10 cars instead of just one, the cars get made so much faster that the coordinated effort is well worth it.

Henry Ford, the great car manufacturer, did not invent assembly-line manufacturing (it was invented by Frederick Taylor, who did time-and-motion studies of machine shops in the 1880s), but Ford was the first one to decide to really implement the process.

Ford was not making fancy cars. His goal was to make cars that everyone could afford. He gave the world the "Tin Lizzie," or Model T. Before Ford implemented his assembly line, it took 12 1/2 hours to build a Model T. Once the Model T was being built on the assembly line, it only took two hours and 38 minutes! As the assembly line improved, production time decreased further to only 93 minutes! Could you build an entire car, putting it all together, in only 93 minutes?

To help his cars sell, Ford also started a financing system. Instead of having to pay for the car all at once, Ford would lend the money to the buyer, who would then pay it back in small monthly payments. Because most cars are bought this way today, it seems funny that at the time Ford started this system it was considered revolutionary.

Questions to Ponder

❏ Ford was born in Dearborn, Michigan. What is the capital of Michigan, and how many of the Great Lakes border Michigan? (*Lansing. Four out of the five Great Lakes border Michigan: Erie, Michigan, Huron, and Superior.*)

❏ What is the only Great Lake that does not border Michigan? (*Lake Ontario is the only Great Lake that does not border Michigan. A good way to remember the Great Lakes is by the word HOMES. Each lake starts with one of the letters in the word HOMES.*)

❏ One of Ford's great passions was bird watching. Can you name 10 types of birds?

❏ Many fast-food restaurants hire consultants who do time-and-motion studies. The consultants analyze how many steps it is to each food section, how long it takes to prepare what, and then they show the restaurant how to serve the food more efficiently and quickly. Why are workers taught to get the drinks first? (*If they got the French fries first, for instance, they would be cold by the time the drinks were poured.*) Out of the fast-food restaurants you have been to, which one has the assembly line down the best?

❏ Why can fast-food restaurants sell food more cheaply than other restaurants? (*Using the assembly line, with the food being the same everywhere it is sold, the company can have everything ready. They buy in bulk so they can buy at cheaper prices. They then sell quickly, and thus sell more. They make their profit from quantity sold. They sell so much that they only have to make a little profit off of each item.*)

Benjamin Banneker

(1731–1806)

When Benjamin Banneker was 20 years old, he was shown a pocketwatch for the first time in his life. His fascination with the watch was so great that the man whose watch it was decided to give it to Banneker. Banneker took it apart and put it back together over and over, learning how it worked, figuring out how all the gears affected the others. Banneker decided that he would make his own clock.

With only a geometry book, a book about the laws of motion, and a journal from London that showed a picture of a clock, Banneker set to work. It took two years. Banneker first had to make the intricate calculations necessary to design the gears, and then he had to carve each gear by hand out of wood. In 1753, Banneker's clock was finished. The clock, the first ever to be made in North America, kept the time perfectly. For over 40 years it struck every hour to the second.

Banneker was also interested in astronomy, the study of the stars. Using his clock, Banneker began to measure the movement of the stars. Banneker predicted a solar eclipse in 1789. A solar eclipse is when the moon passes between the sun and Earth, and a shadow is cast on Earth. No one believed Banneker! Everyone thought, "How can an untrained African American, the son of freed slaves, know how to calculate the time of eclipses?" The eclipse did not occur on the day that two eminent white mathematicians and astronomers had predicted, but it occurred on the exact day that Banneker predicted. Banneker's calculations were the ones that were correct!

By 1792, Banneker had enough information to fill an almanac. His almanac, which he published with the help of abolitionists (people who fought to help abolish slavery), became a trusted resource among farmers and was considered more accurate than Benjamin Franklin's popular almanac.

Banneker's cabin was burned to the ground on the day he was buried. It is believed that it was set on fire by people who wished to destroy any trace of Banneker's career. Fortunately, one of Banneker's relatives had already given most of his research papers, clocks, and other possessions to a friend. Banneker showed us that intelligence comes from how we use our brains, not from how we look.

Questions to Ponder

❏ Banneker was born in Maryland. What is the capital of Maryland, and is Maryland east or west of the Mississippi? (*Annapolis is the capital of Maryland. Maryland is east of the Mississippi.*)

❏ The person George Washington appointed to survey and design Washington, D.C., resigned abruptly and took all the plans with him when he left. Banneker, who had helped with the survey, reproduced the plans and saved the day for Washington, D.C. What does a surveyor do? (*A surveyor, using mathematics, figures out the lines and contours of the earth and puts them to paper. The surveyor can then mark out streets, parks, and other tracts of land.*)

❏ Banneker's predictions for the eclipse were correct, unlike the predictions of two eminent astronomers. What does *eminent* mean? Can you use it in a sentence? (*Eminent means "standing out," "prominent," "famous," etc.*)

Fannie Farmer

(1857–1914)

When Fannie Farmer went to a publisher with her cookbook manuscript, she was told that she would have to pay production costs for the book herself. Why were the publishers so unsure that her book would sell? The publishers felt that no one would be interested in Farmer's "scientific" recipes. They were too novel and different. Farmer took the financial risk, putting out her own money.

Believe it or not, these risky "scientific" recipes were what we see today in every cookbook that we pick up. The year was 1896, and before Farmer printed her cookbook, there was not any compilation of recipes in a standardized way. Instructions were given orally, and people were told to use a "pinch" of salt or a "handful" of flour. Compare the hands in your class: would everyone's handful of flour be the same?

At the age of 16, Farmer's left leg became paralyzed, probably by a mild stroke or polio. Though Farmer could walk, she limped. Unfortunately, due to prejudice against the disabled and frightening ignorance, Farmer's limping meant that most of society put her in the category of "unmarriageable." Because of this, Farmer went to work for a family friend as a "mother's helper." It was while helping to cook for the family and at the same time teach the little girl she was taking care of to cook that Farmer thought up her "scientific" recipes. They provided clear instructions that anyone could follow, and because the measurements were standardized, they could be duplicated by all. To think that saying one needed exactly two cups of flour and exactly one teaspoon of salt would be considered newfangled and "scientific!"

Wanting to become more independent, Farmer left her job as a "mother's helper" when she was 28 and enrolled in the Boston Cooking School. She soon became the school's assistant principal. Farmer worked hard in developing proper nutritional standards for hospital patients, and she also helped one doctor in his research on diabetes. Yet, it is her cookbook—not her teaching, research, or monthly column that she wrote for over a decade—that has made her a household name. The publishers who were sure that Farmer's cookbook would not sell were wrong—several million times over!

Questions to Ponder

- ❏ Farmer was born in Boston. In what state is Boston, and is Boston the capital of that state? (*Boston is the capital of Massachusetts.*)

- ❏ Should one ever be judged by a physical disability?

- ❏ You are told to put in a "pinch" of garlic or really hot pepper. Would it matter to you the size of the pinch?!

- ❏ How many teaspoons in a tablespoon, and how many tablespoons in a cup? (*There are three teaspoons in a tablespoon and 16 tablespoons in a cup.*)

- ❏ Why do we put some form of baking powder in most of our cakes and muffins? (*Baking powders contain an acid and an alkaline material that react in the presence of moisture to form the gas carbon dioxide. The carbon dioxide forms tiny bubbles in the dough. These bubbles quickly expand the dough, which is then set by the heat.*)

George and Robert Stephenson

(1781–1848) and (1803–1859)

Even though George Stephenson was barely able to read and write, George came to be called the Father of Railways, a well-earned and impressive title for someone who could not even retain the simplest engineering theory.

George started in the coal mines of England, following in his father's footsteps. At that time, huge amounts of coal were needed to fuel the factories of the industrial revolution. Typically, George would have toiled for years in the pits, and his children would have followed in his footsteps, just as George had followed his father's. Yet, what set George apart was his supreme confidence, his refusal to surrender to anyone—even when bullied by miners older and stronger than he—and his uncanny intuition about the way mechanical things work. It was almost as if George could sense faults in machines, and then, by trial and error experimentation, he would figure out how to improve them. George even invented a lamp that burned underwater so that he could fish at night!

When George's son Robert began school, a perfect partnership was started. George would invent and improve machines, and Robert would then draw up the plans and specifications. While George built locomotives, Robert designed bridges and railways. George did not build the first locomotive, but he was the one who improved what was there and put into play his idea of piping exhaust steam up the chimney to increase the fire's draft and produce more power.

George said that he could build a railroad for moving cotton and people from the port of Liverpool to the mills of Manchester. No one had ever before thought such a daunting and colossal task possible. Traversing 63 bridges, two tunnels, and an enormous bog that wouldn't bear a man's weight, even just the tracks themselves seemed impossible to build. George built the tracks, standing up to all his opponents and critics, even the farmers with shotguns who felt that steam locomotives would fall apart at 10 miles per hour (16 kph) and wipe out everyone nearby. When one skeptic, thinking a cow could derail the engine if it got on the tracks, told George, "Would not that, think you, be a very awkward circumstance?" George replied in his thick Northern accent, "For the cow."

Robert built the Rocket, the engine his father designed for the job. In 1829 when the tracks and the Rocket were completed, there was a contest between horses and the locomotive. The Rocket, steaming past the astounded judges at the incredible speed of 29 miles per hour (46.7 kph), won a clear and decisive victory.

Questions to Ponder

❏ The Stephensons lived in England. What is the capital of England, and what channel separates England from France? (*London is the capital of England. The English Channel separates England from France.*)

❏ Robert designed bridges as far away as Cairo. In what country is Cairo, and is it that country's capital? (*Cairo is in Egypt, and it is the capital.*)

❏ George invented a revolutionary safety lamp that prevented gas explosions in coal mines. Sir Humphry Davy, an eminent scientist who had himself devised a similar lamp, refused to believe that "an ill-educated, upstart mechanic from the North country could have beaten [him]." It was then that George's life-long contempt for establishment scientists began. Are people still too ready to judge someone by a job title? Do we sometimes put too much emphasis on what schools one attends as opposed to what one has learned?

Ranulph Fiennes

(1944–)

When Ranulph Fiennes woke up in the morning, the first thing that he did was not open his mouth. If he did, he would tear off the scabs that were sealing his lips together, and the pain would be excruciating. Instead, he would smear a tube of greasy lip salve onto the lumpy scabs that had welded together in the night. Then, gently, he would work the tip of his tongue against his lips from the inside until they slowly parted.

Fiennes and his teammate, Dr. Mike Stroud, were in the coldest place on Earth—Antarctica. Still-air temperatures of –126.4°F are common. At this temperature, if one drops a steel bar, it is liable to shatter like broken glass. Mercury turns to solid metal, and tin falls apart into granules.

Attempting to cross the continent completely self-supported, the two men were each hauling a 485-pound sledge. There were no dogs to help them, and there would not be any supplies brought by air. Could you pull a 485-pound sledge?

The men had a terrible time with blisters and frostbite. At one point, Stroud had to operate on his own foot. He gave himself two injections of anesthetic and "then plunged a scalpel blade deep into the swelling with diagonally crossed injections." Once, Fiennes' face mask froze on his face, becoming firmly embedded in his beard. Despite his care, when he removed it, a chunk of skin and beard came away. Fiennes was left with a raw and bloody patch the size of a silver dollar.

Stroud figured out that Fiennes was burning up 10,000 calories a day, but they had only enough rations for 5,200 calories a day. They also knew that towards the end of the trip it would be necessary for them to go down to half-rations. They had planned carefully, but a lot of it would come down to human endurance and the drive to succeed. Needless to say, both men lost a significant amount of weight.

After 1,350 miles, Fiennes and Stroud could travel no further. If they continued, death would be a certainty. They did not have enough food, and their bodies were ulcerating and rotting before them. Only their determination and ability to withstand physical agony allowed them to cover the tremendous distance that they did.

Questions to Ponder

❑ Conditions in Antarctica are so harsh that a simple mistake can mean death. Team cooperation is necessary and vital. When Fiennes wrote about leadership and discipline he said, "Sarcasm must be avoided like the plague." What is sarcasm? (*Sarcastic comments have a biting and stinging wit to them.*)

❑ Fiennes and Stroud are in the *Guinness Book of Records* for the longest totally self-supporting polar sled journey. What would you like to be in the *Guinness Book of Records* for? (Hopefully not for sneezing! The record right now is held by a woman who suffered a sneezing fit for 977 straight days. She sneezed over one million times in the first 365 days alone.)

❑ Fiennes and Stroud were unable to wash for the entire 95-day journey—and they were too exhausted to care. Have you ever been so involved in something that your priorities were forced to change?

Benjamin Franklin

(1706–1790)

Benjamin Franklin was America's first windsurfer. It's true! During one of Franklin's experiments, he used kites to pull himself across a lake! Franklin was also the first to build a second-story toilet. But those two things are not what he is primarily known for. For what is Franklin most known?

Franklin was one of the Founding Fathers of the United States. He was also a diplomat, printer, author, scientist, and inventor. Franklin was known for his quick wit and ability to play with words. He used his talents when he wrote and published *Poor Richard's Almanack*, a periodical that contained common-sense philosophy, general information, and witty sayings. One of the sayings you might be familiar with that Franklin wrote for his almanac is, "Early to bed, early to rise, makes a man healthy, wealthy, and wise."

When Franklin signed the Declaration of Independence, he knew that if the bid for independence was not successful, he and the rest of the men who signed the document would be hanged for treason. Franklin warned his fellow signers with this witty comment, "We must all hang together, or we shall surely all hang separately."

Franklin is famous for his work with electricity. He proved that the lightning we see in the sky during thunderstorms is actually electricity. Franklin proved this by setting up an experiment in which he flew a kite with a sharp, pointed wire at the top in a lightning storm. At the end of the kite string was a key. Lightning hit the wire on top of the kite, and the electrical current flowed down through the string and onto the key. This is actually a very dangerous experiment, and Franklin was very fortunate that no one died.

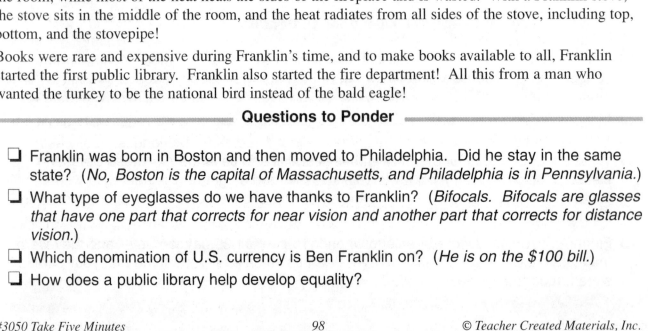

From Franklin's work with electricity came one of his most important inventions: the lightning rod. A lightning rod is placed on the top of a house or building. Since it is the highest point, the lightning strikes the rod rather than the building. The rod channels the electrical current down to the ground where it becomes harmless. Franklin never patented his lightning rod or tried to profit from this great invention that has saved a countless number of lives and homes.

Franklin also invented the Franklin stove. When a fire is lit in the fireplace, only a little heat gets into the room, while most of the heat heats the sides of the fireplace and is wasted. With a Franklin stove, the stove sits in the middle of the room, and the heat radiates from all sides of the stove, including top, bottom, and the stovepipe!

Books were rare and expensive during Franklin's time, and to make books available to all, Franklin started the first public library. Franklin also started the fire department! All this from a man who wanted the turkey to be the national bird instead of the bald eagle!

══════ Questions to Ponder ══════

❑ Franklin was born in Boston and then moved to Philadelphia. Did he stay in the same state? (*No, Boston is the capital of Massachusetts, and Philadelphia is in Pennsylvania.*)

❑ What type of eyeglasses do we have thanks to Franklin? (*Bifocals. Bifocals are glasses that have one part that corrects for near vision and another part that corrects for distance vision.*)

❑ Which denomination of U.S. currency is Ben Franklin on? (*He is on the $100 bill.*)

❑ How does a public library help develop equality?

Chico Mendes

(1944–1988)

Chico Mendes's father was a rubber tapper, and at the age of nine Mendes became one, too. Work was not new to Mendes, for from the age of five Mendes had been responsible for gathering wood, working in the garden, and hauling water from the river to the house. Mendes's house, small and rectangular, had a roof of palm leaves and was built on stilts. It was about three feet above the ground; this helped keep the house free from the crawling insects and animals that abounded in the Amazonian jungle.

Mendes and his father worked an area of about 700 acres (2.8 km²). They would get up before dawn. To see, they would put on a special helmet that had a wick that they would dip in kerosene and then light. The lit wick, positioned before a shiny disk, provided just enough light for them to see their way along the dusky trails.

Mendes and his father would cut the trees for the milky latex, which they sold for rubber. They were careful with how they treated their trees, for they knew that the trees were necessary for their livelihood. They let the tree heal between cuts, and they never cut too deeply. Mendes's cousin said, "Year in and year out, the rubber tree is like our mother." The work was not done when Mendes returned late at night, for once they had collected the latex, they had to cure it over a fire.

Mendes said, "My life began just like that of all rubber tappers, as a virtual slave. . . . The rubber-estate owners would not allow schools because if a rubber tapper's children went to school, they would learn to read, write, and add up—and then they would discover to what extent they were being cheated."

Mendes did learn to read and write despite the lack of schools. Every Saturday for three years he would take a three-hour walk to visit a man with whom he would read newspapers and listen to radio news broadcasts. Mendes began to realize that the rubber tappers could work together to improve their lives. They also needed to unite to save the rainforests and the trees in it that they needed for survival. Many people did not understand the delicate balance in a rainforest, and they were coming in and stripping everything for a quick profit.

Mendes was assassinated one night when he stepped outside his house to walk to where he could take a shower. He was killed because of his struggle to set up extractive reserves to keep the rainforest intact. Yet, Mendes, even in death, could not be silenced. After all, this humble rubber tapper had spoken to environmental groups in Washington, D.C., and met with members of Congress. He had been honored by the United Nations and the Better World Society for his work. Today, people all over the world have taken up Mendes's struggle to preserve the rainforests for generations to come.

Questions to Ponder

❑ Mendes was born in Brazil. Brazil is so large that it occupies nearly half of its continent. Which continent is that? (*Brazil occupies nearly half of South America.*)

❑ What is the capital of Brazil, and what is Brazil's national language? (*Brasilia is the capital of Brazil. Portuguese is Brazil's national language.*)

❑ In the late 1800s and early 1900s, there was a tremendous demand for rubber. Why? (*There was the boom of the automobile industry, and rubber was needed for tires.*)

❑ In the Amazonian rainforest, scientists once found 50 types of ants in 10 square feet of decaying leaves and 400 different types of insects on one tree. What can you find in 10 square feet and on one tree where you live?

Jacques Cousteau

(1910–1997)

Think of exploring the ocean, and one thinks of scuba divers. With their compressed-air tanks on their backs, flippers on their feet, and wet suits to keep them warm, they have entered a different world. Adventures await them: sharks, colossal squids, poisonous sea snakes. None of this would be possible without the scuba equipment—the aqualung. The aqualung has opened up the world to oceanographers and other aquatic scientists. The navy and police departments have skilled scuba divers as part of their team, as do oil companies.

Jacques Cousteau wanted to swim with the fish, exploring the ocean with his hands free. In 1943, with Emil Gagnon, he invented the self-contained underwater breathing apparatus (SCUBA) that scuba divers use today. There have been some slight changes made to it, but it is basically the same tool. When Cousteau first tried it out, wearing just a thin bathing suit (inventing wet suits was to come later), he waded into the frigid waters of the Marne River outside Paris, France. No breathing tubes or guide ropes connected him to the surface. When the bubbles stopped, Gagnon, watching from the river bank, started to strip off his clothes. As he was about to brave the icy waters, his friend emerged. Cousteau said that he could swim horizontally, but he could not stand or swim up or down. The men figured out what was wrong, and they fixed it. From that point on, Cousteau changed how man could interact with the ocean.

Jacques Cousteau *(cont.)*

With his ship *Calypso*, Cousteau studied animals in the ocean all over the world. He developed film techniques for underwater use, and he produced educational films about the world undersea. Three of Cousteau's films even won Academy Awards.

One of the dangers Cousteau learned about was called "rapture of the deep." This is when divers go too deep and an excess of nitrogen gets into their blood. The diver begins to feel great happiness, but also a sense of invulnerability. Believing that nothing can harm them, divers will sometimes pull out their mouthpieces and die. Cousteau taught his divers that, to avoid this, one must never dive alone.

There is a saying that goes like this: People learn from their mistakes. Cousteau built his first shark cage to protect his divers when they started diving in the Atlantic Ocean. When the cage, with its three divers in it (one of whom was Cousteau), was hoisted off the deck and then lowered into the ocean, the three occupants were tossed around, knocking and banging themselves painfully on the iron bars. After they were submerged, they saw a six-foot (1.8 m) barracuda swim past them, and that was when they noticed that the barracuda could have easily swum right inside the cage—as too could a six-foot shark! Needless to say, improvements were made to the cage prior to its return to the sea.

Questions to Ponder

❏ Cousteau was French. What is the capital of France? What bodies of water border Cousteau's homeland? (*Paris is the capital of France. France is bordered by the Mediterranean Sea, the English Channel, and the Atlantic Ocean.*)

❏ Cousteau led an expedition that took place for two years up the Amazon River. On which continent is the Amazon River, and can you name two countries that the Amazon River and some of its tributaries flow through? (*The Amazon River is on the continent of South America. The Amazon River flows through Brazil and Peru.*)

❏ To see if men could live underwater for extended periods of time, Cousteau developed equipment and sent divers below the surface of the water for a month in the Red Sea. Name countries that border the Red Sea. (*The Red Sea is bordered by Egypt, Sudan, Ethiopia, Saudi Arabia, and Yemen.*)

❏ If you threw a yellow hat into the Red Sea, what would it become? (*It would become wet.*)

Mary McLeod Bethune

(1875–1955)

"Praise the Lord you were born free!" These were the words that Mary McLeod Bethune's grandmother often said to her. Bethune's grandmother and parents had been slaves. Some of Bethune's older brothers and sisters were born into slavery. They were sold to other masters. Bethune was born on July 10, 1875, 10 years after the Civil War ended, so she was born free.

Bethune's parents grew cotton. They worked long hours in the field. Cotton was sold by weight, but Bethune's parents could not read the scale. They had to trust what the cotton dealer told them. Bethune and her father suspected that they were never paid enough, but there was nothing they could do: they could not read the numbers. One girl told Bethune, "You can't read. Black children never read."

Five miles (8 km) from where Bethune lived, a school was finally started for children of freed slaves. Bethune walked every day—five miles there, five miles back. There were not any desks. There were only a few books. There were no pencils or paper.

However, the next time Mary's father went to sell his cotton, and the cotton dealer said, "You have 280 pounds." Mary looked and said, "Isn't it 480 pounds?" Word got out about Mary, and pretty soon all the farmers wanted her with them when they sold or bought anything. She made sure they were not cheated.

Bethune won a scholarship to a boarding school. Her fees were paid by a woman who believed that all children, black and white, should be educated. Bethune worked hard, and for the first time she did not have to share a bed with her sisters. Bethune went on to start her own school for girls, and this school is now part of Bethune-Cookman College. President Franklyn D. Roosevelt asked Bethune to be the Director of Negro Affairs for the National Youth Administration. This was the first time an African-American woman had held such a high government post. Bethune also started an organization that worked hard to end the poll tax and promoted the teaching of African-American history in public schools. Bethune even spoke before the United Nations about the needs of African Americans.

Questions to Ponder

- ❏ Bethune was born in South Carolina. What is the capital of South Carolina? (*Columbia*)
- ❏ The sign over the front door of Bethune's school said, "ENTER TO LEARN"; and on the inside of the same door were the words, "DEPART TO SERVE." What did she mean?
- ❏ Bethune opposed the poll tax. What was it? (*The poll tax was a tax people had to pay if they wanted to vote. After the 15th amendment to our Constitution gave the vote to African Americans in 1870, many states instituted poll taxes to prevent poor African Americans from voting. It wasn't until the 24th amendment, adopted in 1964, that the poll tax was prohibited for federal elections.*)
- ❏ What would your school day be like if there were not any desks or paper in the school and only a few books?
- ❏ Bethune also started a hospital in the city where her school was because the hospital there would not treat African Americans. Should a hospital ever be allowed to turn sick people away?

Mother Jones
(late 1830s–1930)

Mother Jones applied for a job in a cotton mill. She was told by the manager that he could not hire her unless she had a family that would work with her. By telling him that her five children would be arriving soon from another town, she was hired and given the "privilege" of renting a rundown shanty with broken windows and a rotten floor.

Conditions for all cotton mill workers were horrible at that time, but Jones had come to do something specifically about the children. Working undercover, she found that "tiny babies of six years old with faces of 60 did an eight-hour shift for 10 cents a day," and that the four-year-olds who had to come to the mills to help their older brothers and sisters did not receive even a penny. Jones witnessed little boys and girls walking up and down the rows of spindles and reaching their hands into the dangerous machinery to fix threads. She saw the children crawling under the machines to oil them. She wrote about how exhausted the children were, arriving at the factory by 5:30 A.M., working without a break until their half-hour lunch break. Often during their break, the children did not eat; instead, they fell asleep on the floor until they were told it was time to start work again. Accidents were common.

When Mother Jones was once asked by a congressman where she resided, Jones replied, "I reside wherever there is a good fight against wrong." Because of the deplorable conditions in the mines, the long hours the miners worked, and the living conditions of the miners, Jones often found herself residing with these poor laborers. Mining companies owned the miners' houses, all of the surrounding land, the schools, and even the churches. Miners were paid by the amount of coal they dug, and it was company men who weighed the coal. Often the miners were cheated. What little the miners were paid was in scrip, meaning that it was not actual cash but rather paper that said they could spend a certain amount. If the miners did not spend this at a company store (where the prices were what the company wanted them to be), the miners were fired.

Today there is a special Mother Jones display in the lobby of the U.S. Department of Labor headquarters in Washington, D.C.

Questions to Ponder

❏ Jones was born in Cork, Ireland. What is the capital of Ireland? (*Dublin*)

❏ Does the Atlantic, Indian, or Pacific Ocean border Ireland? (*the Atlantic Ocean*)

❏ Though we have stringent labor rules in the United States today thanks to the work of people like Mother Jones, many of the products we buy today are made in factories in other countries where labor conditions would not pass our standards. Workers are paid much less than our minimum wage. Company owners claim that if their products were made in the U.S., they would be much more expensive. Others feel that the companies want too much of a profit. Some consumers boycott companies that they feel take advantage of their workers, whether the products are made in the U.S. or abroad. What does boycott mean? (*When one boycotts the products from a particular company, one refuses to buy them.*)

❏ There was one law to "protect" children in Pennsylvania that said that a working child be at least 13 years old and work no more than 10 hours a day, six days a week. In reality, most children were much younger. Does your school day suddenly seem quite short?

Rene T.H. Laennec

(1781–1826)

When you think of a doctor, what is one of the first things that comes to mind? What does a doctor always have? A stethoscope! Stethoscopes are medical instruments that are used for listening to body sounds. We usually think of the doctor using them to listen to our heart and lungs, but doctors will use stethoscopes to listen to other body sounds also. For example, a doctor can apply it to a patient's stomach and the area where the intestines are and listen for the appropriate gurgling. If there is only silence, a doctor will know that there is a possible blockage. Many diseases and heart conditions can be diagnosed with the use of the stethoscope, and it has become such an important tool that every doctor and nurse has been trained to use one.

This is the truth: the first stethoscope was nothing more than some rolled up sheets of paper! But what a discovery it was! Rene T.H. Laennec needed to listen to a young woman's heart. At that time, doctors would tap on people's chests. If someone's chest was filled with fluid, it would sound different from someone's chest whose lungs were clear and healthy. Yet, the tapping method (or the percussion method, as it was more formally called) was not effective with Laennec's patient.

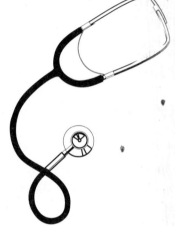

The story goes that, after seeing his patient, Laennec went out for a walk. He saw two young boys playing a game in which each child stood at a long piece of wood, each holding up an end to their ears. Then one boy would scratch the wood with a pin, and the other boy could hear the scratching through the wood loud and clear. Laennec realized that he could perhaps amplify chest sounds. Going back to his patient, he rolled up some papers and tried. Sure enough, through the end pressed against his ear, he could hear the woman's heart thumping.

Laennec soon got tired of rolling up papers and experimented with different types of woods. Through experiments, Laennec discovered that if a hollow channel ran through the center of a wooden tube, the sounds heard were much greater and clearer. He found that light woods, such as beech, made better stethoscopes than dark woods and other materials like metal or glass. Laennec wrote a two-volume book on how to diagnose diseases of the lungs and heart by using the stethoscope. Doctors all around the world today are helped by Laennec's invention.

Questions to Ponder

❑ Laennec was born in France. Can you name the capital of France, and does part of France border the Mediterranean Sea? (*Paris is the capital of France. Yes, France does border the Mediterranean Sea.*)

❑ Most things can be improved. The stethoscope doctors use today is a much better instrument than it was when Laennec invented it in 1816. A great improvement to the stethoscope was making it binaural. An American doctor named Camman made the first binaural stethoscope in 1855. What is a binaural stethoscope? (*A binaural stethoscope is one that can be listened to with both ears.*)

❑ Can you make a simple stethoscope and listen to someone's heartbeat?

Sequoyah
(1766–1843)

Sequoyah was a Cherokee Native American who was born in Tennessee. He learned to hunt, grow corn, trap animals, and find his way with ease through the Cherokee Hills (which we know today as the Great Smoky Mountains).

Cherokee history, traditions, and beliefs were carried to each new generation by the spoken word. Every bit of information about the tribe had to be memorized, even down to who was related to whom and how to make medicine from plants. Healing secrets and special myths were told only to a few, and those individuals who were told the secrets had to work hard to remember all the details. If they forgot and did not teach the next person, it was gone forever.

The Cherokee language did not have a word for writing. They referred to the messages on paper that they saw the new settlers using as "talking leaves." Some Cherokees felt that the "talking leaves" were a type of magic that Cherokees could never understand.

Sequoyah knew that it was only a problem that needed solving. Sequoyah created a written language for the Cherokees. He made an alphabet in which 85 symbols were used for Cherokee sounds. Sequoyah's written language helped unite the Cherokee people. This language is still being taught and used today.

What is amazing about Sequoyah is that he is the only individual in over 5,000 years of recorded history known to have created a writing system without first being literate (able to read and write) in some language! What also makes his alphabet even more phenomenal than it first appears to be is the fact that the Cherokee language is one of the most structurally complex languages in North America. According to one author, "In the Cherokee language, multiple units of meaning are linked together to form words. Every regular Cherokee verb has over 21,000 forms."

Questions to Ponder

❏ What tree is named after Sequoyah? (*The giant sequoia. Giant sequoias can be found in Sequoia National Park, CA. One tree named General Sherman had a girth of over 83 feet. The bark alone had been estimated at places to be 24 inches thick. It was also estimated that there was over 600,120 board feet of lumber in General Sherman and enough wood to make over 5 billion matches.*)

❏ Can you find the Great Smoky Mountains on the map? How many of you have been to the Great Smoky Mountains?

❏ If we did not have an alphabet, would it be harder to learn at school? How would we keep records of our history? Would we be able to write to our friends or relatives? (*We would rely on oral historians. Our lives would be very different. We would have to send live messengers to our friends and relatives and trust that they said what we wanted them to.*)

❏ The Cherokees were forced to give up their land and move to Oklahoma. Thus, Sequoyah went from Tennessee to Oklahoma. What are the capitals of Tennessee and Oklahoma, and can you see how far away they are from each other on the map? (*Nashville is the capital of Tennessee, and Oklahoma City is the capital of Oklahoma.*)

❏ Can you invent an alphabet?

David Doubilet
(1946–)

When Dr. Eugenie Clark discovered a type of flounder that repels sharks by exuding a poison, David Doubilet took the pictures. Doubliet is a professional underwater photographer. Doubliet has to plan ahead for every photo shoot. Because he cannot change lenses or film underwater, he may dive with 10 cameras. He also has to bring electronic flash equipment with him underwater. His diving mask, with glasses built into them, is one of a kind. It is so important to him that when he travels from location to location, he carries it with him on the plane. He can make do with someone else's wet suit, but he needs his own personalized mask.

Doubilet has to plan ahead with his equipment, packing carefully and bringing extras of everything; but he also has to think about what he is photographing. Once, while photographing Great White sharks in Australia, Doubilet was outside his shark cage. His foot was right next to it so that he could quickly get back in if he needed to, but he wanted to lie down in the algae so that he could get a perfect shot. As the shark got closer, it began to get more and more agitated. Doubilet continued to take pictures. Finally, Doubilet knew it was time to get in the shark cage.

One problem: there was no shark cage! A swell had moved the boat, cage, and anchor 50 yards (45.7 m) away! Because he was not wearing fins, Doubilet could not swim. He began to bounce along the bottom, backing up and pushing the shark away as hard as he could with his camera when it got close. The shark would dart away and then come back for another pass. When Doubilet got to the cage, his friend pulled him inside and slammed the door. Doubilet made it just in time, for the furious shark smashed against the cage with its teeth.

Questions to Ponder

❏ Doubilet photographed Great White sharks off the coast of Australia. Is Australia the smallest continent or the second to smallest? (*It is the smallest. Australia is also the only continent that is occupied by a single nation.*)

❏ Which oceans surround Australia? (*The Indian and Pacific Oceans surround Australia.*)

❏ Doubilet grew up in New York City. Is New York City the capital of New York? (*No, Albany is the capital of New York.*)

❏ Which is more dangerous to people: a shark or a bee? (*Of course this depends on your personal situation, but more people are killed annually by bee stings than by sharks! Every year, hundreds of millions of people swim in oceans all around the world, but only about six people are reported killed each year by sharks.*)

❏ If you are ever attacked by a shark, what should you do? (*Don't panic! Sharks are excited by things that thrash around, so you must try to stay calm. Hit the shark on the nose as hard as you can. This may confuse the shark's senses. The shark may lose track of where you are and break off the attack. If you can, stick your fingers in the shark's eyes or nostrils. This too sometimes causes the shark to break off the attack. Most people who die from a shark attack die from loss of blood. So the faster you can get to a doctor, the better your chances of surviving.*)

Jan E. Matzeliger

(1852–1889)

Look down at your feet. You and everyone in your class is wearing shoes—maybe not the brand or the specific kind you wanted, but everyone has them. Shoes in the United States are plentiful. Many people have more then one pair, and sometimes, people will buy a pair just to go with a particular dress or outfit.

This has not always been the case. Shoes used to be expensive and rare. Many people would not wear them except in the winter, and often several children would share one pair. They would take turns wearing them outside.

Think for a moment what freedom shoes allow us: we can walk across snow, through thorns and brambles, and across hot surfaces. Our feet are protected, and it is less likely that we will get cut and grow ill from infections. And with our feet covered, we spread less disease.

Shoes were very expensive because they had to be made completely by hand. The sewing machine, invented in 1846, made shoe production faster; but it was still a slow process because of the problem of attaching the upper part of the shoe to the sole. There had been no machine invented that could do this part, though many people had tried to invent one.

When Jan E. Matzeliger arrived in the United States from Suriname, he was looked down upon because of his dark skin and his lack of English. Matzeliger taught himself to speak and write English, and he found a job as an apprentice in a shoe factory. He went on to work at other jobs, but at night he worked on a machine that could sew the upper part of the shoe to the sole. Turning down offers to buy his models while he was improving them, Matzeliger spent over four years working every evening and spending all of his money on parts. Often, he subsisted on nothing but cornmeal mush.

Usually when one requests a patent, it is awarded on the blueprints sent in with the application. In Matzeliger's case, the patent officials could not believe that the machine could really do what he said it could do. They traveled to his home to see for themselves. Matzeliger got his patent.

Before, working a 10-hour day, a skilled professional could produce about 50 pairs of shoes. With Matzeliger's machine, one could turn out 150 to 700 pairs of shoes in the same amount of time, depending on the quality of work. The price of producing a pair of shoes was cut in half.

Questions to Ponder

❏ Matzeliger was born in Suriname. His father was a Dutch engineer who had been sent there, and his mother was a black Surinamese whose ancestors probably came from West Africa. On what continent is Suriname, and what is Suriname's capital? (*Suriname is on the eastern coast of South America. Its capital is Paramaribo.*)

❏ When Matzeliger first started working on his machine, he tried to keep it a secret. Why do you think he did so? (*Some of his first inventions were patented by others who had the money to apply. Also, if the skilled people sewing the uppers to the sole knew what he was doing, they would probably have tried to have him fired. As it was, these skilled sewers could shut down a factory if they decided to stop working.*)

❏ Could you design a pair of shoes?

Helen Keller and Anne Sullivan

(1880–1968) and (1866–1936)

Helen Keller was born in 1880 in the state of Alabama. When she was only 19 months old, she developed a high fever. As a result of this fever, Keller became deaf and blind. Think about how we learn to talk—we listen to people around us and copy them. We begin to understand the world by watching what is going on. Keller could not listen or look.

When Keller was five, she realized that she was different from other people. She would feel people's lips moving, their expressions changing, and somehow she sensed that they were doing something without her. She would move her lips, but still she could not communicate with those around her. She would kick, scream, punch, and hurl her body about in a violent frenzy. She became uncontrollable. One uncle thought she should be put away in an institution.

Anne Sullivan was chosen to teach Keller in 1887. Sullivan was a woman who had known hard times. She and her brother were sent to the poorhouse when their mother died. When her brother died in the poorhouse, Sullivan was on her own. Sullivan had poor vision due to several eye infections, and despite several operations, she became blind. Sullivan attended a school for the blind where she learned the manual alphabet and how to read Braille. After several more operations, some of Sullivan's eyesight was restored.

Sullivan was shocked at the way Keller behaved. During mealtimes, Keller would not even take a seat. She would wonder around the table grabbing food off of anyone's plate. Sullivan would not let her. Keller threw such a violent temper tantrum, punching and biting, that the rest of the family fled in horror.

Sullivan worked hard to teach Keller how to behave. At the same time, she constantly finger-spelled the letters for whatever item they were touching or to explain what they were doing in Keller's hands. Keller did not understand that these finger touches were language. Then one morning, about a month after Sullivan had arrived, Sullivan took Keller's hand and held it in the water that was coming from the spout of a water pump. Into Keller's other hand, Sullivan spelled w-a-t-e-r over and over. Suddenly, Keller understood. She rushed around touching all that she could, eagerly waiting for the finger spelling that gave them a name. As a baby learns by listening, so Sullivan taught Keller by constantly spelling proper sentences.

Keller went on to graduate from Radcliffe College with honors. Sullivan went with her to translate lectures and books and write what Keller spelled into her fingers. Keller published her autobiography, and she lectured widely to promote education for the blind and other social causes. During World War II, Keller visited wounded soldiers. She wanted them to see that even if they were maimed and damaged, they were not defeated. They could fight back, as she had.

Questions to Ponder

❑ Keller was born in Alabama, and Sullivan was born in Massachusetts. What are the capitals of these two states? (*Montgomery, Alabama; Boston, Massachusetts*)

❑ Some people felt that Keller did not really go to college, but rather Sullivan did. Both Keller and Sullivan adamantly disagreed. What do you think?

❑ Do you think Sullivan was a better teacher because of her years of being blind?

David Bushnell

(1740–1824)

The local postmaster was a British spy. He copied down a letter in which David Bushnell's friend described Bushnell's invention after he had viewed it with Benjamin Franklin. When the governor received the information, the governor thought it was a joke. Oh, right! Men traveling underwater in a "Sub-Marine Vessel" presenting a danger to English battleships? The governor didn't pay any attention at all to the reports. He was sure that it was impossible.

Yet, there was a submarine! Bushnell, a farmer and not a shipbuilder, thought up his "Sub-Marine Vessel" and constructed it without any fancy tools in a friend's shed. The Turtle, the name Bushnell gave to his underwater boat, was the world's first working submarine, and it was used in the Revolutionary War.

Bushnell's Turtle could hold about a 30-minute supply of air, and it could move, if there wasn't any current or tide to work against, at the mighty speed of three miles per hour (4.8 kph). About six feet (1.8 m) high, three feet (.9 m) long and four feet (1.2 m) wide, it was made of heavy, oak planks, with the spaces in between the planks sealed with tar to make it watertight. There was room for only one man, and he entered, feet first, through the brass top. Bushnell designed the top so that there were small glass windows in it so that light could enter when the Turtle was above water. Today, this same design is used in our submarines: we call it a conning tower.

The driver had to turn a propeller crank to get the ship to move, and he controlled his underwater depth by pushing a valve down at his feet that allowed water into a tank at the bottom of the boat to make it heavier. When he wanted to go up, he had to use two hand pumps (they looked a little like our bicycle hand pumps) to pump the water out of the tank. Submarines today use this same ballast system— though when they pump the water out, they don't do it by hand! The air system was made up of two tubes that floated on the surface of the water. When it was time to submerge, the tubes could be stopped with cork valves, and there was about a 30-minute air supply. The boat stayed upright during all of this maneuvering because of hundreds of pounds of lead on the bottom.

The Turtle did take a man underwater and under an enemy ship, exactly as it was designed to do. It carried a keg mine on a timer (also designed by Bushnell) that successfully exploded—just not where it was supposed to! George Washington, when writing to Thomas Jefferson about the Turtle, summed it up well with these words, "I then thought, and still think, that it was an effort of genius." What do you think?

Questions to Ponder

❑ Bushnell was born in Saybrook, Connecticut. What is the capital of Connecticut, and is Connecticut considered a New England state or a Midwestern state? (*Hartford; New England; Connecticut was one of the original 13 colonies.*)

❑ When one is claustrophobic, one has a great fear of closed-in or narrow places. Mark out the space one would have inside the Turtle. Remember that at eye level one would see only oak beams. Small glass windows in the brass top would let light in, but only when the boat was above water. How would the darkness and close quarters affect you? Would you feel confined and claustrophobic, or would you not be bothered at all?

❑ Bushnell didn't go to college until he was about 30. Are you ever too old to get an education?

Douglas Mawson

(1882–1958)

They recorded winds of over 200 miles per hour (322 kpl). When they went outside to service their instruments, they had to wear long-toothed steel crampons attached to the bottoms of their thick leather boots. Even with the crampons (spikes that dug into the ice) and bending as low as they could, sometimes they could not stand; they would end up crawling on hands and knees. Ice masks would form over their entire faces because of their breath, and they would have to continually break off the ice.

Mawson's explorations enabled Australia to claim 2,500,000 square miles (6,474,970 km^2) of the Antarctic continent. Mawson's will to survive horrendous events and incredible physical endurance has made him a hero that all other polar explorers refer to. In 1912, Mawson, as part of his expedition to explore and gather scientific facts about unexplored territory, went with two other men eastward into the continent. They had 17 dogs and three sledges. They had enough provisions to last nine weeks. They had to cross endless fields of *sastrugi*, hard ridges of ice carved by polar winds. They had to deal with menacing crevasses, many of which could not be seen until they were at the precipice of, or beginning to founder into, that were hundreds of feet deep. And, of course, there was always the weather—fierce, biting, and relentless. During the worst of the storms, all they could do was hunker down in their canvas tent and wait it out.

Disaster struck on December 12, five weeks out. One of Mawson's men, with the sledge carrying most of their supplies and pulled by their strongest dogs, fell into a crevasse, an abyss of at least 150 feet (45.7 m). Mawson and his remaining man were 320 miles (515 km) away from their base hut. Ice-torn glaciers, unstable ice, and unfathomable cold separated them. No help would ever come for them. They were completely on their own. All that was left to them was enough rations for three men for a week. They had lost all their food reserves, dog food, heavy weather tent, waterproof clothes, plates, mugs, spoons, etc.

Only Mawson made it back. Surviving off of the remaining dogs, crawling much of the way on his hands and knees, his skin falling off of him in strips, his right nostril continually streaming blood, his hands and feet rotting at the ends, he made it home. The first man to reach him lifted Mawson's emaciated body and knocked the ice mask off from around his face. He stared at the sunken eyes and the fissured face, and he cried, "My God! Which one are you?"

Questions to Ponder

❏ Mawson was Australian. What is the capital of Australia? (*Canberra is the capital of Australia.*)

❏ Mawson traveled to the magnetic South Pole on January 16, 1909. He made this landmark journey by sledge with one other man. Is the magnetic South Pole marked on your map?

❏ Mawson normally weighed 15 stone. He was less than 8 stone when he returned. How much did he lose? (*A stone is a British unit of measure equal to 14 pounds. Mawson went from 210 pounds to less than 112. He lost about 100 pounds.*)

❏ Why do you think some people never give up?

❏ It has been said that Mawson's story is one of the greatest survival stories ever to be written. Do you agree?

Guion Bluford

(1942–)

Aerodynamics deals with the motion of air and other forces acting on bodies in motion. When cars and planes are designed, aerodynamics comes into play. What shape will allow the vehicle to go faster? What tilt of the wings or windshield gives the least resistance? The albatross is a bird with spectacular aerodynamics. Because its body is quite small in relation to how big its long, narrow wings are, the albatross can soar over the sea like a glider, riding the wind currents without even flapping its wings once!

Guion Bluford did not even know the word *aerodynamics* yet, but he was already testing its effects. Bluford had a paper route, and he would never just toss the papers onto his customers' front lawns. Instead, he would experiment by practicing different ways of aiming and throwing them. He did the same type of experimenting when he played table tennis. How did hitting the ball differently with the paddle every time effect where the ball where was going, its arc, and its speed. One positive side effect of his experiments with the table-tennis paddle was that he became an expert at the game!

Wanting to design aircraft, Bluford studied aerospace engineering in college. While there, he joined the Air Force ROTC (Reserve Officers Training Corps). After graduating, Bluford became an Air Force pilot. He served in the Vietnam War, receiving 10 Air Force medals for his distinguished service. Bluford taught other pilots how to fly, but he never gave up on his own education. As part of his work toward his Ph.D., Bluford developed a computer program that could calculate air pressure, density, and velocity on any part of an aircraft wing. Pretty impressive for a man whose high school guidance counselor said was not college material!

Bluford went on to become an astronaut. He was one of 34 people chosen out of 8,878 applicants. In 1983, as a member of a five-person crew aboard the space shuttle *Challenger*, Bluford became the first African American in space.

Questions to Ponder

❏ Bluford was born on November 22, 1942. How old is he today? Can you figure this out down to months and days?

❏ Bluford was born in Philadelphia, Pennsylvania. Is Philadelphia the capital of Pennsylvania? (*No, Harrisburg is.*)

❏ Bluford went into space four times, spending almost a total of 700 hours. About how many days is that? (*That is a little more than 29 days.*)

❏ Bluford once said, "If I had been the second or third [African American in space], then I probably could have enjoyed it more." What do you think Bluford meant by this?

❏ While in space for the first time, the president called the *Challenger*. His message was relayed via a ground transmitter in Hawaii. After congratulating all of the astronauts, he told Bluford, "You, I think, are paving the way for many others. You are making it plain we are in an era of brotherhood here in our land." Who was the president in 1983? (*Ronald Reagan was the president of the United States in 1983.*)

❏ Bluford flew fighter planes on 144 combat missions in Vietnam. Can you find Vietnam on the map, and do you know its capital? (*Hanoi is the capital of Vietnam.*)

William Shakespeare

(1564–1616)

"To be, or not to be, that is the question . . ." "My kingdom for a horse!" "O Romeo, Romeo! Wherefore art thou Romeo?" Do you recognize any of these lines? All three come from William Shakespeare's plays—*Hamlet, King Richard the Third,* and *Romeo and Juliet,* respectively. Shakespeare was an English playwright, actor, and poet. He is generally considered to be the greatest writer in history.

Shakespeare was a prodigious writer. When one is prodigious, one produces an extraordinary amount. Shakespeare produced a total of 38 plays. It has been said that his fellow actors bragged that Shakespeare "never blotted a line"—in other words, Shakespeare rarely had to revise or change what he had written. Knowing and liking his fellow actors as well as they liked him, Shakespeare would even write parts specifically for the actors that he knew would play them. Shakespeare's fellow actors must have enjoyed working with him, because not only did they brag about him, but they also took care to publish a complete collection of all of his plays after he died. We are fortunate they did this, for many plays written at that time have not been preserved.

Very little is known about Shakespeare's life, but we do know that he was married at the age of 18 to a woman who was eight years older than he was. They had three children. Shakespeare left his wife and children at home for the years he was in London writing, acting, and producing. He would visit them about once a year until, at the age of 46, he retired there to live the life of a country gentleman. It is an interesting note of history that Shakespeare actually made very little money from his writing. He accumulated his modest fortune by money earned acting and then investing it shrewdly in real estate.

Questions to Ponder

❑ Shakespeare was born in Stratford-on-Avon in England. What is the capital of England, and does England have a president or a prime minister? (*London is the capital of England. England has a prime minister.*)

❑ Outbreaks of the plague occasionally closed down everything in London, including the theaters. Some people even said the plague was God's punishment for theater! What was the plague? (*The bubonic plague, also known as the Black Death, was an acute infectious disease caused by a specific bacterium transmitted to humans by fleas from infected rats. One epidemic that struck Europe and parts of Asia in the 14th century killed as much as three quarters of the region's population in less than 20 years.*)

❑ Most serious actors consider Shakespeare the ultimate test of their skill. Which type of Shakespearean play would you choose to try—a comedy, a tragedy, a drama?

❑ Shakespeare wrote over 150 sonnets. One of his most famous starts with "Shall I compare thee to a summer's day?" What is a sonnet? (*A sonnet is a poem in the pattern of 14 lines that rhyme to a particular scheme and contain a certain beat.*)

❑ We use the term "star-crossed lovers" today. This phrase was first used by Shakespeare in the prologue of the play *Romeo and Juliet.* What do we mean when we refer to someone as star-crossed lovers? (*We mean that fate prevents the lovers from being together—as is the case of Romeo and Juliet.*)

Maya Ying Lin

(1959–)

How many of you have ever been to Washington, D.C., and seen the Vietnam Veterans Memorial? It is a black V-shaped wall that is tucked into the side of a small hill. Carved on the wall's black granite surface are the names of the men and woman who died in Vietnam—over 58,000 of them.

Many of the monuments in Washington are large and majestic. The Washington Monument is a white tower that reaches a bit over 555 feet into the sky. The Lincoln Memorial is styled after a Greek temple, and it houses a colossal statue of Abraham Lincoln.

When Maya Ying Lin walked over the ground that had been set aside for the Vietnam Memorial, she felt that she had to design a memorial that did not compete with the other memorials around her. Her design, one of the 1,420 submitted, was chosen for its simplicity and strength. As people trace over the names of those who have died, feeling the indentations of the letters with their fingers, their own faces and bodies are reflected back at them in the shiny, black granite. Many people are so affected that they feel compelled to leave flowers, medals, or letters at the memorial to those who died.

Lin was only 21 years old and a senior at Yale University when her design was chosen for the Vietnam Veterans Memorial. Lin continued to study at Yale as a graduate student in architecture. Lin did not think that she would ever design any more memorials. Instead, she wanted to focus on her career as an architect and as a sculptor. However, after the Southern Poverty Law Center in Montgomery, Alabama, asked her to design a civil-rights memorial, Lin changed her mind.

For months, Lin read and studied all that she could about the civil-rights movement. She was struck by a biblical phrase that Martin Luther King, Jr. used in two of his speeches: "We will not be satisfied until justice rolls down like waters and righteousness like a mighty stream."

Lin's memorial is a time line of the civil rights movement's major events, including the killings of 40 men, women, and children. The time line is covered with a layer of water, clear and fine enough that the time line can easily be read through it. Visitors are free to put their hands in the water and feel the letters etched into the granite.

Questions to Ponder

❑ Lin's parents fled Shanghai, China, in the 1940s to settle in Ohio. Is Shanghai the capital of China, and can you find it on the map? (*No, Beijing is the capital of China.*)

❑ Why should an architect always consider where something is going to be built before he or she designs it? (*The architect would not like the building to look out of place or to be overpowered by its surroundings. It would not make sense for an architect to put large windows on the side of a building that faces an ugly brick wall!*)

❑ Would Lin have been able to use water in her civil-rights memorial if she had been designing it for an open plaza in Alaska instead of the open plaza she designed it for in Alabama? (*No, the water would freeze!*)

❑ How could the architect who designed your school improve it? Make sure you consider the flow of students through the building, as well as noise, social actions, safety, and comfort!

Leo Baekeland

(1863–1944)

How many times in your life have you been in a situation where, when it was all said and done, you realized that you would have been a lot better off if you had just kept your mouth shut? In the 1890s Baekeland invented a photographic paper called Velox that could be developed in artificial light rather than sunlight. George Eastman, of Kodak camera fame, realized instantly that there would be a great market among amateur photographers for this paper. Eastman asked Baekeland if he would consider selling the rights to it. Baekeland hoped that he might get $50,000 for it but then decided that he would settle for $25,000. But before Baekeland could state his price, Eastman offered him $750,000! Baekeland was quite relieved that he had kept his mouth shut!

Baekeland was a man who changed our world. He made the first commercial batch of synthetic plastic. Look around you: plastic, a manmade fiber, is everywhere. We find plastic in our pens, our cars, our computers, our water bottles, and even in our artificial organs.

What made Baekeland successful was turning his thinking inside out. Baekeland was working on creating a way to dissolve the rock-hard substance produced by the reaction between phenol and formaldehyde. Baekeland thought that this resin might produce a substitute for shellac. Shellac was a highly prized natural substance harvested from insects in Southeast Asia. Then, instead of trying to dissolve the rock-hard resin, Baekeland thought, "Can I make use of this frustrating resin?" By controlling the conditions of the reaction between the phenol and the formaldehyde, Baekeland eventually did it. He turned it into Bakelite, a hard, clear solid that was impervious to acids, electicity, and heat and that could be dyed with bright colors. Bakelite was made into thousands of things: insulators, heat shields, knife handles, telephones, etc.

Baekeland once arrived home with four heavy suitcases. His grandson remembers that all four of the suitcases were locked. So that he would have to carry only one bulky key, Baekeland had locked the first suitcase and then put its key into the second suitcase. After locking the second suitcase, he put the key to that suitcase in the third case. The key to the third case was locked in the fourth case. Sounds great, but Baekeland had lost the key to the fourth case—the one key he was supposed to carry! When the key finally turned up and the cases were opened, they were full of books, papers, notebooks, and manuscripts. Baekeland had forgotten to pack clothes!

Questions to Ponder

❏ Baekeland was born in Belgium. What is the capital of Belgium, and can you name one country that borders Belgium? (*Brussels; Belgium is bordered by the Netherlands, Germany, France, and Luxembourg.*)

❏ Baekeland's work set the world into a new age—one that featured man-made materials and fibers. How has fashion been affected by man-made fibers? How many of you are wearing rayon, polyester, or nylon right now?

❏ When Baekeland needed to cool off, he would walk into a swimming pool with all of his clothes on—white sneakers, white shirt, duck trousers, and sun hat. He said, "The evaporation keeps you cool." Do you agree? How do you cool down?

❏ After reading Benjamin Franklin, Baekeland immigrated because he decided that America was the place of great promise for an educated man of low birth. Do you agree?

Captain James Cook

(1728–1779)

Captain James Cook was an English explorer who traveled around the world, charting vast areas of the Pacific Ocean, Australia, New Zealand, Tahiti, and the Arctic Ocean. Before his travels, many myths existed about these uncharted waters. Cook came back with stories of exotic people and animals.

Cook was the son of a poor farm laborer. He had only a few years of elementary schooling, but in his few spare hours from working, Cook taught himself mathematics, navigation, and astronomy. Cook was one of the first sea captains ever to keep his men free from scurvy and other diseases. He made his men eat fresh food, and there is an account of his lashing of two men for refusing to eat their fresh beef. Cook made his men air their bedding daily, and he even examined their hands! If anyone's hands did not pass his inspection, they missed their daily allowance of grog! Cook was very proud of his ships never becoming "hospital ships" or "death ships." Cook was the first man to sail across the Antarctic Circle. They saw hundreds of icebergs and plenty of penguins. Because Cook's men did not know that penguins could live far out at sea for months, the men were given false hope that land was close by.

When Cook first landed on the Hawaiian Islands, it was believed by the natives that he was a god. Great feasts and religious ceremonies were held for him. When he sailed away, the king and head priest were relieved because they had been concerned about the great quantities of food they had felt obligated to supply to him. Cook had to return just a week later, though, because a strong gale had ripped their sail and broke the mainmast. This upset the islanders because it did not seem right that a god's ship would need repairing. Perhaps Cook was not a god after all, they reasoned. After a misunderstanding in which it appeared that Cook was challenging another god, Cook was killed. Cook's men fought back and insisted that Cook's remains be brought back to them. Cook's bones were delivered "very decently wrapped in a large quantity of fine cloth." Cook's flesh had been burned as a sacrifice to the gods, and his bones had been treated as any high chief's would be—as sacred relics.

Questions to Ponder

- ❏ One of Cook's ship was called *Endeavor*. What does the word *endeavor* mean? (*Endeavor, when used as a verb, means to strive to achieve or reach. As a noun, endeavor means a serious, determined effort.*)

- ❏ Cook visited New Zealand, Australia, and Tahiti. Can you name their capitals and find them on the map? (*Wellington, New Zealand; Canberra, Australia; Papeete, Tahiti*)

- ❏ Cook was the first European to visit Hawaii. What is the capital of Hawaii, and what number state was it when it joined the Union? (*Honolulu is the capital. In 1959 Hawaii became the 50th state to join the Union.*)

- ❏ Cook and his men were intrigued by and ate a marsupial that is unique to Australia. What is a marsupial, and can you guess which one Cook saw? (*A marsupial is an animal that has a pouch in which to carry its young. Cook was seeing kangaroos. The first picture of a kangaroo was published in 1773 in the book* Voyages, *which described Cook's first voyage.*)

- ❏ How would you let people who had never seen anyone of your hair, eye, or skin color know you were friendly if you could not speak the same language?

Abigail Adams

(1744–1818)

"Remember the Ladies." These famous words were part of a letter that Abigail Adams sent to her husband, John Adams, when he was a delegate to the Continental Congress in March 1776. As the delegates worked to form the new nation of the United States, Abigail wrote, "I long to hear that you have declared an independency. And by the way, in the new code of laws, which I suppose it will be necessary for you to make, I desire you would remember the ladies, and be more generous and favorable to them than your ancestors." These words were written long before women gained the right to vote in this country. Women could not vote until the 19th amendment to the Bill of Rights passed in 1920!

Throughout her life, Abigail wrote hundreds and hundreds of letters. Her letters not only documented her love for and marriage to John Adams, but they also documented the birth of a nation—the United States. John Adams was a politically active lawyer, and he later became the United States's first vice president and its second president. Through her husband, Abigail met many of the major figures of her day, including George Washington, Thomas Jefferson, Ben Franklin, and King George III. In her letters, Abigail discussed all of them. Despite all the time that has passed, even today Abigail is considered to be one of the most distinguished and influential of the first ladies.

Abigail's spirit and sense of fairness is exemplified by her action during the Boston Massacre, which took place on March 5, 1770. British soldiers fired on a hostile crowd, and five people were killed. A British officer and eight soldiers were charged with murder. No lawyer, British or colonial, would counsel them. After Abigail gave her approval, Adams volunteered to defend them. Both Abigail and her husband strongly believed that all people had a right to legal counsel and a fair trial. This right was later written into our Bill of Rights: our sixth amendment guarantees the right to a speedy, fair trial, an impartial jury, and the right to counsel in all criminal cases. Adams argued the case brilliantly, and the men were found innocent. Adams believed that his defending the men would stop him from being elected to the Massachusetts legislature; but he was wrong. Even though Adams's election would leave him open to charges of treason from the English government, Abigail was pleased. She believed in independence as strongly as her husband.

Questions to Ponder

❑ Abigail was born in Massachusetts. Which of these three states—New York, Pennsylvania, and Vermont—does not border Massachusetts? What is the capital of Massachusetts? (*Pennsylvania does not border Massachusetts. The capital of Massachusetts is Boston.*)

❑ John Adams, Abigail's husband, was the first vice president of the United States. Who was the first president? What was his wife's name? (*George and Martha Washington*)

❑ John Adams was the second president. The sixth president was John Quincy Adams. Was John Quincy Adams related to John Adams? (*Yes, they were father and son.*)

❑ Historians learned much about the relationship between Abigail and her husband by studying their correspondence. They also learned about the United States and key figures in its development. With the development of the telephone and electronic mail, will historians have a harder time documenting the 21st century?

Stephen Hawking

(1942–)

A black hole is a region in space where gravity is so strong that not even light can escape. Stephen Hawking is a theoretical physicist who studies black holes. A physicist is a scientist who studies matter and energy and the interactions between them. Hawking's work on black holes has changed how we view and understand the universe.

Hawking's mind is not the only thing about him to admire. His courage and fortitude when it comes to combating a great physical handicap adds to what makes him a hero to many. Hawking has amyotrophic lateral sclerosis, a disease that is more commonly called ALS or Lou Gehrig's disease. ALS causes the nerves that control muscle movement to grow steadily weaker and weaker. Because of ALS, Hawking has been confined to a wheelchair since his late 20s. Unable to walk, stand, or feed himself, Hawking can move his left hand only enough to work the controls of his wheelchair and the computer that is his only means of communication. Hawking, with a twinkle in his eye, apologizes to people for how his voice synthesizer sounds: because it was programmed in California, it has an American accent!

When Hawking leaves his office late at night, he often runs his wheelchair at full speed down the dark paths to his home. His nurse and assistant have to run after him! Hawking has even taken his wheelchair onto the disco floor and turned and twisted his wheelchair amidst the dancers. Hawking is married and has children.

Questions to Ponder

❑ Hawking was born in Oxford, England, in 1942. Is Oxford the capital of England, and is 1942 before, during, or after World War II? (No, *London is the capital of England. World War II took place between 1939 and 1945, and thus Hawking was born during the war.*)

❑ Hawking studies our universe. The universe contains billions of galaxies. A galaxy contains billions of stars, as well as gas and dust clouds. If you were an interstellar traveler (a traveler journeying between stars), and you got lost, could you recite your address—up to your galaxy—to the Universal Lost and Found Police Department? (*address, country, continent, planet Earth, Milky Way galaxy*)

❑ What is cosmology, and what does a cosmologist study? (*Cosmology is the study of the origin, evolution, and fate of the universe. A cosmologist studies cosmology. Cosmo is a Greek prefix meaning universe. The Russian word for astronaut,* cosmonaut, *is derived from this prefix.*)

❑ Hawking says, "If you are disabled physically, you cannot afford to be disabled psychologically." What does Hawking mean by this?

❑ Hawking's work had to take into account *escape speed.* Escape speed is the speed an object must have to move away from another object forever, despite the pull of gravity. What do you think Earth's escape speed is compared to the sun's? (*Earth's escape speed is about 25,000 miles per hour or 7 miles per second. The sun's gravity is much stronger than that of Earth's. Its escape speed is about 400 miles per second.*)

Harry Houdini

(1874–1926)

No one, it was said, could ever escape from Scotland Yard's "darbies" (what British handcuffs were called at that time.) The police superintendent was more than happy to show the brazen American escape artist Harry Houdini that he was a fool for even thinking he could escape. The superintendent wrapped Houdini's arms around a pillar, and then left, saying that he would let "the American lad" stay there for a while. Only seconds after the superintendent reached his office, Houdini showed up.

Back in the United States, Houdini had himself stripped, searched, and locked into a jail cell in Washington, D.C. He was out within two minutes. He then opened up all the other cells and moved prisoners around to different cells! Another time, Houdini had his hands shackled behind his back, attached to leg irons, and then fastened to 10 pairs of handcuffs that were cuffed together to form a chain linking his hand and leg fetters. As if this was not enough, he was then placed in a closet. The police had searched the closet thoroughly to make sure that it was completely empty. It took just 10 minutes for Houdini to walk out. All the handcuffs and other manacles were still locked, but not on Houdini! The police then made Houdini try again, this time with a thick belt used to restrain violent patients around his arms and body. A padlocked straitjacket was placed over that! Once again, it took Houdini only a short time to escape.

How did Houdini do it? One of the most important reasons behind Houdini's success was his vigorous and relentless training. Houdini wrote how he trained every muscle, not just a group of muscles, to be "a responsive worker, quick and sure for its part, to make my fingers super-fingers in dexterity, and to train my toes to do the work of fingers." Houdini was born right-handed, but he forced himself to use the left hand until he could use it as well as the right. Houdini could use his toes as well as most people can use their fingers. For preparation for Houdini's underwater escape feats, he installed an oversized bathtub in his home so that he could practice holding his breath for several minutes. Houdini also studied ahead of time, learning about different locks and practicing on them. For example, when Houdini performed his escape from the Scotland Yard, Houdini had already figured out how to open the cuffs. For that type of cuff, he had to rap a certain spot on them against a hard surface.

Questions to Ponder

❑ Houdini told reporters that he was born in Appleton, Wisconsin. What is the capital of Wisconsin, and do any of the Great Lakes touch Wisconsin? (*Madison is the capital of Wisconsin. Both Lake Superior and Lake Michigan border Wisconsin.*)

❑ Houdini was an American, but he was actually born in Hungary. What is the capital of Hungary, and is Hungary in Asia, Europe, or South America? (*The capital of Hungary is Budapest. Hungary forms part of Europe.*)

❑ Houdini's birth name was Ehrich Weiss. Houdini took his stage name from the famous French magician Houdin. Many famous stage people and authors have changed their names. Why? (*There are many reasons: privacy, glamour, easier to pronounce and remember, to aid in promoting a particular image, etc.*)

❑ What exactly is Scotland Yard? (*Scotland Yard is the headquarters of the Criminal Investigation Department of the London Metropolitan Police.*)

Thurgood Marshall

(1908–1993)

Brown vs. the Board of Education of Topeka is one of the most famous cases that ever went before the Supreme Court. The decision the court made on this case changed the entire education system in the United States.

Before 1954, the policy in the United States was that "separate but equal" schools were all right. Children could be kept out of school simply because of the color of their skin. Even if a child lived next door to a school, if their skin color was not the right color, they would have to go to a different school, even if it were miles away.

What made this policy even worse was that the schools were not equal. Some schools, those with white student bodies, received more funding. They had better buildings, facilities, books, equipment, and transportation. Other schools were overcrowded, without enough books, and often with much lower standards simply because there were not enough teachers or materials.

Thurgood Marshall argued this case in front of the Supreme Court. He said, "The only thing [segregation] can be is an inherent determination that the people who were formerly in slavery, regardless of anything else, shall be kept as near that stage as is possible. And now is the time, we submit, that the Court should make it clear that that is not what our Constitution stands for."

The Court agreed unanimously. It concluded that the segregation of children in public schools solely on the basis of race deprives the children of the minority group of equal educational opportunities.

Known as "the little man's lawyer," Marshall argued 19 cases before the Supreme Court. He won 14 of them. Then, in 1967, Marshall was appointed to the Supreme Court. Marshall was the first African American to become a Supreme Court justice. The Supreme Court, part of our judicial branch of government, is the highest court in the land. There is one chief justice and eight associate justices. Justices are appointed for life. They are chosen by the president, but they must be confirmed by the Senate. Justices cannot be taken off the court just because there is a new president. The only way to relieve a justice from his duty is to successfully impeach him. Decisions that are handed down by the Supreme Court are rendered by majority vote. Supreme Court decisions have an extreme impact on social policy.

Questions to Ponder

❑ Marshall was born in Baltimore, Maryland. Is Baltimore the capital of Maryland, and can you find it on the map? (*The capital of Maryland is Annapolis.*)

❑ Was Maryland one of the 13 original colonies? (*Yes. Maryland was the 7th state to ratify the Constitution.*)

❑ The Supreme Court meets in Washington, D.C. What is Washington, D.C., and what does the D.C. stand for? (*Washington, D.C., is the capital of the United States. The D.C. stands for District of Columbia. The District of Columbia is not a state, although some people want it to be one. Residents of the District of Columbia could not even vote in presidential elections until 1961.*)

❑ What are the three branches of our federal government? (*The three branches are the executive, legislative, and judicial.*)

Orville and Wilbur Wright

(1871–1948) and (1867–1912)

On December 17, 1903, a heavy, ungainly looking glider with a heavy engine rose from the ground and flew. It was the first time in history that an engine-powered machine had ever elevated itself off the ground and covered distance. In addition, because Orville and Wilbur Wright had designed moveable wing assembly parts to direct the craft, they could direct and steer where the machine was going.

This event did not come quickly or easily. It took years. When they were young, the Wright brothers' mother taught them that, "If you get it right on paper, it'll be right when you build it." The brothers wanted a sled, and their mother helped them design one. Their mother encouraged them to think about what the sleds the other children owned looked like, how fast they went, how much they could hold, and their measurements. She introduced them to the concept of wind resistance: a low sled, with them leaning down on it, would give much less wind resistance than a high sled with someone sitting upright. When the Wright brothers first showed up with their sled, the other children laughed at them because the sled was long, narrow, and looked as though it wouldn't hold anyone. Challenged to a race, they not only left the others far, far behind them, but they traveled an extra 100 yards (91.4 m) farther down the slope than any of the other sleds had ever gone!

Orville and Wilbur Wright (cont.)

When Orville and Wilbur returned from Kitty Hawk after the successful flight, no one believed them! They were laughed at! The brothers ignored the winks and continued to improve their plane. They flew in a neighbor's cow pasture, and people began to believe them only when their father, a bishop, said that he had timed them staying aloft for 39 minutes. President Roosevelt read about the machine and insisted that he wanted to see a demonstration. The brothers were told that they could demonstrate the plane in private so that they would not be embarrassed if it didn't fly or crashed. The brothers said, "Ask a thousand, ask a million. . . . We don't care." The plane flew for over an hour on a guided flight, and then, as if that was not enough, the brothers went up again with a lieutenant who weighed 180 pounds (81.6 kg) as a passenger. Every newspaper headlined the story the next day. No longer did the Wright brothers have to worry about neighbors not believing them!

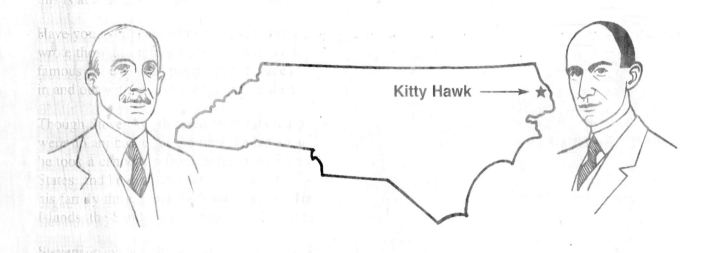

Questions to Ponder

❑ Orville was born in Dayton, Ohio, and Wilbur near New Castle, Indiana. What are the capitals of these two states, and how close are they to each other? (*Columbus, Ohio; Indianapolis, Indiana. Indiana is west of Ohio; they border each other.*)

❑ The first four controlled, sustained flights in a power-driven airplane took place at Kitty Hawk, North Carolina. What is North Carolina's capital, and does part of the Appalachian Mountain chain run through North Carolina? (*Raleigh. The Blue Ridge and Great Smoky Mountains, both part of the Appalachian chain, are in North Carolina.*)

❑ Why do jockeys lean as close to their horses as they can during a race? (*to cut down on wind resistance*)

❑ Why did the Wright brothers try their machine at Kitty Hawk? (*The United States Weather Bureau had told them that at Kitty Hawk there were steady winds and no trees.*)

❑ How have planes changed our lives? (*They have, in a sense, made the world much smaller.*)

Jim Thorpe

(1888–1953)

The pentathlon and decathlon are considered to be two of the most difficult and prestigious events to win during the Olympic Games. When Thorpe entered these events in the 1912 Olympics, the pentathlon consisted of the running broad jump, the javelin throw, the 200-meter dash, the discus toss, and the 1500-meter run. The decathlon was the pentathlon minus the 200-meter dash but plus the 100-meter dash, the pole vault, the high jump, the 110-meter hurdles, the shot put, and the 400-meter run. Thorpe won gold medals in both events.

Thorpe had a rough time when he was young. Born in what was then known as Indian Territory (present day Oklahoma), Thorpe was forced to go to schools that did not allow him to speak his native language or wear Native-American clothes. Thorpe often ran away. The only person who seemed to calm Thorpe down was his twin brother. But when they were almost 10, Thorpe's twin died. Thorpe's father then sent him to a boarding school far away in Kansas so that Thorpe could not run away again. Thorpe ran away anyway, so next he was sent to Carlisle, an Indian school in Pennsylvania. This is where Thorpe's athletic abilities began to show up. Thorpe was simply a phenomenal athlete when it came to football, baseball, and track. The first time Thorpe attempted high jump, he was in his heavy work overalls. He set the school record with a single jump! With Thorpe playing football, his tiny team beat several highly rated college teams.

Thorpe was forced to surrender his Olympic medals after it was revealed that Thorpe had played semi-professional baseball. Thorpe was ignorant of the Olympic rules, and he was devastated when the medals were taken from him. Many people objected, and over the years they fought for Thorpe's medals to be returned. Many other athletes had done what Thorpe had done, but it seemed as if Thorpe was singled out for punishment. Some countries even paid their athletes to compete in the Olympics, a practice that was definitely against the rules. During research of the 1912 Olympic bylaws, one woman discovered that protests regarding the qualifications of an Olympic competitor had to be made in writing and received by the Olympic committee within 30 days of the distribution of the medals. The newspaper report that caused Thorpe's medals to be taken from him wasn't published until seven months after the Olympics. The Olympic committee had for years told Thorpe that ignorance was no excuse, and now their own words were turned against them. They had stripped Thorpe of his medals, ignorant of their own bylaws! Thorpe's medals were restored to him posthumously (in other words, after his death); they were presented to his children.

Questions to Ponder

❏ Some people say that the decathlon is for athlete's who aren't really good enough in any single event. Most people, though, think the decathlon is the ultimate test of speed, strength, and stamina, and that the one who wins this event is the best all-around athlete in the world. What do you think?

❏ The beginning of decathlon is *deca. Deca* can also be seen in "decade" and "decagon." What does *deca* stand for, and what are a decade and a decagon? How about a decimeter? (*Deca is a Greek prefix meaning "ten." A decade is 10 years, and a decagon is a 10-sided figure.* Deci *is a Latin prefix meaning "tenth," and a decimeter is a tenth of a meter. A deciliter would be a tenth of a liter. Think about the prefix* deci *and our decimal system.*)

❏ What is the capital of Oklahoma? (*Oklahoma City is the capital of Oklahoma.*)

Maria Gaetana Agnesi

(1718–1799)

The Witch of Agnesi was named after Maria Gaetana Agnesi. However, the Witch of Agnesi is not a witch; it is a mathematical formula. Agnesi was a brilliant mathematician who figured out how to duplicate precisely the volume of a cube. How did her formula, still used today, get its name? Agnesi had published a book in 1748 that was so popular that it was translated into several different languages. Through a misunderstanding in translation, the formula became known in English as the Witch of Agnesi.

Does sleep help genius? Agnesi's biographers write that Agnesi would often awaken from a deep sleep and write down the solution to a problem that she had been working on earlier in the day—yet Agnesi could not recall waking up and writing down the solution! When Agnesi would become fully awake in the morning, she would be surprised at the conclusion that was written out in detail.

Agnesi was a child prodigy. A child prodigy is a child who is naturally and extraordinarily gifted at something. Agnesi wasn't just gifted in math: she was also amazing when it came to languages. At the age of five, Agnesi, an Italian, spoke fluent French; and by the age of 11, she could translate Greek, Latin, German, Spanish, and some Hebrew. She was first published at the age of nine, when her defense of higher education for women (written in Latin, by the way!) was printed. By the age of 20, Agnesi had published a book on differential calculus.

After Agnesi's father died in 1752, Agnesi devoted her life to helping the sick and the poor. She converted her home into a public hospital, and she was appointed director of a charitable institution that provided care for the elderly and homeless.

Questions to Ponder

❑ Agnesi was born in Milan, Italy. What is the capital of Italy, and what seas border Italy? (*Rome. Italy is surrounded by the Adriatic Sea, the Tyrrhenian Sea, the Ligurian Sea, and the Mediterranean Sea.*)

❑ Agnesi was brilliant when it came to math. How are you? Try these math-related riddles:

—A dog is on a leash. The leash is four feet long, but the dog can eat from a bowl six feet away. How is this possible? (*No one is holding the leash, and the leash isn't tied to anything either.*)

—Sarah has 10 coins that add up to 50¢. Five of the coins are nickels. What are the other five coins? (*The other five coins are nickels, too.*)

—If it takes three minutes to boil eggs for breakfast, how long would it take to boil 10 eggs? (*three minutes*)

—It's cloudy and cold tonight. Will it be sunny in 48 hours? (*Probably not. If one measures 48 hours from tonight, it will still be night. It is usually not sunny at night.*)

—How many months have 28 days? (*All 12 have 28 days. February has only 28 days.*)

❑ When Agnesi published the book *Analytical Institutions* in 1748, Empress Maria Theresa sent Agnesi a casket of jewels in recognition. If women had been allowed, Agnesi would have been made a member of the French Academy of Science. Should organizations be allowed to keep out males or females?

Yo-Yo Ma

(1955–)

Yo-Yo Ma gave his first concert when he was five years old; he played both the cello and the piano. Ma's education had started young. When he was only four, his cello instructor was astonished when Ma started playing a Bach suite. Ma's father had assigned two measures a day of the suite to Ma to memorize. Then the next day, Ma would have to memorize the next two measures. This would continue until the entire suite was memorized. Ma said learning in this way enabled him to recognize patterns, their similarities and their differences, and he soon developed a feeling for musical structure. Ma's father used this same type of instruction when it came to Ma learning Chinese calligraphy. Ma learned two characters, and the next day he had to learn two more.

Though Ma gave many concerts while quite young, Ma feels that it is a good thing that he did not perform too much as a child. Ma says, "It's risky to create careers for 'geniuses' at age nine. The tendency is to make do with your technical limitations in order to get through your performances. The weaknesses then easily become ingrained."

Ma's family moved to New York when he was seven. Though Ma continued to excel with his cello, he found it hard to reconcile his traditional Chinese home life with being an American teenager. Ma went wild, and he says he put his parents through some very rough years.

When Ma travels around the world performing, he must take his cello with him. Ma's instruments are one of a kind, rare and expensive, and he cannot risk having them put in the regular baggage hold. Ma always pays full price for an extra seat so that his cello can have its own chair. One time a plane was completely booked, and even though Ma had paid for two seats, the airline could not find the reservation for the second seat. Ma was told that his cello would have to go in the hold. Ma insisted that the cello had to travel with him. Finally, in desperation, Ma asked to see the flight list. After scrutinizing it, he found his cello's reservation at last: "Mr. Cabinba," short for "cabin baggage."

Questions to Ponder

❑ Ma was born in Paris. Of what European country is Paris the capital? (*Paris is the capital of France.*)

❑ Many child geniuses and performers have private tutors. Do you think that this is appropriate? (Note: Ma feels that part of the reason he became the world-class musician that he is today is because he went to Harvard and limited himself to one performance a month while he was there as a student.)

❑ Isaac Stern first heard Ma perform when Ma was only five or six. Stern said, "The cello was literally larger than he was." About how large is a cello, and how many strings does it have? (*The cello is about 47 inches long, including the neck. The body is usually about 27.5 inches. The cello has four strings.*)

Guglielmo Marconi

(1874–1937)

Guglielmo Marconi once took apart his cousin's sewing machine so that he could make a mechanical roasting spit. While she wept, he put it back together again, and much to her relief, though disassembled and reassembled, it still worked! It wasn't so easy when it came to the dinner plates! Marconi concocted an elaborate contraption of string and dinner plates that he shot high-voltage electricity into. Marconi's father was enraged with Marconi's "smashing" and irreparable results.

Marconi was shy and withdrawn as a child, and though he read avidly the books in his father's library, when he went to school he did very poorly. Marconi put everything that he read to the test—for example, he constructed a still after reading about how they worked; but Marconi's constant tinkering did not improve his school grades. Marconi ended up flunking out of secondary school, and he did not pass the entrance examinations to the Italian Naval Academy or to the University of Bologna. Marconi ended up going to a technical school, and it was there that two very important things happened: a teacher introduced Marconi to electrophysics, and a blind telegrapher taught Marconi Morse code.

While on vacation, Marconi read about some experiments by Heinrich Hertz that dealt with the transmission of electromagnetic waves. Marconi believed that the Hertzian waves could be adapted to a system of wireless telegraphy. Obsessed, Marconi worked in his parent's attic for months. During that time, he rarely came out, and his mother took to leaving trays of food by the door.

Then, late one summer night, Marconi woke up his mother and took her to the attic. He tapped on a telegraph key and, from the far end of the attic, a bell tinkled. There was not a wire between the bell and the key—only air. What would eventually become wireless telegraphy, radios, televisions, and radar was discovered by a 20-year-old loner.

Marconi then increased the distance, from attic to garden to open fields, all the while improving his equipment. On December 12, 1901, all doubters were silenced: Marconi's receiving station at Signal Hill, St. John's, Newfoundland, picked up the signal transmitting across the Atlantic from Cornwall at the tip of England. Marconi was awarded the Nobel Prize for his pioneering work in 1909.

Questions to Ponder

❑ Marconi was born in Italy. Sicily and Sardinia belong to Italy. What are Sicily and Sardinia, and what is Italy's capital? (*Sicily and Sardinia are islands. Rome is the capital of Italy.*)

❑ Can you spot Newfoundland on the map?

❑ When Marconi was not playing hooky and did attend school, he was often made fun of by the other students and his teacher for his English-accented Italian. Marconi's mother was Scotch-Irish. She met Marconi's father when she was visiting Italy. Her parents had sent her there to prevent her from singing at London's Covent Garden—something that nice girls did not do! Should one ever tease someone because of his or her accent? Have you ever been somewhere where it is you with the accent, and not the other way around?

❑ How often do you listen to the radio? How has the radio changed the world? (Consider information, speed, and communication.)

❑ Some states require high-school exit exams. Would this Nobel Prize winner pass?

Marian Anderson

(1902–1993)

Marian Anderson had sung in most of Europe's capitals. She had performed all over Scandinavia to packed concert halls. She sang before kings and queens. The world famous Toscanini told her, "Yours is a voice such as one hears once in a hundred years." Yet, Anderson was told that she could not sing in her own nation's capital. In 1939, Washington, D.C., was still a segregated city. Washington's famous Constitution Hall was owned by the Daughters of the American Revolution (DAR), and they would not allow Anderson to sing because they said that her skin was the wrong color.

Mrs. Roosevelt, the First Lady and wife of President Roosevelt, took action: she resigned from the DAR. Newspaper headlines all over the United States reported the story. It was discussed on radio stations. The ladies of the DAR did not apologize, and they did not change their minds.

Officials of the Department of the Interior invited Anderson to sing at the Lincoln Memorial. Carved into the Lincoln Memorial are the words from Lincoln's Emancipation Proclamation: " . . . a new nation conceived in liberty and dedicated to the proposition that all men are created equal."

When Anderson sang on Easter Sunday, the number of people who had come to hear her, Americans of all colors, was so great that the crowd stretched all the way from the foot of the Lincoln Memorial to the Washington Monument. The Secretary of the Interior introduced Anderson by saying, "Genius, like justice, is blind. Genius draws no color lines." Anderson's first song began "My country 'tis of thee / Sweet land of liberty."

Questions to Ponder

❏ Anderson was born in Philadelphia. In what state is Philadelphia, and what is that state's capital? (*Philadelphia is in Pennsylvania. The capital of Pennsylvania is Harrisburg.*)

❏ Anderson gave concerts in Scandinavia. Scandinavia is a region of Northern Europe. Can you name two of the countries that make up Scandinavia? (*Scandanavia is comprised of Norway, Sweden, Denmark, Finland, and Iceland.*)

❏ Once during the performance of a song in German, Anderson forgot the words; and so, without stopping her singing, she made some up. The experience frightened her so much that she decided that she had to learn German. Would you have been able to make up words if you forgot them?

❏ Anderson's range was so wide that she could sing alto, soprano, and tenor. What is the difference? (*In four-part harmony, the range of notes goes in this order: bass, tenor, alto, soprano.*)

❏ Anderson's mother taught her that as soon as she went out on stage, even before she started to sing, she had made her first impression. Anderson always dressed impeccably (excellently, neatly) and stood proudly. Was Anderson's mother right? How does the way you dress and how you stand affect the way people treat you?

Hans Christian Anderson

(1805–1875)

It is normal to be nervous while one is taking an examination. Your hands might get a little sweaty, and you might feel a little hollow at the bottom of your stomach; but have you ever gotten so nervous that you accidentally sprayed your professor's face with ink? Hans Christian Anderson did.

Anderson is known today as a writer of fairy tales. His power of description coupled with his sense of fantasy and highly developed sensitivity contributed to his mastery. How many of you have heard of "The Little Mermaid," "The Ugly Duckling," "The Emperor's New Clothes," "The Red Shoes," "The Snow Queen," and "The Nightingale?" Anderson wrote a total of 168 fairy tales. Anderson's tales were made up, but there were things in Anderson's own life that read like a fairy tale. For example, Anderson desperately wanted to get married, but he had a problem with the women he chose. The first woman Anderson wanted as his wife he had never even met! Even more odd was the fact that she wasn't even living—but that would be the case when the person with whom you fell in love was the ancestor of a friend and you had only seen a portrait of the person!

When one is frugal, one is sparing when it comes to using up his or her resources. Anderson was frugal when it came to dressing himself. He would wear his clothes and shoes long after he outgrew them. If someone gave him a coat that was too big, Anderson would not get rid of it. Instead, he would stuff it with newspapers to make it fit.

Questions to Ponder

❑ Anderson was born in Denmark. What is the capital of Denmark, and is Denmark closer to Sweden or Italy? (*Copenhagen is the capital of Denmark. Denmark is closer to Sweden than it is to Italy.*)

❑ When Anderson was feeling really melancholy, he would get horrible toothaches. Anderson even got these toothaches in his false teeth after he had lost all of his teeth! What does *melancholy* mean? (*When one is melancholy, one is dejected, sad, and feeling dismal. A melancholy song is one that makes you feel sad.*)

❑ Anderson was described as awkward and unattractive. He once wrote of himself, "His nose as mighty as a cannon, / His eyes are tiny, like green peas." Do you think Anderson put some of his feelings about his own appearance into the story "The Ugly Duckling"?

❑ During the Denmark nights, there can be 17 hours of darkness. Would that seem strange to you?

❑ Anderson was a nature lover who was known to hug trees. There are some people who teach young children who are lost in the woods to "hug a tree." Why do you think they do this? (*There is a better chance of being found if you remain in one place. Searchers travel through the woods systematically, and if the lost child keeps moving, they often end up going in circles and walk through places that have already been searched. If a child sees a tree as a friend and stays by his friend, there is less chance of him being missed.*)

❑ Anderson loved traveling. Instead of staying in his own house, he would always stay with friends or in hotels. The minute he had enough money, he would travel. Where would you travel to if you had enough money?

Cleopatra
(69 B.C.–30 B.C.)

Cleopatra desperately wanted to meet Julius Caesar. Caesar, ruler of Rome, was in Egypt, having pursued one of his enemies there to kill him. Cleopatra wanted Caesar's help. Cleopatra was the daughter of Ptolemy XI, and, as was the custom at that time, she was married to her younger brother, Ptolemy XII. Marriage between siblings took place among royal families so that the lineage would remain pure. When they married, Cleopatra was 17, and her brother was 10. Now, three years later, both Cleopatra and her brother were fighting over who would be supreme ruler of Egypt. Cleopatra knew that with Caesar's army behind her she could reign without fear of her brother.

Intelligent and forward, Cleopatra sped to Caesar's palace. Wanting to enter the palace undetected, Cleopatra rolled herself up into a carpet. Her servant then draped the carpet over his shoulder and boldly walked past the palace guards to the room where Caesar was! He presented the carpet as a gift from Cleopatra. When Cleopatra emerged, she spoke in Latin, the language of the Romans to Caesar. Historians have written that Caesar was overwhelmed by her charm, boldness, courage, and stories. By the time Caesar left, Cleopatra was firmly on the throne of Egypt.

After Caesar was killed, Cleopatra aligned herself with Marc Antony. Cleopatra presented herself to Antony quite differently from the way she introduced herself to Caesar. Dressed as Venus, attended by beautiful children draped in jewels, she sailed down the Nile on a splendid barge. Everything on the barge was perfumed, and Cleopatra had servants playing drums, flutes, and harps. The oars were silver, and the sails were purple. Antony was as wildly attracted and taken in as Caesar.

Antony's rule was challenged by Octavian. When it became apparent that Octavian was going to win, Antony and Cleopatra fled. Despite Antony's forces momentarily succeeding in pushing back Octavian's army, when Antony heard the rumor that Cleopatra was dead, he flung himself on his sword. He did not die instantly, and Cleopatra had time to have him carried into her temple, where he died in her arms. Octavian was afraid that Cleopatra would kill herself, too, in her desire to join her lover. It has been said that when he confronted Cleopatra to tell her that he would parade her as a prisoner in Rome, he kept his eyes on the floor so that he would not be taken in by her charms.

Cleopatra succeeded in never being shown as a prisoner. Cleopatra had her servants bring her a couple of asps, sacred and deadly snakes. Some legends claim that the snakes were brought in a basket of figs. Regardless of the way she obtained the snakes, Cleopatra died dressed in her jeweled and perfumed best.

Questions to Ponder

❏ Cleopatra was queen of Egypt. What is the capital of Egypt? (*Cairo*)

❏ Was Cleopatra audacious? (*Audacious means adventurous, reckless, bold, and daring. Think of Cleopatra in the rug. One could certainly say that she was audacious!*)

❏ Why was Rome so interested in Egypt? (*Bread. Roman leaders gave out free bread made from Egyptian wheat. Egypt also provided wild beasts and sand for the arena floors for the disgusting gladiator fights.*)

Oscar De La Hoya

(1973–)

Oscar De La Hoya was walking five blocks from his home to his girlfriend's house when five men with guns jumped out of a pickup truck and stole his wallet. When Oscar returned home two hours later, he found his wallet (and the $150 he had in it) there. The robbers must have realized who he was from his I.D. and returned it. Who was Oscar de la Hoya?

Oscar was born on February 4, 1973, in East Los Angeles. Just blocks away from the modest home he lived in with his parents, siblings, and grandparents, were rough neighborhoods. Crimes, drugs, and gangs abounded. Oscar's father took Oscar to a boxing gym at the age of six, and Oscar was on his way.

In 1992, Oscar flew to Barcelona, Spain, to compete in the Olympics. Oscar didn't only worry about beating his opponents; he worried about beating the computer too. Judging has never been completely fair, especially with judges often favoring certain countries. In the 1988 Olympic Games in Seoul, Korea, everyone was sure that a U.S. boxer had beat his South Korean opponent. To everyone's surprise, the majority of the judge's had voted for the South Korean. Even the South-Korean boxer thought that the American had won. Perhaps there was an anti-American bias. Perhaps the judges had been bribed.

To deal with this, a new computer system was set up. The computer system was just as messy and unfair. Each judge is given a keypad with two buttons. Every time a boxer from the red corner scores a blow, the red keypad is pushed. Every time the boxer from the blue corner scores a blow, the blue keypad is pushed. Sounds good so far, but at least three of the five judges had to press the button within one second for a blow to be recorded by the computer. What if the boxer scoring the blows has his back to the judge?! What if the punch was thrown with such lightning speed that the judge did not see it? What if the judges could not keep up with the fight? What if the judge hit the wrong button? What if the judge was cheating, and so was purposefully not punching the button? If the judge was questioned, he could say that the computer made the error!

Oscar beat his opponents and the computer! He was the only American to win a gold metal in boxing in 1992. After his triumph, Oscar ran around the ring with the flags from the United States and Mexico. He waved the United States flag because he was a U.S. citizen, and he waved the Mexican flag to show respect to the country where both his mother and father had been born.

Questions to Ponder

❑ De La Hoya was born in California. What is the capital of California? Is it to the north or south of Los Angeles? (*Sacramento is north of Los Angeles.*)

❑ What ocean borders California? (*The Pacific Ocean borders California.*)

❑ If you could compete in an Olympic event, what event would you choose?

❑ What is the capital of Spain? (*Madrid is the capital of Spain.*)

❑ The Strait of Gibraltar separates Spain from what continent? (*Africa*)

❑ Could you be a fair judge, even if you were judging your friends?

❑ Some people feel that when there are many judges, the highest and lowest scores should be thrown out. Do you think that this would make the final score more fair?

Henry Stanley and David Livingston

(1841–1904) and (1813–1873)

Henry Stanley was abandoned to the "workhouse." The workhouse was a place where Britain's homeless, unemployed, elderly, and anyone who was needy, could have a place to stay as long as they worked for it. It was hard living: the food was bad and there was not enough of it; the work was hard; and everyone slept in underheated, overcrowded dormitories. Stanley hated it and left at the age of 15. He sailed to America, where he worked for a man in New Orleans. Stanley took the name of this man, saying that the man had adopted him. Before, Stanley was known as John Rowlands.

Stanley went on to become a newspaper reporter, and in 1871, Stanley was sent to Africa to look for David Livingston. Livingston was a missionary medical doctor who had gone to work in South Africa. He had become famous because of his exploring. He was the first European to travel the Zambezi River, see Victoria Falls, and cross the Kalahari Desert. Livingston went to check out the source of the Nile in 1866, but by 1871, many people in Britain thought he was dead. Even the government was not sure as to whether or not a rescue party should be sent out. An American newspaper hired Stanley to see if he could find Livingston.

Livingston was not lost. He knew where he was, but he was quite ill and quickly running out of food and supplies. When Stanley met up with him beside Lake Tanganyika, Stanley uttered his now famous greeting, "Dr. Livingston, I presume?" Stanley and Livingston have become linked in history, but they actually only traveled together for a few months. They were two very different individuals. One of Livingston's objectives was to document the slave trade. He found it abhorrent, and he wanted it stopped. He witnessed and documented violent attacks by Arab slavers, and he brought back slave chains to England as proof of the cruelty of the slave trade. Stanley, in contrast, used some of these slave chains on his other expeditions when he wanted to keep his men from running away. Because of the way he dealt with obstacles by using explosives, Stanley became known as Bula Matari which means "smasher of rocks."

While traveling, both Stanley and Livingston had to watch out for mosquitoes and tsetse flies. The mosquitoes carried malaria, and the tsetse flies could transmit the disease *trypanosomiasis*, or sleeping sickness as it is commonly referred to. This name came about because it makes its victims weak and tired.

Questions to Ponder

❑ Stanley was born in Wales. What country is Wales part of? (*Wales is a political division of Great Britain and Ireland.*)

❑ Livingston was born on the outskirts of Glasgow, Scotland. What is the capital of Scotland? (*The capital of Scotland is Edinburgh.*)

❑ Stanley sailed to New Orleans when he left the workhouse. In what state is New Orleans, and what is the capital of that state? (*New Orleans is located in Louisiana. Baton Rouge is the capital of Louisiana.*)

❑ Livingston was the first European to cross the Kalahari Desert. Can you find the Kalahari Desert on the map, and do you spell desert with one s or two? (*One wants more dessert, so dessert needs more s! Desert has only one.*)

❑ Stanley found Livingston beside Lake Tanganyika. Can you find this lake on the map?

Susan B. Anthony

(1820–1906)

In 1872, Susan B. Anthony was arrested. Her crime? Voting. Anthony had read an advertisement in the newspaper that said, "Citizens, register now! If you were not permitted the right to vote, you would fight for the right, undergo all privations for it, face death for it. You have it now at the cost of five minutes' time to be spent in seeking your place of registration, and having your name entered." Putting this with the Fourteenth Amendment that said, "All persons born or naturalized in the United States . . . are citizens of the United States," and the Fifteenth Amendment that said, "The right of citizens of the United States to vote shall not be denied or abridged . . . on account of race, color, or previous condition of servitude (slavery)," Anthony knew that she should vote. Thus, she went down, registered herself, and voted.

Yet, women were not allowed to vote in the United States until April 26, 1920, when the Nineteenth Amendment was adopted. This amendment proclaimed, "The rights of citizens of the United States shall not be denied or abridged . . . on account of sex." Women who worked for the right to vote were called suffragists. Suffragists worked for the Suffrage Movement, the movement for the right to vote.

When the deputy marshal knocked on Anthony's door to tell her that she was under arrest, he told the dignified silver-haired woman that she could just meet him at his office when she was ready. He did not need to escort her. Anthony dramatically extended her arms out for handcuffs, but the deputy didn't put any on. He escorted her to the streetcar where the conductor then asked her for her fare. She said so that everyone could hear, "I am traveling at the expense of the government. This gentleman is escorting me to jail. Ask him for my fare." The deputy reluctantly paid!

Released on bail, Anthony spoke everywhere she could to publicize her cause. When she went to trial, though, the judge was so angry that a woman dare think that she had rights that he immediately proclaimed Anthony guilty. He did not allow Anthony to speak, saying that women were not competent to be witnesses in court, and he ordered the jury to pronounce a guilty verdict, and then dismissed them before they could open their mouths! He fined Anthony $100 plus court costs. Anthony told the judge that she would never pay it. She never did, and the judge knew if he did imprison her, she could appeal to the Supreme Court (and possibly win). Thus, Anthony went free.

Questions to Ponder

❑ Anthony was born in Adams, Massachusetts. What is the capital of Massachusetts, and can you name another state that borders Massachusetts? (*Boston is the capital. New York, Vermont, New Hampshire, Rhode Island, and Connecticut all border Massachusetts.*)

❑ What piece of American money pictured Susan B. Anthony? (*For two years (1979 and 1981), the Susan B. Anthony dollar coin was minted. It was silver, with eleven sides. It was discontinued because everyone thought that it was a quarter! Have you seen one?*)

❑ Many countries have one-dollar coins. Why would a government be interested in dollar coins? (*They last a lot longer.*)

❑ Are there countries today where women cannot vote? (*Yes*)

❑ Even though voting is a privilege that Americans fought and died for, very few Americans actually vote on election day. Why do you think this is?

❑ Australia charges fines if one does not vote. Should we?

Frederick McKinley Jones

(1892–1961)

You're at the fair, the beach, a park, a store, and all of a sudden you have a craving for ice cream. No problem. You simply go up to the counter clerk and buy one. But how did the ice cream get there? How did it get to the store without melting?

Frederick McKinley Jones' supervisor was playing golf with a man who was complaining that an entire truck load of chickens had spoiled because the ice in which they were packed had melted before he could reach his destination. Jones' boss had said that he would make him a truck that could keep them cool, but he had not meant the man to take it seriously! When a truck was dropped off at Jones' work, Jones' boss had to call up the owner and tell him that he was just kidding when he said that he could build a refrigerator for the truck.

Enter Jones. Jones was a mostly self-educated African American who was resourceful and curious. He never had the opportunity to go to high school, but he used the library extensively. Whenever anything interested him, he would check out every book on the subject and study them until he understood every part of them completely and thoroughly. Jones climbed into the truck, started measuring, and spent most of the night making calculations. The next day he told his boss that he could build the kind of air-cooling unit that the owner of the truck wanted. He did it.

From there, he and his boss started a company that manufactured a compact, automatic shock-proof air conditioner for truck transportation of foods. Jones kept on improving his machine, and over the years, Jones has been awarded more than 60 patents, 40 of them being for refrigeration equipment alone.

Jones's cooling units changed the way Americans ate. He also helped his country greatly during World War II. Jones designed refrigerator units that were sent to army hospitals and battlefields in the South Pacific. Jones's units were used to keep the blood serum needed for transfusions at the correct temperature. Needed medicine and food could also be kept at the right temperature for the soldiers. Some of Jones's units were installed on the army planes so that when wounded soldiers were transported out, supplies were available to the medical staff on board. Jones's units were so advanced, that some could even produce heat if needed.

═══════════════ **Questions to Ponder** ═══════════════

❑ Jones was born in Cincinnati, Ohio. Is Cincinnati the capital of Ohio? (*No, Columbus is the capital of Ohio.*)

❑ Orphaned at the age of ten, Jones moved to Kentucky. What is the capital of Kentucky, and do Ohio and Kentucky share a border? (*Frankfurt is the capital; and yes, they share a border.*)

❑ Jones spent most of his life in Minnesota simply because he once took a wrong train and instead of going straight back explored the town, found a job at a hotel, found another job from a guest at the hotel who was from Minnesota, and from that job found others. What is the capital of Minnesota? (*St. Paul is the capital of Minnesota.*)

❑ Name some things that are transported in refrigerated trucks. (*medical supplies, blood, food, certain chemicals, etc.*)

❑ Without refrigerated trucks and refrigerated train cars, how different might the inside of your local supermarket look? (*The time of year would make a big difference! There would be a lot less fresh fish, meat, dairy products, and even vegetables; and there would be a lot more canned goods and higher prices.*)

Jean Craighead George

(1919–)

You walk into your summer home and on the second floor, smack in the middle of a bed, there is a five-foot (1.5 m) black snake peacefully sleeping. What do you do? Jean Craighead George and her father gently tugged at the bedspread so that the snake would wake up. After watching it uncoil and slither off the bed, exiting through a hole in the wall, they kept it a secret. Even though the snake was an excellent housekeeper, keeping the mice and rats at bay, Jean knew that it would be best if her mother never found out!

All of her life, Jean was entranced with animals. When she was six, she raised a vulture. At first Jean was revolted by what the vulture ate: carrion (dead meat). Then she realized that vultures play a very important part in the ecological cycle. Vultures are on the "clean-up" crew. Built for this type of eating, most vultures have bald heads. This is so when they grab their food, even if they are reaching inside ribs, they remain clean—there are no head feathers to mess up. Many vultures defend themselves by regurgitating, or vomiting, their food. The smell is enough to drive most any beast away!

Jean also raised up a kestrel, a small falcon that she named Bad Boy. One night, while there were guests for dinner, one of the guests took a biscuit and started to reach for the strawberry jelly. At that moment, Bad Boy flew straight into the bowl of jelly, and then squawking, flew to a perch—the top of the guest of honor's head!

Jean has written many children's books, most of them dealing with animals and nature. Her two most famous ones are probably *My Side of the Mountain* and *Julie of the Wolves*. In *My Side of the Mountain*, a 13-year-old boy runs away from home and lives in a tree. When Jean first submitted this book, it was rejected because the publishers didn't think parents should encourage kids to leave home. Jean's editor told the publisher that it was better to run to the woods than to the city, and the publishers changed their mind.

Jean had originally gone to Alaska to learn all that she could about wolves so that she could write an article about them. After all her research and time, she was told that the magazine had bought an article about wolves from someone else. At first Jean was upset, but then she took all that she had learned and used it in her book *Julie of the Wolves*.

Questions to Ponder

❑ George was born in Washington, D.C., on July 2, 1919. In what state was she born? (*Washington, D.C., is the capital of the United States, but it is not a state. Washington, D.C., is coextensive with the District of Columbia. George Washington selected the exact site, and it was chosen as a compromise between northern and southern interests.*)

❑ The Craigheads lived in Ottawa, Canada, for a few years while Jean's father studied bark beetles for the Canadian Government. Is Ottawa or Ontario the capital of Canada? (*Ottawa is the national capital of Canada. Ontario is a province (sort of like our states) of Canada, and its capital is Toronto. Ottawa is in the province of Ontario.*)

❑ While in Alaska, Jean saw a family freezer—a large deep pit beside the house. One climbed down a ladder to enter it. Why was no electricity needed? (*In many cold areas, there is permafrost, a permanently frozen layer below the earth's surface.*)

❑ When Jean learned she had won the Newbery Award, she accidentally offered her neighbor dog food instead of cookies. Have you ever been too excited to think properly?

Nathan Hale

(1755–1776)

Nathan Hale was an American Revolutionary soldier who was captured by the British while attempting to return to his regiment. He had been sent to Long Island to gather information about the British there. He had successfully penetrated British lines, but he never made it back. He was hanged the next day after his capture without a trial. The last words he spoke prior to his execution not only comprise one of the most famous quotations in the history of the United States, they also exemplify the ultimate in one's love and loyalty for one's country.

Even though it was known that the punishment for spying was death by hanging, Hale volunteered. Hale knew that General Washington and the other revolutionary leaders did not have enough men to defend all the places they could be attacked. Washington needed to know where the British were going to attack so that all their men could be placed there to defend themselves. If the Revolutionary forces were spread out everywhere, they would be vulnerable and weak. They needed to know where to position themselves.

When Hale crossed into British territory, he posed as a Tory schoolmaster who could not find work because the revolutionaries in his town had chased him off due to his support for the British. Hale hid all the information he had gathered about the British in the loose inner sole of his shoe. When he was picked up for questioning, the papers were found. Hale knew that the end had come. Hale's last words, though, will remain in our hearts and be part of our history forever:

"I only regret that I have but one life to lose for my country."

Questions to Ponder

❏ Hale was born in Pennsylvania. Pennsylvania borders one of the Great Lakes. How many Great Lakes are there, what are their names, and which one borders Pennsylvania? (*There are five Great Lakes. Many people remember them by thinking of the acronym HOMES. An acronym is a word formed by the first letters of a series of words. H for Lake Huron, O for Ontario, M for Michigan, E for Erie, and S for Superior. Lake Erie is the Great Lake that borders Pennsylvania.*)

❏ Hale was born on June 6, 1755, and he died on September 22, 1776. How many years, months, and days old was he when he died? (*21 years, 3 months, 16 days*)

❏ Hale joined a regiment from Connecticut. It has been said that Connecticut is one of the most difficult states to spell. Can you spell it?

❏ Hale was a true patriot. A patriot is someone who loves his country and zealously supports it. *Pater* or *patris* is Latin for father. Do you think our word "patriot" was derived or developed from the Latin word for "father"? (*Yes. A patriot is like a father to his country.*)

❏ Knowing that *pater* and *patris* are Latin for "father," who are your paternal grandparents—your mom's parents or your dad's parents? (*They are your father's parents. Your maternal grandparents would be on your mother's side.*)

❏ Can you think of any other famous quotations that are particularly important to the history of the United States?

Robert Peary

(1856–1920)

"A few toes were not much to give to achieve the Pole." These words were written by Peary after a failed attempt on the North Pole. Mathew Henson, an African American, who was vital to and went on all of Peary's expeditions, had peeled off Peary's boots to discover that some of Peary's toes were so frostbitten that they simply came off with the boots!

Peary never gave up on the North Pole. Having learned how to survive and travel in Polar regions by the Inuit, or native people, of Greenland where Peary led several expeditions, Peary felt that it was a very possible feat. He was determined that he would accomplish it. The loss of his toes did not stop his determination. Peary wrote, "There is no time to pamper sick men on the trail."

Peary left for his final assault on the Pole in the winter of 1909 on March 1. Though the hours of daylight were short and the cold was intense, the ice was firmer. Remember that the North Pole does not rest on a continent. It rests on a layer of ice over sea water. Oftentimes, Peary had to deal with ice ridges over 65 feet (19.8 m) high, and sometimes the ice they were on would split open. They would have to cross the water on an ice raft, make a time-consuming detour, or wait for the ice to be pushed together again. Peary enlisted the help of many Inuits, and at night, they all slept in igloos. For the final leg of the journey, though, only six men went: Peary, Henson, and four Inuit named Ukkujaak, Oodaaq, Iggianguaq, and Silluk. On April 6th, they reached the North Pole!

But when Peary and Henson returned, they were told that they were not first. Just six days before, Frederick Cook announced that he had reached the Pole a year before Peary. Cook said that he had traveled with two Inuit and 26 dogs from Axel Heiberg Island in northern Canada, journeyed to the Pole, and then made his way to Denmark where he reported the news.

To this day the controversy remains. Cook made an epic journey, yes, but did he reach the Pole? In 1911 Congress listened to hearings and studied the documents of both men and decided that it was indeed Peary who was first. But there have been some recent doubts as to whether or not Peary actually made it to the Pole. Peary returned so quickly from the Pole that it does not seem possible that he could have traveled that long distance in such a short amount of time. In addition, Peary's diary entry for April 6th, where he claims to have reached the Pole, is written on a separate piece of paper. In the diary itself, there were four blank pages. Had Peary written the entry after the event?

Questions to Ponder

❏ Peary was born in Pennsylvania. He also spent some time in Nicaragua surveying the site of a proposed canal. Can you name the capitals of Pennslyvania and Nicaragua and then find them on the map? (*Harrisburg, Pennsylvania; Managua, Nicaragua*)

❏ Peary led three expeditions to Greenland. What did Peary establish about Greenland for the first time? (*Peary established that Greenland is an island. In fact, Greenland is the largest island in the world.*)

❏ What is frostbite? (*Frostbite is when your body literally becomes frozen. This usually happens first to the extremities—the nose, fingers, toes, cheeks, and earlobes. Blood cannot circulate, and the tissue dies. If infection then sets in, amputation may be necessary.*)

The Ringling Brothers

To learn tightrope walking, Al Ringling strung a rope between two trees. The rope was only a few inches above the ground. Once Al could walk the length of the rope without falling off, he raised the rope a few inches. This continued until he could walk confidently on a rope that could only be reached with a tall ladder.

Yet, Al knew that this was not enough to entertain people. He had to make it look scary. Al practiced looking as if he were losing his balance and about to fall off. Sure enough, when he performed this trick for the first time in front of an audience, they gasped in terror when he started to totter back and forth.

The Ringling brothers grew up in a poor family. They did not have enough money to see a circus, but that was what they wanted to see more than any other thing in the world. When a circus finally came to town, they went down to the river and waited. They could not buy tickets and see the show, but they could watch the animals and equipment being unloaded from the boat. Finally, they would see an elephant.

The Ringling Brothers (cont.)

Later that evening, their father surprised the brothers. He had a pass for the entire family. One of the acrobats needed a belt fixed; and Mr. Ringling, a harness maker, was able to fix it. The belt went around the waist of one of the performers, and a metal cup was attached to the belt. A long pole rested in the metal belt. An acrobat climbed the pole, and from his precarious position, he twisted and turned, looking as if he were going to smash to the ground at any moment.

From that moment, the Ringling Brothers were hooked. They put everything they had into owning a circus. When they started out, they had to do everything, including all the juggling, trapeze work, and clowning. After 20 years, their circus had over 1,000 performers and workmen. It had 350 of the world's finest horses, 30 elephants, and lions and tigers. They were the second biggest circus in the world, but then after Mr. Barnum and Mr. Bailey died, the Ringling Brothers bought their circus. The circus is now seen all over the world and goes by the name of "Ringling Brothers and Barnum and Bailey Circus." If anyone ever says to you, "Your dream is too big," think of the Ringling Brothers! They could not even afford tickets to see a circus, but they ended up owning the world's biggest circus!

Questions to Ponder

❏ The Ringling brothers' father was born in Germany. Did he immigrate or emigrate to the United States? (*He immigrated. Immigration is when one enters a country that one is not native to for permanent residence. When one emigrates, on the other hand, one leaves their country to go live in another.*)

❏ Which one has only one **m**, *immigrate* or *emigrate*?

❏ What is the capital of Germany, and does Germany border the Mediterranean Sea or the Baltic Sea? (*The capital is Berlin. Germany borders the Baltic and the North Sea.*)

❏ The Ringling brothers lived in Wisconsin and Iowa when they were young. What are the capitals of these states, and do they share a border? (*Madison is the capital of Wisconson, and Des Moines is the capital of Iowa. Iowa is bounded by the Mississippi River, across which lies Wisconsin.*)

❏ It has been said that when one walks a tightrope one should not look down; one should look straight ahead to where he or she is going. How would this help?

❏ What is your favorite circus act?

❏ Some circuses have stopped using trained animals. What do you think about this?

Leonardo da Vinci

(1452–1519)

Take your pick: was Leonardo da Vinci a genius at painting, sculpting, architecture, music, engineering, science, or inventing? Any answer would be correct. Da Vinci was a true Renaissance man, meaning that he was a person who had wide interests and was an expert in many areas. Born in Vinci, a little town near Florence, Italy, da Vinci showed at an early age great skill in drawing. Though da Vinci was able to write and draw with either hand, he preferred the left. Da Vinci could write backward with his left hand, from right to left, so that the writing didn't look right unless it was read in a mirror. Da Vinci could read it easily though without a mirror.

When da Vinci painted the Archangel Gabriel in his painting *Annunciation*, he used the actual wings of a bird as a model for Gabriel's wings. Da Vinci also prepared carefully for each painting, making dozens of sketches for separate parts of his paintings. If da Vinci even painted a blossom on the canvas, it wasn't until he had sketched it several times and gotten the proportions perfect. Da Vinci felt that art was mathematical, and he even established a formula for the perfect proportions of an ideal human body.

Da Vinci actually replanned the city of Milan. He designed a model city with two levels of streets and underground canals. Da Vinci would not be surprised at all to see our network of underground subways today! In da Vinci's notebooks were also architectural drawings of domed churches. When da Vinci was chief military engineer, he drew up plans to fortify towns, drain marshes, and build canals to divert a river.

Da Vinci was born at a time when helicopters, tanks, parachutes, submarines, bicycles, and airplanes did not exist. Yet, in his notebooks, da Vinci left sketches that anticipate the creation of these things. He would not be surprised at the sight of these inventions today. He would probably wonder what took us so long!

Da Vinci had only one problem: he often did not finish what he started! Perhaps da Vinci always found life too interesting to just narrowly focus on one project. Perhaps when he started something, it just made him realize how much more there was to learn. What is certain is that through his paintings and by the richness and originality expressed in his notebooks, we know that da Vinci possessed one of the greatest minds of all time.

Questions to Ponder

❏ What is the capital of Italy? Is it north or south of Venice? (*Rome, the capital, is south of Venice.*)

❏ The Mona Lisa is one of da Vinci's most famous paintings. Why didn't Mona Lisa smile? (*It is now believed that she may have been hiding her black and rotting teeth. Think of what your teeth would look like without proper dental care!*)

❏ If one is ambidextrous, as da Vinci was, one can use both hands equally well. Is anyone in your class ambidextrous? How would being ambidextrous help a carpenter, baseball player, or surgeon?

❏ Can you write your name backwards so that when it is held up to a mirror it looks correct?

I. M. Pei

(1917–)

What do the Rock and Roll Hall of Fame in Cleveland, Ohio, the Louvre Art Museum in Paris, France, and the National Gallery of Art, East Building, in Washington, D.C., all have in common? All three of these buildings exhibit the work of Ieoh Ming Pei. I.M. Pei, as he is more commonly known, was the architect when it came to designing or adding on to these buildings.

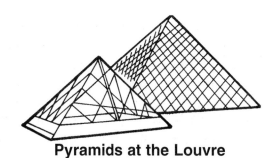

Pyramids at the Louvre

Every time a building is built, whether it is a house, a bank, a skyscraper, or a school, someone has to design it. Plans need to be drawn up that builders can follow. Will there be enough windows, electrical outlets, bathrooms, and safe exits? Will the ceiling beams be strong enough to support the floors above them? Will it be earthquake proof? Will it look beautiful? Will it blend into the surroundings? Will it be energy efficient? How many people are expected to use this building and for what purpose? The person who draws up these plans, hopefully dealing with all these questions satisfactorily, is the architect. Architects have to go to a special school for many years. They have to learn how to draw and design, but they also have to learn about the materials needed to construct buildings and what types of supports their buildings will need.

I.M. Pei's father wanted Pei to become a doctor, but Pei got sick every time he saw blood. Pei studied architecture instead! When Pei was asked to add on to the National Gallery of Art, he had to make sure that his new work complemented the old. The original National Gallery was visually similar to many of the other historical buildings in the city. Using the surrounding buildings as a guide to the height, Pei used the same pink Tennessee marble for the new building that had been used in the original. Yet his innovations were breathtaking. On the lower level, there is even what appears to be a wall of water. It is actually a waterfall that starts outside, but on the lower level, inside the building, the water is enclosed by a sheet of glass. There is a skylit roof formed by 25 glass tetrahedrons, and several glass pyramids that rise from the plaza. Pei has become known for his glass pyramids, and he has used them in many of his designs.

Questions to Ponder

❏ Pei was born in Canton, China. At the age of 10, Pei moved with his family to Shanghai. Is either one of these two cities the capital of China? If not, what is the capital of China? (*No, the capital of China is Beijing.*)

❏ Of North Korea, Vietnam, and Thailand, which one of these countries does not share a border with China? (*Thailand does not share a border with China.*)

❏ Both Pei and his wife became American citizens. Wanting their children to become assimilated and blend into American life, Pei and his wife did not teach their children to speak Chinese. Pei says now that he regrets this decision. If you were a new American citizen, and you spoke your native language as well as English, would you teach your children to speak your native language?

❏ How might a design for an elementary school be different from a school designed for a high school? How would the number of students attending change the plans?

Semiramis, Queen of Assyria
(ca. 800 B.C.)

Believe it or not, every time you put on a pair of trousers, you are doing something that is related to Semiramis, Queen of Assyria. Assyria was an ancient empire of Western Asia that originated around the city of Ashur on the upper Tigris River. In its heyday, its leadership spread throughout the Middle East, and it even conquered Egypt. Semiramis was a bold queen who traveled and fought with her army. According to the Greek historian Diodorus, Semiramis was about to set off on a long and difficult journey when she invented the trousers. She wanted to camouflage herself. From a distance, while riding horseback and wearing trousers, she knew it would be impossible to tell whether she was a male or a female.

There is a famous story about Semiramis and her hair. All Assyrians, both men and women, wore their hair long and elaborately cut, layered, styled, oiled, and curled. Assyrians braided and corn-rowed their hair. Tight curls were glued to foreheads with perfumed gel; and as if this was not enough, men wore spit curls in their beards! One can imagine how long it would take to have one's hair done. The story goes that Semiramis was getting an elaborate braided hairstyle when she was told that fighting had started in Babylon. With only half of her head braided and styled, the other half uncombed and wild, Semiramis went to battle. She refused to have her hair finished until the rebellion had been squelched. In this way, she showed her troops her resolve. Later, a statue was put up of Semiramis with half of her hair done, and the other half sticking out all over the place.

Semiramis was not Assyrian by birth. She was a princess of Chaldea, a region south of Babylon between the Euphrates River and the Persian Gulf. The King of Assyria married her for political reasons. It makes sense geopolitically to have families sharing borders. Semiramis's husband died about 811 B.C., and Semiramis built up the kingdom and ruled it until their son became of age. She is credited with developing and building up a large canal and irrigation system between the Tigris and Euphrates Rivers. She also built roads nonstop and erected a monument made out of a massive piece of stone in an obelisk shape (like the Washington Monument.) It was about 135 feet (41 m) tall and about 25 feet (7.6 m) square.

Questions to Ponder

❏ Egypt was once part of Assyria's territory. What is the capital of Egypt, and what famous river flows through Egypt? (*Cairo; the Nile*)

❏ Just as Semiramis knew, it is often our dress that gives us away. If you saw two small babies, both wearing identical suits, would you be able to tell which one was the boy and which one was the girl?

❏ Archaeologists have found markers that prove that Semiramis traveled from Babylon to India, Turkey, and the Arabian Peninsula. What are the capitals of India and Turkey? (*New Delhi, India; Ankara, Turkey*)

❏ Semiramis was credited with creating the Hanging Gardens of Babylon, one of the Seven Wonders of the Ancient World. The Hanging Gardens of Babylon were actually created for a queen 300 years after Semiramis. Which is the only one of the Seven Wonders of the Ancient World that can be seen today? (*the Pyramids of Egypt*)

George Washington Carver

(1864–1943)

Dr. George Washington Carver was kidnapped when he was only an infant. He and his mother, stolen also at the same time as Carver, were slaves. They had been kidnapped from his owner's plantation by a band of slave raiders. Carver was ransomed for a horse, but Carver's mother was sold and shipped away.

When the Civil War ended, Carver had no idea where his mother was. Despite being completely alone, Carver never gave up or lost his determination when it came to obtaining an education. He worked as a field hand, and then he worked his way through Simpson College where he was the first African-American student to be admitted. From there, he went on to Iowa Agricultural College (now Iowa State University), and after graduating, was hired to teach and conduct research at Tuskegee Institute, an agricultural and industrial school founded for African-American students in 1881.

At that time, "King Cotton" dominated southern agriculture. Cotton was grown year after year in the same fields, and the soil was becoming depleted of its nutrients. Diseases and insect pests were numerous. Carver wanted to diversify, to develop a variety of crops that could be grown in the South. He also wanted to figure out uses for the plants that could be grown, thus making sure that there would be a market for them.

Think for a moment about the peanut, sweet potato, and the pecan. Carver found over 350 uses for them! From peanuts alone, Carver developed meal, instant and dry coffee, bleach, wood filler, metal polish, paper, ink, shaving cream, rubbing oil, linoleum, and synthetic rubber. During World War I, sweet potato flour became an important product; and it was developed by Carver—along with postage stamp glue—from sweet potatoes! Reflect a moment about the products listed—they are all very different from each other. Carver let nothing limit the scope of his inventions!

Carver was never able to patent the new strains of plants that he developed because the U.S. Patent Office did not permit plants to be patented until 1930. In fact, despite all of his inventions, because of his desire to help people, Carter only took out three patents in his entire life. Yet, Carver changed the economy of the South, and when he died in 1943, the entire nation mourned him.

Questions to Ponder

- ❏ Carver was born in Diamond Grove, Missouri. What is the capital of Missouri and what two great rivers helped shape the state? (*Jefferson City; the Mississippi and Missouri*)
- ❏ Tuskegee Institute, where Carver taught and worked, is in Alabama. What is the capital of Alabama and does either the Mississippi or Missouri River flow through Alabama? (*Montgomery is the capital of Alabama. The Mississippi and Missouri rivers do not flow through Alabama. The Alabama and the Tombigbee rivers do.*)
- ❏ It has been said that Americans are at their worst when it comes to geography and their dates in history. Can you name the years of the Civil War? (*1861–1865*)
- ❏ Carver once said, "No man can drag me down so low as to make me hate him." What do you think Carver meant by these words?
- ❏ Why was it "King Cotton"? (*Cotton dominated the South's economy. When one is dependent on only one thing, if that crop fails—whether it is due to weather, insects, or the market—the entire economic system falls apart.*)

William Roentgen

(1845–1923)

On December 22, 1895, William Roentgen took an X-ray of his wife's hand. This was the world's first X-ray. Roentgen's wife did not think about what this would mean when it came to diagnosing broken bones. She also did not think about how X-rays would make it easier for surgeons to perform surgery. For example, now if a doctor wanted to remove something, he or she could find out exactly where it was lodged before cutting into a patient.

Instead, Roentgen's wife's reaction was to get very upset. She felt that looking at her own bones was like seeing herself already dead. Initially, many other people felt the same fears as Roentgen's wife. Because X-rays could "see" through walls and clothing, many people worried about their privacy. One London company even went as far as selling what they claimed to be X-ray-proof underclothes!

Roentgen discovered X-rays by accident. He was experimenting with cathode rays, invisible streams of electrons emitted by the cathode in a vacuum tube. While performing one experiment, Roentgen noticed a faint green light glowing from a bench about three feet from the tube. The light was coming from a barium platinocyanide screen. This was a surprise and completely unexpected because it was thought that cathode rays could not travel farther than an inch or two.

Roentgen worked ceaselessly, testing over and over these astonishing penetrating rays that caused the light. During one test, Roentgen placed objects between the tube and the screen where the green light appeared. A piece of paper did not dim the screen, and a thick book only dimmed it a little. But when Roentgen held up a sheet of lead, the lead not only stopped all the rays, but around the shadow of the lead sheet, was an outline of Roentgen's own bones! In the paper where Roentgen described his work and sent copies of his bone pictures, Roentgen called the rays "X-rays" because they were so mysterious. X-rays were used for the first time in the U.S. on February 3, 1896. A doctor brought a patient to a laboratory in Dartmouth College. The doctor wrote later that the image showed "the fracture of the ulna very distinctly." For his discovery of X-rays, Roentgen was awarded the first Nobel Prize in physics in 1901.

Questions to Ponder

❏ Roentgen was born in Germany, and when he was three, he moved with his parents to Holland. Do these countries share a border and a language, and what are their capitals? (*Yes, they share a border but not a language. In Germany, the German language is spoken. In the Netherlands (popularly known as Holland), Dutch is spoken. The capital of Germany is Berlin, and the capital of the Netherlands is Amsterdam.*)

❏ Is the ulna a leg or arm bone? (*The ulna is an arm bone.*)

❏ Are X-rays the only way we have of scanning the human body today? (*No. Doctors also use ultrasonic scanners that produce pictures called sonograms. Ultrasonic waves are sound waves above the normal range of hearing. These waves bounce off objects (like a baby in a mother's womb), causing echoes that are then converted into electronic signals to form an image. MRI machines, or magnetic resonance imaging machines, use incredibly strong magnets to make pictures that are much more detailed than X-ray pictures.*)

Einstein and E = mc^2

One of the most famous equations in the world is Albert Einstein's $E = mc^2$. Physics is a science that deals with matter and energy and how they interact in the fields of electricity, radiation, atomic structure, heat, magnetism, and nuclear phenomena. Einstein is recognized as one of the most famous physicists of all times. Einstein is famous for his work on relativity, which included gravitation as a determiner of the curvature of a space-time continuum.

Einstein was born in Germany, but when the Nazi government confiscated his property in 1934 and revoked his German citizenship because he was Jewish, Einstein decided to become an American. Einstein worked at the Institute for Advanced Study in Princeton, New Jersey.

When Einstein was little, he was not a good student at school. He always did well in mathematics, but he had little interest in other subjects. He was even asked to drop out of one high school. Einstein was working in a patent office when he wrote the three famous papers that changed the way scientists look at the world. Einstein showed that when we think about our world, we cannot think with only the dimensions of length, width, and thickness. We have to add the dimension of time. Einstein also wrote a paper that said that light bends as it travels through space. In 1919 when there was a total eclipse of the sun, scientists took pictures that showed that Einstein's calculations were correct. As the light from the stars passed near the sun, the light bent.

Questions to Ponder

❏ What does $E = mc^2$ mean? (E *represents units of energy*, m *represents units of mass, and* c^2 *is the speed of light squared (or multiplied by itself). The speed of light is a very large number, and it is multiplied by itself. Thus, this equation points out that a very small amount of matter can release a huge amount of energy. Think of nuclear reactions.*)

❏ What is the speed of light? (*Light travels through a vacuum at about 186,000 miles per second. A light year, or the distance light can travel in a year, is over five trillion miles.*)

❏ Einstein was born in 1879 and died in 1955. In which century was he born in, and in which century did he die? (*He was born in the nineteenth, and he died in the twentieth.*)

❏ Einstein received a Nobel Prize for his work in theoretical physics in 1921. What is the Nobel Prize? (*Alfred Nobel, the inventor of dynamite, was a Swedish chemist who was worried about the potential uses of the explosives he had invented. He established a fund to provide annual awards in science, literature, and for the promotion of international peace. Nobel Prizes have now become one of the highest and most respected honors in the world.*)

❏ What is an eclipse of the sun as compared to an eclipse of the moon? (*An eclipse is the blocking out of light from one object by the intervention of another object. An eclipse of the sun is when the sun's light is blocked by the moon, and an eclipse of the moon is when sunlight on its way to the moon is blocked by the earth.*)

❏ If you had not learned how the world worked, and no one could tell you what was happening and why, would suddenly having the sun's light disappear or the moon disappear frighten you?

Helen Thayer and the Magnetic North Pole

At the age of 50, Helen Thayer became the first woman to ski to the magnetic North Pole. It took her 27 days to travel the 345 miles (555 km). She had to deal with gale-force storms, treacherous ice floes, brutal weather, and polar bears. Though she was picked up by airplane a few days after she reached her destination, to get there she had to pull a sledge that carried all of her supplies. Her only contact with other people was during her nightly radio transmissions. For companionship and to help protect her against polar bears, Thayer traveled with Charlie, a large husky dog who pulled a sled that contained his own food.

Our compasses point to the magnetic north pole, but the magnetic North Pole cannot be defined as just a dot on a map. The magnetic pole is in constant motion, and sometimes it changes its position as much as 100 miles (161 km) a day. It travels in an elliptical path in a clockwise direction. To make sure she reached her goal, Thayer skied in a wide expanse around the calculated pole area. Her compass, as everyone else's would be too, was useless at the pole vicinity. Close to the pole, the compass needle just turns lazily and unpredictably in all directions because of the lack of horizontal magnetic pull.

Thayer's big concern was polar bears. Polar bears have excellent eyesight, and their sense of smell is phenomenal. With the longest head and nose out of all the bears, a polar bear can sniff out seals in dens that are covered by three or four feet of snow and ice. Thayer learned from the Innuit, the native people of the region, that if one did meet a polar bear, that one should maintain eye contact and not back up. She was also cautioned that just because it appeared that a bear had left, she should not trust that it was so. Often, a bear would circle around and come back on the attack at a different angle. Thayer needed Charlie, the dog, to alert her to the presence of polar bears. Charlie proved invaluable at this, and his presence allowed Thayer to sleep in relative safety. Once spotted, Thayer kept the bears away by shooting flares at them with a flare gun.

There were several close calls. One bear got so close that it knocked over the sled. If it were not for Charlie, Thayer would have died. Several bears were not intimidated by the flare gun that Thayer carried for protection. One bear left only after a flare landed on and burned its paw.

Questions to Ponder

❏ Thayer was born in New Zealand. In what ocean does New Zealand lie, and what is New Zealand's capital? (*New Zealand lies in the Pacific Ocean. Wellington is the capital of New Zealand.*)

❏ Why do polar bears sometimes cover their noses and mouths with a paw when they are stalking their prey? (*Camouflage! The nose and mouth are black. It is the only part of them that can be seen in the white world in which they live.*)

❏ Why do polar bears have such tiny ears? (*Not only are they tiny, but they do not stick out. This is so they will not freeze. Think of how much colder your ears and fingers get when it is cold out and they are not covered.*)

❏ Thayer was the U.S. National Luge Champion in 1975. What does a luger do? (*A luger competes in luge, an Olympic event. On a very small sled, one races down curving, steeply-banked chutes. One steers by shifting one's weight, using one's feet, and pulling straps attached to the runners of the sled.*)

Niagara Falls and Annie Taylor

Niagara Falls is an internationally famous waterfall on the United States and Canadian border. Niagara Falls is where the Niagara River drops from Lake Erie to Lake Ontario. Though Niagara Falls is only 49th in the world when it comes to height, when measured in terms of how much water flows over the falls and how much power this water has, Niagara Falls jumps up in ranking to third greatest in the world. Why would anyone even think of going over these falls in a barrel?

Annie Taylor was 63 years old when she decided to go over the falls in a barrel. She told people that she was only 43 because she did not think anyone would believe that a 63-year-old woman could be strong enough to survive going over the falls in a barrel. The only other woman who had tried this feat before Taylor hadn't made it. She suffocated from lack of air while her barrel swirled around for hours in the middle of Whirlpool Rapids before it could be retrieved.

Taylor designed her four-and-a-half-foot (1.4 m) oak barrel. The top was 36" (91 cm) in diameter, and it tapered to 15" (38 cm) at the bottom. For strength, there were 10 iron hoops bolted around it at regular intervals. Hoping that it would help keep the barrel upright and minimize battering by the current, a 100-pound (45 kg) anvil was placed at the bottom of the barrel. In total, the barrel weighed 160 pounds, (72.6 kg) the same as Taylor.

Taylor had to wiggle her way into the barrel and into a harness that was attached inside the barrel. It was hoped that the harness would keep her feet down and her head from hitting the lid of the barrel. There were large cushions to protect her body. The cover had rubber around the rim for a watertight fit.

When Taylor was first put into the barrel, with the cover fastened tightly, she saw light! Instead of stopping, Taylor just had her helper plug the hole. He did this by merely pushing a strip of cloth into it! The helper then pumped air into a rubber hose using a bicycle pump. The rubber hose had a spout near Taylor's mouth.

Taylor survived, but she was so weak that she had to be cut out of the barrel. She had lots of bruises and a slight concussion. None of her bones were broken, but she did need stitches for a scalp wound. Taylor said, "It was a terrible nightmare, and I'd sooner be shot by a cannon . . . than do it again. But I'm not sorry I did it if it helps me financially." Unfortunately for Taylor, though she was famous briefly, she died penniless in 1921.

Questions to Ponder

❑ Niagara Falls is in the state of New York on the U.S. side. What is the capital of New York? (*Albany is the capital of New York.*)

❑ In what province of Canada is Niagara Falls? Do you know the province's capital, and the capital of Canada? Can you find Niagara Falls and these cities on the map? (*Niagara Falls lies in the province of Ontario. Toronto is the provincial capital of Ontario. Ottawa is the capital of Canada.*)

❑ If Annie died in 1921, and she was 63 when she went over the Falls in 1901, how old was Annie when she died? (*She was approximately 83 years old.*)

❑ In your opinion, was Annie foolish?

Code Heroes of World War II

Codetalkers were special Marines. They went behind enemy lines, were directly involved in fighting, and were essential to providing the lifeline of communication for their units during deadly combat for Japanese-held islands. Working in pairs, they were assigned throughout the combat regions wherever they were needed in the Pacific. Their code was top secret, and it was never broken. What was the code and who were the codetalkers?

Philip Johnston grew up among the Navajo Native Americans. At that time, he was one of only 28 non-Native Americans who had mastered the complex Navajo language. There were not any Germans or Japanese included in this 28. Knowing firsthand how difficult the language was to learn, Johnston went to the commanding officer of the Marines in February 1942 and suggested using Native Americans fluent in both their native language and English as codetalkers.

The first 30 recruits, fluent in both Navajo and English, underwent special training that included radio communications procedures. They memorized a list of specialized military terms, and they had to come up with Navajo phrases that would cover words and phrases that did not exist in their language. For example, the Navajo words meaning "sparrow hawk" substituted for "dive bomber," "our mother" for "America," and "iron fish" for "submarine."

When the codetalkers were shipped out to battle zones in the fall of 1942, it became immediately clear how vital they were to the military operation. Dispatches could be coded, transmitted, and decoded twice as fast as what had been previously possible by other coding methods. In addition, their code was unbreakable. More codetalkers were wanted. Codetalkers who were fluent in Navajo, Comanche, or Choctaw as well as English were recruited. Hunched over their equipment in the midst of bedlam and fighting as they and their fellow Marines fought for control of the islands, the codetalkers provided crucial support in a horrible war.

Over 25,000 Native Americans fought to protect the United States during World War II. Four hundred of these 25,000 soldiers were involved in the special marine unit of codetalkers. These brave and heroic men kept their contribution a secret for the entire war.

Questions to Ponder

❏ Who were the Allies and who were the Axis powers in WWII? Which side did the United States belong to? (*The United States belonged to the Allies, which consisted chiefly of Great Britain, the U.S., and the Soviet Union. The Axis powers were Germany, Japan, and Italy.*)

❏ When did WWII begin and end? What event directly caused the U.S. to become involved in the war? (*WWII lasted from 1939–1945. The U.S. entered the war on December 7, 1941, when Japan attacked Pearl Harbor.*)

❏ Why was it so important that it be kept a secret who the codetalkers were? Can you keep a secret? (*If it were known publicly, a person who spoke these languages could be captured or kidnapped and then forced to translate or send incorrect messages. If a codetalker revealed to just one person what he was doing, then that one person could tell one person, and that one person could tell one other person, etc.*)

❏ Only 28 non-Native Americans could speak Navajo. How many non-native English speakers can speak English? How many people in your school are bilingual?

❏ Can you make up a code? Do you think you could break one?

Cowboys

Don't trust the movies! Movies make being a cowboy glamorous, romantic, and fun. Instead, being a cowboy was a hard and dirty job. Movie cowboys are usually white and English speaking. In real life, one out of seven cowboys was African American, and the working language of nearly all cowboys was Spanish. After the Civil War, many men in discharged troops who could not find work when they returned home, including 200,000 ex-slaves, signed up to work as cowboys.

Cowboys rounded up the cattle into herds of about 5,000 three- and four-year-old steers. After branding the animals that didn't have brands, the cowboys moved the herds up north, about 15 miles (24 km) a day. By the 1870s, the trails used were well-worn tracks up to 750 miles (1207 km) long and 400 miles (644 km) wide. They stretched out over hot, dusty prairie. To avoid attacks from rustlers, cowboys tried to stay away from hills and woods.

Few cowboys owned their own horses. Horses were very expensive, and a cowboy had to change mounts several times during a day. Many cowboys tried to buy their own saddles though. Even though a saddle cost about a year's wages, a saddle would last a cowboy his lifetime.

At the time of the large cattle drives, people traveled by stagecoach. There was one robber who was better than the movies! Charles E. Bolton, or "Black Bart," prided himself on never spilling a drop of blood while he robbed only coach companies. "Black Bart" always wore a sack over his head with two eye-holes cut into it, spoke with an educated accent, and left poetry in the boxes he had robbed!

"Chuck" was the cowboy slang for food, and the chuck wagon did indeed carry food as well as water, cooking utensils, medicine, bedding tents, tools, and spare saddles. Cowboys usually had enough to eat—beef, bread, and beans—but it was the same food over and over. As a matter of fact, the meat was served hot and spicy to hide the taste of old meat! If a cowboy was lucky, he got biscuits and dried fruit.

Questions to Ponder

❏ Many cattle drives ended in Abilene or Dodge City where the cattle were sold and herded into wagons for transport to the slaughterhouse. In which states are Abilene and Dodge City found? What are their capitals? (*Abilene is in Texas. The capital of Texas is Austin. Dodge City is found in Kansas. The capital of Kansas is Topeka.*)

❏ Stray cows were called mavericks. This term originated in about 1870 from Samuel A. Maverick who did not brand his cows. Any unbranded range animal today or one that is separate from the herd is considered a maverick. Today, we call some people mavericks. What type of person would we call a maverick? (*An independent person who refuses to conform with the group might be called a maverick.*)

❏ Cowboy boots cost a cowboy a week or two's wages. Yet, they were worth it. Why? (*The high heels helped keep the feet in the stirrup, and the spurs off the ground. The sides protected the cowboy from rattlesnakes and thorns. Though spurs look cruel, they were used very carefully. Spur marks on a horse were a sign of poor horsemanship.*)

❏ What did a cowboy use his hat for? (*Made of felt, a cowboy hat was used to keep off sun and rain, and it served as a pail and a fan.*)

❏ The neckerchief had many uses. Can you name some? (*It can be protection from the sun, a bandage, a face mask, a handkerchief, a filter, etc.*)

Mammoth Cave

Mammoth Cave is not a place to get lost in! The largest cave in the world, Mammoth Cave has passages on five different levels, some going as deep as several hundred feet. There is an underground river where eyeless fish live, and there is even an enormous cathedral-like room with a ceiling that is 200 feet (61 m) high. About 330 known passageways have been mapped, but there are at least a couple hundred more.

This colossal cave was created by rainfall trickling through cracks in a ground surface of limestone. Over many years, the water seeped through underlying layers of softer stone. The cave's passages were formed when the water hit harder stone and flowed along the harder stone's surface.

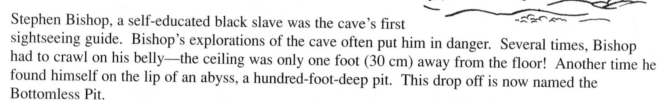

Stalactites and stalagmites are formations found in caves. Stalactites (think of the "c" in stalactite for ceiling) hang from the ceiling. Stalagmites (think of the "g" in stalagmite for ground) rise up from the ground.

Stephen Bishop, a self-educated black slave was the cave's first sightseeing guide. Bishop's explorations of the cave often put him in danger. Several times, Bishop had to crawl on his belly—the ceiling was only one foot (30 cm) away from the floor! Another time he found himself on the lip of an abyss, a hundred-foot-deep pit. This drop off is now named the Bottomless Pit.

The temperature in Mammoth Cave is always the same, even in the winter and the summer. It is 54 degrees Fahrenheit (12.2°C). The fish that swim in the river in Mammoth Cave do not have eyes. There are also blind shrimp, crayfish, crickets, and beetles. All of these creatures have highly developed other senses to make up for their lack of vision.

Questions to Ponder

❏ Mammoth Cave is in Kentucky. What is Kentucky's capital? Find it on the map! (*Frankfurt is the capital of Kentucky.*)

❏ Would you be able to see your hand in front of your face if you did not have any means of artificial light in Mammoth Cave? (*No, and the answer would still be "No" even if it were only half an inch away!*)

❏ Kentucky was the birthplace of the two presidents who served on opposing sides during the Civil War. Can you name the two presidents? (*Abraham Lincoln was president of the Union, and Jefferson Davis was president of the Confederacy.*)

❏ If you could choose to live somewhere where the temperature was always constant, as in Mammoth Cave, what temperature would you choose and why?

❏ When some people enter caves, they feel claustrophobic. Claustrophobia is the fear of closed-in places. Would you feel claustrophobic in a cave? Have you ever suffered from claustrophobia?

The Highest Mountain in the World

The highest mountain in the world is Mt. Everest. Mt. Everest is in the Himalayan range, and it is 29,028 feet (8,848 m) high. This mountain borders Nepal and Tibet. On May 29, 1953, Edmund Hillary and Tenzing Norgay were the first men to reach the top. The first woman to reach the top was Ang Tsering of Nepal on May 16, 1975.

Mt. Everest reaches up so high through the earth's atmosphere (about two-thirds) that the air at the top of the mountain is very thin. There is not enough oxygen to sustain life. Many climbers use bottled oxygen. Reinhold Messner was the first man to climb Everest without bottled oxygen. He was also the first to climb it solo, or by himself. He did not use any guides.

Why do people climb mountains? George Mallory, a climber who died on Mt. Everest in 1924 while attempting to be the first on the top, answered "Because it's there."

Questions to Ponder

❑ Can you find Nepal, Tibet, and Mt. Everest on the map?

❑ Does it ever rain on the top of Mt. Everest? (*No, it is so cold that precipitation only falls as snow.*)

❑ If a polar bear was flown to the top of Everest, would it be able to survive? (No, the air is very thin there and there is not enough oxygen to sustain life. Even if the bear could breathe, he would not be able to live. Because of the extreme cold and powerful winds, nothing can grow. The bear would find nothing to eat.

❑ If you climbed Mt. Everest, would you use a guide? Bottled oxygen?

The Great Wall of China

Look at a wall in your classroom. How long do you think it is? Now think about the Great Wall of China. The Great Wall of China is 1,500 miles (2,414 km) long, and it averages about 25 feet (7.6 m) in height. The Great Wall of China is the only man-made thing on Earth that can be seen from outer space.

The wall is an amalgamation of many walls. When something is amalgamated, it is united or put together from separate parts. Many shorter walls were connected together to make the Great Wall.

Why was this wall built? In ancient times, it was thought that this wall would help fortify the border. When something is fortified, it is made stronger. It is strengthened. The emperors thought that the wall would help stop enemies from crossing into China.

Questions to Ponder

❑ Can you find China on the map? Is the Great Wall marked on the map? (*The Great Wall is in the northern part of China.*)

❑ The wall did not work when it came to stopping attacks. Why do you think it didn't work?

❑ The Great Wall is now one of the biggest tourist attractions in China. Would you like to go see it?

❑ How long would it take you to walk this wall?

Fortuitous Mistakes

How many of you have ever eaten a chocolate chip cookie? If you haven't, you are certainly in the minority. Over 7 billion are consumed annually, and it is estimated that half the cookies baked in American homes are chocolate chip. Did a great cook set out to create this recipe? No, it was a mistake.

In 1930, Ruth Wakefield was busy running her Toll House Inn, located on the toll road between Boston and New Bedford, Massachusetts. She mixed up a batch of cookies and then discovered that she was out of baker's chocolate. She broke up some chocolate into small pieces, thinking that when she added them to the dough the chocolate bits would melt and then be absorbed into the dough. Instead, when she took them out of the oven, the chocolate had not melted into the dough. She did not have her chocolate cookies; she had chocolate chip cookies!

Today many people who are blind use trained guide dogs to help them get about. The dogs are trained to learn hand gestures, simple commands, and to exercise good judgement. They also have to learn when to disobey and show "intelligent disobedience." For example, if the dog is given the command to go forward, but there is a hole or other obstacle in the way such as a low hanging limb, the dog must disobey.

No one set out to start a training program for these dogs. It all started out as a mistake. Near the end of World War I, a doctor in Germany was walking outside a hospital with his dog and a blind patient. The doctor was called into the hospital, and when he came out, his dog and the blind man were gone. The dog had led the blind man clear across the hospital grounds! The amazed doctor decided to see how well a trained working breed of dog could lead a blind person. The doctor's results were so successful that the German government expanded the program. The first American guide dog school was started in 1929 after an American reporter wrote about Germany's program. Today, we have many schools, and blind people everywhere use guide dogs to help them lead independent and fulfilling lives.

Questions to Ponder

❏ What is a toll road? (*A road that, in order to travel on it, one has to pay a toll or a fee. The toll is usually for the upkeep of the road.*)

❏ Can you guess the three most popular breeds of dogs trained as guide dogs? (*German shepherds, golden retrievers, and Labrador retrievers are the three breeds of dogs most likely to be guide dogs.*)

❏ There is a French proverb that goes like this: "Only he who does nothing makes a mistake." Could you explain what this proverb means to someone who is having trouble understanding it?

❏ Do you think Cinderella wearing glass slippers was a mistake? (*It is believed that a Cinderella fairy story probably began in China. In Europe alone, over 500 different versions have been told. Most of us are familiar with the French version written by Charles Perrault in 1697. It is believed that Perrault made a mistake and changed Cinderella's slippers to glass. Before, Cinderella's slippers were made of fur, and "vair" is an old French word that means "a type of fur." "Vair" is pronounced the same as "verre," the French word that means "glass"! Perrault got the two words mixed up when he put the story down in writing!*)

"One If by Land, and Two If by Sea"

There is a famous poem by Henry Wadsworth Longfellow titled "Paul Revere's Ride." This poem, with great drama and embellishment (that means with lots of details added) tells the story of Paul Revere, a hero of the Revolutionary War. Paul Revere was a silversmith who on the night before the battle of Lexington and Concord, rode across the Massachusetts countryside warning the other colonists that the British troops were moving toward them. The British wanted to seize military supplies and arrest revolutionaries.

One if by land, and two if by sea are the words Longfellow used to describe the signal used to guide the midnight ride of Paul Revere (more of Longfellow's descriptive words). Revere had received his information about the British through signal lights placed in a church tower by a friend. Everyone that Revere warned that night was ready to fight the British the next day.

Questions to Ponder

❑ Is it acceptable to embellish true events in poems? How about when one is telling someone else a story? What if one is writing a textbook to be used in school?

❑ Can you find a copy of the poem "Paul Revere's Ride"?

❑ Can you think of anything you have ever read which is based on true facts but then turned into a fictionalized, or made-up, story?

"I Have Not Yet Begun to Fight"

John Paul Jones was a naval leader in the Revolutionary War. Jones became known for his attacks on British ships across the ocean. Jones was once battling a British ship when his own ship became badly damaged. The commander of the British ship then called over, asking if Jones would surrender. Instead of giving up, Jones answered back, "I have not yet begun to fight." Jones and his crew ended up capturing the British ship, and instead of Jones surrendering, it was the British captain! Two days later Jones's ship sank because of the damage wrought during the battle.

The words "I have not yet begun to fight" have come to represent how human beings can overcome all odds. They demonstrate the spirit of those who will never give up, no matter how terrible and horrible the situation seems to be. When one says, "I have not yet begun to fight," they are remembering John Paul Jones. They are telling one, "Don't count me out! It may seem as if I do not have a chance in the world, but not only am I not done, but I won't be done until I have won and you are out!" These words mean that defeat is not an option. Defeat cannot and will not happen.

Questions to Ponder

❏ In which ocean would John Paul Jones have fought against the British? (*John Paul Jones fought the British in the Atlantic Ocean.*)

❏ What are some of the things we have done because of our "I have not yet begun to fight," attitude? (*Examples might include the following: gone to the moon; sailed around the world; performed organ transplants; mapped human genes; etc.*)

❏ Is one more likely to lose if one feels that he or she doesn't have a chance?

"The Shot Heard Round the World"

Can a shot be heard around the world? Ralph Waldo Emerson wrote a poem about the Battle of Lexington and Concord. The Battle of Lexington and Concord was the first battle of the Revolutionary War. This battle is the one where Paul Revere made his famous ride. Revere rode through the countryside alerting the Americans that the British were coming. The British met resistance from the Minutemen. The Minutemen were armed civilians who were named Minutemen because they were ready to fight alongside regular soldiers at a minute's notice.

Emerson wrote,

> *Here once the embattled farmers stood*
> *and fired the shot heard round the world.*

Emerson was born in 1803 and died in 1882. He was one of America's most influential authors and thinkers, and he wanted his words to show how ordinary men can change the world. These farmers stood up for their right to be free, and their determination helped to establish a new nation, a nation where "all men are created equal." Our fight for our freedom has encouraged worldwide movements toward democracy.

Questions to Ponder

❑ Emerson was born in 1803 and died in 1882. This means that he lived his entire life in which century? (*He lived in the 19ᵀᴴ century.*)

❑ The Battle of Lexington and Concord was fought in Massachusetts. Massachusetts is one of the most difficult state names to spell. How many of you can spell it correctly before you find it on the map?

❑ We celebrate our Independence Day as July 4, 1776. How many days after the Battle of Lexington and Concord, fought on April 19, 1775, was this? (*442 days: April 19, 1775–April 19, 1776 = 366 (1776 was a leap year); April 19–April 30 = 11; May = 31; June = 30; and July = 4. Therefore, 366 + 11 + 31 + 30 + 4 = 442.*)

❑ The Minutemen made a difference. When can a minute make a difference? (*missing a train, brain damage if a heart has stopped, etc.*)

❑ The United States Postal system has a two-letter abbreviation for every state. Is MA the postal abbreviation for Maryland, Massachusetts, or Maine? (*MA is the postal abbreviation for Massachusetts. Maryland's postal abbreviation is MD, and Maine's is ME.*)

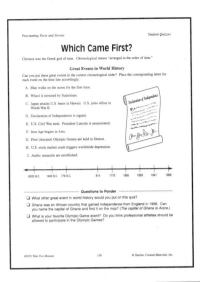

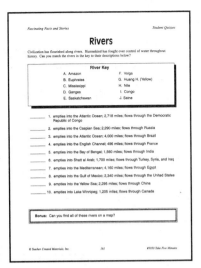

Student Quizzes

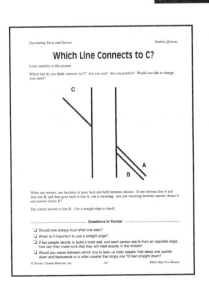

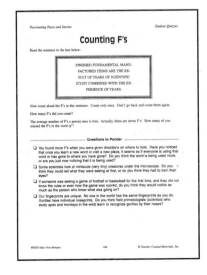

Which Came First?

Chronos was the Greek god of time. *Chronological* means "arranged in the order of time."

Great Events in World History

Can you put these great events in the correct chronological order? Place the corresponding letter for each event on the time line accordingly.

A. Man walks on the moon for the first time.

B. Wheel is invented by Sumerians.

C. Japan attacks U.S. bases in Hawaii. U.S. joins Allies in World War II.

D. Declaration of Independence is signed.

E. U.S. Civil War ends. President Lincoln is assassinated.

F. Iron Age begins in Asia.

G. First (Ancient) Olympic Games are held in Greece.

H. U.S. stock market crash triggers worldwide depression.

I. Arabic numerals are established.

6500 B.C.   1400 B.C.   776 B.C.   814   1776   1865   1929   1941   1969

Questions to Ponder

❏ What other great event in world history would you put on this quiz?

❏ Ghana was an African country that gained independence from England in 1956. Can you name the capital of Ghana and find it on the map? (*The capital of Ghana is Accra.*)

❏ What is your favorite Olympic Game event? Do you think professional athletes should be allowed to participate in the Olympic Games?

Which Came First? (cont.)

Chronos was the Greek god of time. Chronological means "arranged in the order of time."

Inventions

Can you put these inventions or discoveries in the right chronological order? Place the corresponding letter for each event on the time line accordingly.

A. multiplication sign (x)

B. bar code system

C. ballpoint pen

D. woven cloth

E. stainless steel

F. frozen food

G. sewing machine

H. wheelbarrow

I. X-ray research showing first photographs of the human brain recalling a word

J. printing press with moveable type

| 5000 B.C. | 230 A.D. | 1450 | 1631 | 1846 | 1913 | 1929 | 1938 | 1970 | 1991 |

Questions to Ponder

❏ How have these inventions changed our lives?

❏ Would you like to be known as a chronic complainer? When something is chronic, it happens all the time. A chronic complainer complains all the time.

❏ Which came first, the chicken or the egg?

When Did Each Become a State and Join the Union?

There are 50 states in the United States. There is a star for each state on our flag. The 13 stripes on our flag represent the original 13 colonies. Can you put these states in the order of when each became an official state of the United States of America?

State Key

Texas	California	Hawaii
Rhode Island	North Dakota	Kansas
Alaska	Missouri	Mississippi
Colorado	Nevada	Georgia

1. _____

2. _____

3. _____

4. _____

5. _____

6. _____

7. _____

8. _____

9. _____

10. _____

11. _____

12. _____

Questions to Ponder

❏ When did your state join the Union?

❏ Should there be a stripe for every state? (At first, with every new state, a new star and stripe were added to the flag. There got to be too many stripes, though, and so it was changed to just the original 13 stripes for each original colony, and each new state got a new star.)

❏ Will we ever have more states? Will some of our territories and commonwealths—like Puerto Rico, American Samoa, Guam, and the Virgin Islands—ever become states?

❏ Can you find any of the above territories and commonwealths on the map?

Non-Capital Cities and Their States

It has been said that American students perform abysmally when it comes to geography. When something is abysmal, it has immense or fathomless extension downward. Thus, if one is abysmal when it comes to geography, one is horrible! One is at the bottom! One knows very little.

Look carefully at the word *abysmal*. How many of you know what *mal* means in Spanish? *Mal* means bad, and if one does an abysmal job, one does a job badly. If one is malnourished, one is not properly nourished. If one is maladjusted, one is not adjusted properly. The Latin prefix *mal* means "bad" or "evil," and many of our English and Spanish words we use today are derived from Latin. Some educators believe our education system is abysmal because Latin is no longer a required subject. For those of you who are word experts, what does *abyss* mean? (An abyss is a bottomless pit.)

Back to geography! It is a given that every student should know state capitals, but students should also be able to place major metropolitan or high commerce areas to the region or state they are in. A common mistake is to speak of Chicago as the capital of Illinois—even television news anchors and radio announcers have made this error. (Springfield is the capital of Illinois.)

So how will you do on this quiz? Will you earn an abysmal score or a superior one?

All of these cities are not state capitals, but they are big and often mentioned in newspapers, books, and magazines or mentioned on radio and television. Can you match the city to the state?

State Key

California	Louisiana	Missouri	Ohio	Texas
Florida	Maryland	Nevada	Pennsylvania	Washington
Kentucky	Michigan	New York	Tennessee	Wisconsin

---

1. Las Vegas _____

2. San Francisco _____

3. Houston _____

4. Pittsburgh _____

5. Seattle _____

6. Los Angeles _____

7. Louisville _____

8. Baltimore _____

9. Cleveland _____

10. San Diego _____

11. Miami _____

12. New Orleans _____

13. Milwaukee _____

14. St. Louis _____

15. Philadelphia _____

16. Detroit _____

17. Cincinnati _____

18. New York City _____

19. San Antonio _____

20. Memphis _____

Capitals of the World

While it is important to learn about the history and geography of one's own country, it is just as essential to be aware of the other countries of the world. For instance, most Americans know that the capital of the United States is Washington, D.C. How many, however, can name the capital of China—the most populated country in the world? When we read the newspaper or watch television, the names of different countries and the major (and often, capital) cities of those countries reoccur often. To better understand what one is reading or hearing, it is vital to be able to match cities with the countries to which they belong.

See how many of these major capital cities you can match to their countries. Write the name of each capital on the line next to its corresponding country.

Capital Key

Athens	Cairo	Paris
Baghdad	Lima	Rabat
Bangkok	London	Rome
Beijing	Madrid	Stockholm
Berlin	Moscow	Taipei
Brussels	New Delhi	Tokyo
Buenos Aires		Vienna

1. Argentina _____
2. Austria _____
3. Belgium _____
4. China _____
5. Egypt _____
6. France _____
7. Germany _____
8. Great Britain _____
9. Greece _____
10. India _____
11. Iraq _____
12. Italy _____
13. Japan _____
14. Morocco _____
15. Peru _____
16. Russia _____
17. Taiwan _____
18. Thailand _____
19. Spain _____
20. Sweden _____

Rivers

Civilization has flourished along rivers. Humankind has fought over control of water throughout history. Can you match the rivers in the key to their descriptions below?

River Key

A. Amazon	**F.** Volga
B. Euphrates	**G.** Huang H. (Yellow)
C. Mississippi	**H.** Nile
D. Ganges	**I.** Congo
E. Saskatchewan	**J.** Seine

_____ 1. empties into the Atlantic Ocean; 2,718 miles (4,374 km); flows through the Democratic Republic of Congo

_____ 2. empties into the Caspian Sea; 2,290 miles (3,685 km); flows through Russia

_____ 3. empties into the Atlantic Ocean; 4,000 miles (6,437 km); flows through Brazil

_____ 4. empties into the English Channel; 496 miles (798 km); flows through France

_____ 5. empties into the Bay of Bengal; 1,560 miles (2,511 km); flows through India

_____ 6. empties into Shatt al Arab; 1,700 miles (2,736 km); flows through Turkey, Syria, and Iraq

_____ 7. empties into the Mediterranean; 4,160 miles (6,695 km); flows through Egypt

_____ 8. empties into the Gulf of Mexico; 2,340 miles (3,766 km); flows through the United States

_____ 9. empties into the Yellow Sea; 2,295 miles (3,693 km); flows through China

_____ 10. empties into Lake Winnipeg; 1,205 miles (1,939 km); flows through Canada

---

Bonus: Can you find all of these rivers on a map?

Who Said That?

How many of these famous lines can you match to the people who said them? Choose from the names listed in the key.

Famous Person Key

Abraham Lincoln

John F. Kennedy

Sojourner Truth

Daniel Boone

Mark Twain

Muhammad Ali

Franklin D. Roosevelt

Thomas Alva Edison

Louis Armstrong

Susan B. Anthony and
Elizabeth Cady Stanton

---

1. "Float like a butterfly, sting like a bee."_____

2. "The only thing we have to fear is fear itself." _____

3. "Name the greatest of all inventions. Accident."_____

4. "Ain't I a woman?" _____

5. "Ask not what your country can do for you; ask what you can do for your country."

   _____

6. "I've never been lost, but I was bewildered once for three days."

   _____

7. "Men their rights and nothing more; women their rights and nothing less."

   _____

8. "Government of the people, by the people, and for the people."

   _____

9. "Man, if you have to ask, you'll never know."_____

10. "Genius is one percent inspiration and ninety-nine percent perspiration."

   _____

Bonus: Why do think these people would say these particular things?

Which Line Connects to C?

Look carefully at this picture.

Which line do you think connects to C? Are you sure? Are you positive? Would you like to change your mind?

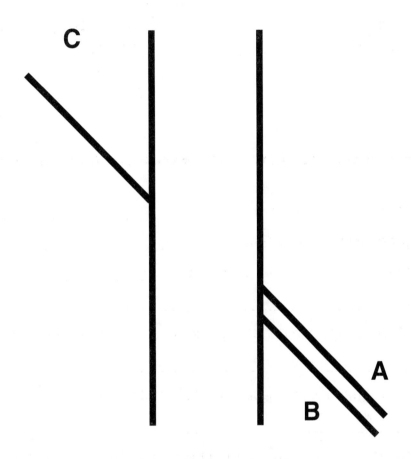

When one wavers, one hesitates or goes back and forth between choices. If one chooses line A and then line B, and then goes back to line A, one is wavering. Are you wavering between answer choice A and answer choice B?

The correct answer is line B. Use a straight edge to check!

Questions to Ponder

❏ Should one always trust what one sees?

❏ When is it important to use a straight edge?

❏ If two people decide to build a brick wall, and each person starts from an opposite edge, how can they make sure that they will meet exactly in the middle?

❏ Would you waver between which one to take—a roller coaster that takes one upside down and backwards or a roller coaster that drops one 70 feet straight down?

Counting F's

Read the sentence in the box below:

> FINISHED FUNDAMENTAL MANU-
> FACTURED ITEMS ARE THE RE-
> SULT OF YEARS OF SCIENTIFIC
> STUDY COMBINED WITH THE EX-
> PERIENCE OF YEARS.

Now count aloud the F's in this sentence. Count only once. Don't go back and count them again.

How many F's did you count?

The average number of F's a person sees is four. Actually, there are seven F's! How many of you missed the F's in the word *of* ?

Questions to Ponder

❑ You found more F's when you were given directions on where to look. Have you noticed that once you learn a new word or visit a new place, it seems as if everyone is using that word or has gone to where you have gone? Do you think the word is being used more, or are you just now noticing that it is being used?

❑ Some scientists look at miniscule (very tiny) creatures under the microscope. Do you think they could tell what they were seeing at first, or do you think they had to train their eyes?

❑ If someone were seeing a game of football or basketball for the first time and he or she did not know the rules or even how the game was scored, do you think he or she would notice as much as the person who knew what was going on?

❑ Our fingerprints are unique. No one in the world has the same fingerprints as you do. Gorillas have individual noseprints. Do you think field primatologists (scientists who study apes and monkeys in the wild) learn to recognize gorillas by their noses?

Who Do You See?

When some people look at this picture, they see an old woman. When others look at this picture, they see a young lady. Who do you see? Can you spot both?

This is called an optical illusion. *Optical* is a word that means "relating to vision." An illusion is something that is deceiving. An optical illusion is something that is deceiving or playing a trick on your eyes.

Many people can spot either the young or the old lady very quickly. What is difficult for them is then finding the second lady. It is as if their eye wants them to see only one thing.

Questions to Ponder

❏ Oftentimes, the police use eyewitnesses (people who have seen or witnessed the crime) to help them find the criminals. Do you think it would help the police to have more than one eyewitness?

❏ People in deserts often see mirages. Are mirages optical illusions?

❏ Have you ever heard of the saying, "He can't see the forest because of the trees?" Can you relate that saying in any way to this picture? (How about if one can only see the old lady or the young lady?)

Proverbs

Proverbs are a collection of sayings that often reflect the accumulated wisdom, prejudices, and superstitions of a particular culture. Different societies, even ones that do not use a written language system, have proverbs. Can you fill in the blanks on these?

1. _____ speak louder than words.

2. _____ is thicker than water.

3. Don't cut off your _____ to spite your face.

4. Don't put all your _____ in one basket.

5. _____ never strikes twice in the same place.*

6. A man is known by the _____ he keeps.

7. Make _____ while the sun shines.

8. You can lead a horse to water, but you can't make him _____.

9. Where there's a _____, there's a way.

10. People who live in glass houses shouldn't throw _____.

11. _____ wasn't built in a day.

12. Better _____ than never.

* Lightening actually can strike more than once! Ex-park ranger Roy C. Sullivan was struck seven times. In 1942, he lost his big toenail. In 1969, his eyebrows. In 1970, his left shoulder was seared. In 1972, his hair was set on fire. In 1973, his hair was set on fire again and his legs were seared. In 1976, his ankle was injured. In 1977, he had to go to the hospital with chest and stomach burns.

Questions to Ponder

❏ Can you explain any of these proverbs?

❏ Does an apple a day really keep the doctor away?

❏ Can you make up a proverb with some of the "new" things from this century—like computers, e-mail, cell phones, airplanes, space travel, etc.?

Writing Your Own Entry

It's your turn to create an entry that would fit into the format of this book. Here are some hints that one might find useful for completing this task:

☞ First Paragraph

Start with a line that will capture the reader's attention. For example, "The plane engine sputtered," or "The yellow eyes of the beast glared at him out of the darkness." Try to hook your reader in your first paragraph.

☞ Second Paragraph

Provide some biographical information about the person, animal, or event. For example, "A reticulated python held in captivity was once measured at 28 and one-half feet (8.7 m). She weighed 320 pounds (145 kg)," or "His father was a farmer."

☞ Third Paragraph

If you need this paragraph, describe another event or accomplishment your subject witnessed or performed.

Reminder: You don't have to put in everything that you learned about your subject!

Questions to Ponder

❏ Remember geography! Ask these questions:

　—Where was your subject born?

　—If the subject is an animal, where is it found?

　—Is an ocean nearby?

　—What are the neighboring countries?

　—What is the capital?

　—One can usually get at least two questions using geography.

❏ Think vocabulary!

　—Is there a vocabulary word that describes the person or event you are writing about?

　—Can you ask if another person or animal could be described with the same word?

❏ Think about feelings and opinions!

　—Would you like to do what this person did?

　—Was the person right?

　—Would this animal make a good pet?

　—How would you feel in this situation?

Writing Form

Name_____

Date_____

Period _____

Name of person, animal, or event you will be describing:_____

_____

_____

_____

_____

_____

_____

_____

_____

_____

_____

———— Questions to Ponder ————

-
-
-
-
-

Bibliography

Aaseng, Nathan. *Better Mousetraps, Product Improvements that Led to Success.* Lerner Publications Company, 1990.

Adler, David A. *Easy Math Puzzles.* Holiday House, 1997.

Altman, Susan. *Extraordinary Black Americans from Colonial to Contemporary Times.* Childrens Press, 1993.

Anderson, LaVere. *Mary McLeod Bethume: Teacher with a Dream.* Chelsea House Publishers, 1991.

Avery, Susan, and Linda Skinner. *Extraordinary American Indians.* Childrens Press, 1992.

Balcavage, Dynise. *Ludwig Van Beethoven: Composer.* Chelsea House Publishers, 1997.

Bickel, Lennard. *Mawson's Will.* Stein and Day, 1977.

Blum, David. *Quintet: Five Journeys Toward Musical Fulfillment.* Cornell University Press, 1999.

Blumberg, Rhoda. *The Remarkable Voyages of Captain Cook.* Bradbury Press, 1991.

Bowen, Andy Russell. *A World of Knowing: A Story about Thomas Hopkins Gallaudet.* Carolrhoda Books, Inc. 1995.

Bredeson, Carmen. *Jonas Salk Discoverer of the Polio Vaccine.* Enslow Publishers, Inc. 1993.

Brown, Pam. *Florence Nightingale.* Gareth Stevens Publishing, 1989.

Burleigh, Robert. *Who Said That? Famous Americans Speak.* Henry Holt and Company, 1995.

Camp, Carole Ann. *Sally Ride: First American Woman in Space.* Enslow Publishers, Inc., 1997.

Carson, Ben. *Ben Carson.* Zondervan Publishing House, 1992.

Cary, Alice. *Jean Craighead George.* The Learning Works, Inc., 1996.

Collins, David R. *Farmworker's Friend: The Story of Cesar Chavez.* Carolrhoda Books, Inc., 1996.

————. *Mark Twain! A Story About Samuel Clemens.* Carolrhoda Books, Inc., 1994.

Crowley, Carolyn Hughes. "The Man who Invented Elsie, the Borden Cow." *Smithsonian Magazine* (September, 1999): 32–34.

Cummings, Pat, and Linda Cummings. *Talking with Adventurers.* National Geographic Society, 1998.

De Kruif, Paul. *Microbe Hunters.* Harcourt, Brace and Company, Inc., 1966.

DeStefano, Susan. *Chico Mendes: Fight for the Forest.* Twenty-First Century Books, 1995.

Dingle, Derek T. *First in the Field: Baseball Hero Jackie Robinson.* Hyperion Books for Children, 2000.

Famighetti, Robert, Editor. *The World Almanac and Book of Facts.* Funk and Wagnalls., 1994.

Fargis, Paul and Bykofsky, Sheree (editorial directors). *The New York Public Library Desk Reference, 2nd Edition.* Prentice Hall General Reference, 1993.

Ferris, Jeri. *Native American Doctor: the Story of Susan LaFlesche Picotte.* Carolrhoda Books, Inc., 1991.

————. *What I Had Was Singing: the Story of Marian Anderson.* Carolrhoda Books, Inc., 1994.

Fiennes, Ranulph. *Mind Over Matter, the Epic Crossing of the Antarctic Continent.* Delacorte Press, 1993.

Foster, Leila Merrel. *Benjamin Franklin: Founding Father and Inventor.* Enslow Publishers, Inc., 1997.

Foster, Ruth. *A Word a Week Vocabulary Program.* Teacher Created Materials, Inc., 1999.

Frankl, Ron. *Duke Ellington: Bandleader and Composer.* Chelsea House Publishers, 1989.

Freedman, Russell. *Eleanor Roosevelt: A Life of Discovery.* Clarion Books, 1993.

————. *Martha Graham: A Dancer's Life.* Clarion Books, 1998.

————. *Out of Darkness: the Story of Louis Braille.* Clarion Books, 1997.

Bibliography *(cont.)*

Galdikas, Birute M.F. *Reflections of Eden, My Years with the Orangutans of Borneo.* Little, Brown, and Company, 1995.

Glendinning, Richard and Sally. *The Ringling Brothers, Circus Family.* Chelsea House Publishers, 1991.

Glubok, Shirley. *Painting.* Charles Scribner's Sons, 1994.

Gorrell, Gena K. *North Star to Freedom: The Story of the Underground Railroad.* Delacorte Press, 1997.

Green, Robert. *Cleopatra.* Franklin Watts, 1996.

Greenfield, Eloise. *Rosa Parks.* HarperCollins, 1996.

Hammontree, Marie. *Albert Einstein: Young Thinker.* Macmillan Publishing Company, 1986.

Hargrove, Jim. *Diego Rivera, Mexican Muralist.* Children's Press, Inc., 1990.

Haskins, Jim. *Black Eagles: African Americans in Aviation.* Scholastic Inc., 1995.

————. *Outward Dreams: Black Inventors and Their Inventions.* Walker and Company, 1991.

Hayden, Robert C. *Eight Black American Inventors.* Addison-Wesley, 1972.

Hirsch Jr., E.D., Joseph Kett, and James Trefil. *The First Dictionary of Cultural Literacy.* Houghton Mifflin Company, 1996.

Hunt, John. *The Conquest of Everest.* E.P. Dutton and Company, 1954.

Italia, Bob. *Great Auto Makers and Their Cars.* The Oliver Press, Inc., 1993.

Jeffrey, Laura S. *Guion Bluford, A Space Biography.* Enslow Publishers, Inc., 1998.

Jones, Charlotte Foltz. *Mistakes That Worked.* Doubleday, 1994.

Kastner, Joseph. *John James Audubon.* Harry N. Abrams, Inc., 1992.

Kendall, Catherine Wolf. *More Stories of Composers for Young Musicians.* Toadwood Publishers, 1988.

Kent, Zachary. *The Story of Geronimo.* Children's Press, 1989.

————. *The World's Great Explorers, Marco Polo.* Children's Press, 1992.

Kittredge, Mary. *Jane Addams.* Chelsea House Publishers, 1988.

Klausner, Janet. *Sequoyah's Gift: A Portrait of the Cherokee Leader.* HarperCollins Publishers, 1993.

Knudson, R. R. *Babe Didrikson, Athlete of the Century.* Viking Kestral, 1985.

Kraft, Betsy Harvey. *Mother Jones: One Woman's Fight for Labor.* HM, 1995.

Kramer, Barbara. *Neil Armstrong: The First Man on the Moon.* Enslow Publishers, Inc., 1997.

Krull, Kathleen. *Lives of the Writers.* Harcourt Brace and Company, 1994.

Kudlinski, Kathleen V. *Rachel Carson: Pioneer of Ecology.* Puffin, 1989

Lampton, Christopher. *Thomas Alva Edison.* Franklin Watts, 1988.

Lansing, Alfred. *Endurance: Shackleton's Incredible Voyage.* Carroll and Graf Publishers, Inc., 1989.

Lasky, Kathyrn. *A Brilliant Streak: The Story of Mark Twain.* Harcourt Brace and Company, 1998.

Leon, Vicki. *Outrageous Women of Ancient Times.* John Wiley & Sons, Inc., 1997.

Levey, Judith, and Agnes Greenhall, Editors. *The Concise Columbia Encyclopedia.* Avon Books, 1983.

Levin, Pamela. *Susan B. Anthony, Fighter for Women's Rights.* Chelsea House Publishers, 1993.

Levinson, Nancy Smiler. *Chuck Yeager: The Man Who Broke The Sound Barrier.* Walker and Company, 1988.

Lipstyte, Robert. *Jim Thorpe: Twentieth-Century Jock.* HarperCollins Publishers, 1993.

Lovell, Jim and Jeffrey Kluger. *Lost Moon, the Perilous Voyage of Apollo 13.* Houghton Mifflin, 1994.

Mann, Martha. *Nathan Hale, Patriot.* Dodd, Mead, and Company, 1951.

Bibliography *(cont.)*

Markham, Lois. *Jacques-Yves Cousteau: Exploring the Wonders of the Deep.* Raintree Steck-Vaughn Publishers, 1997.

Mason, Antony. *Peary and Amundsen: Race to the Poles.* Steck-Vaughn Company, 1995.

Matthews, Peter (editor). *The Guinness Book of Records, 1994.* Bantam Books, 1994.

Mayer, Ann Margaret. *Sir Frederick Banting, Doctor Against Diabetes.* Creative Education, 1974.

McGovern, Ann. *Shark Lady. Scholastic, 1991.*

McPherson, Stephanie. *The Workers' Detective: A Story about Dr. Alice Hamilton.* Carolrhoda Books, Inc., 1992.

Meachum, Virginia. *Jane Goodall: Protector of Chimpanzees.* Enslow Publishing, Inc., 1997.

Meltzer, Milton. *Dorothea Lange, Life Through the Camera.* Viking Kestrel, 1985.

Morey, Janet Nomura, and Wendy Dunn. *Famous Asian Americans.* Cobblehill Books, 1992.

Morrow, Mary Francis. *Sarah Winnemucca.* Pinnacle Press, Inc., 1990.

Mulcahy, Robert. *Medical Technology: Inventing the Instruments.* The Oliver Press, Inc., 1997.

Newhouse, Elizabeth, L. (editor). *Inventors and Discoverers, Changing Our World.* The National Geographic Society, 1988.

Osborne, Angela. *Abigail Adams.* Chelsea House Publishers, 1989.

Parker, Steve. *Galileo and the Universe.* Chelsea House, 1995.

———. *Marie Curie and Radium.* Harper Collins Publishers, 1992.

Patrick, Diane. *Martin Luther King, Jr.* Franklin Watts, 1990.

Perl, Lila. *It Happened in America: True Stories from the Fifty States.* Henry Holt and Company, 1992.

Prentzas, G.S. *Thurgood Marshall: Champion of Justice.* Chelsea Juniors, 1993.

Rappaport, Doreen. *Living Dangerously, American Women Who Risked Their Lives for Adventure.* Harper Collins Publishers, 1991.

Reynolds, Quentin. *The Wright Brothers, Pioneers of American Aviation.* Random House, Inc., 1981.

Restak, Richard. *The Brain.* Bantam Books, 1984.

Ross, Stewart. *Cowboys.* Copper Beech Books, 1995.

Sanford, William R., and Carl R. Green. *Sacagawea: Native American Hero.* Enslow Publishers, Inc., 1997.

Scordato, Ellen. *Sarah Winnnemucca, Northern Paiute Writer and Diplomat.* Chelsea House Publishers, 1992.

Sheridan, Simon. *Stephen Hawking: Unlocking the Universe.* Dillon Press, 1991.

Shirley, Angelica, and Jean Shirley. *Robert Louis Stevenson, Finding Treasure Island.* Lerner Publication Company, 1997.

Shore, Nancy. *Amelia Earhart.* Chelsea House Publishers, 1987.

Shorto, Russell. *Geronimo.* Silver Burdett Press, 1989.

Simmons, Alex. *Ben Carson.* Steck-Vaughn Company, 1996.

Sinnott, Susan. *Extraordinary Asian-Pacific Americans.* Children's Press, 1993.

Sipiera, Paul P. *The World's Great Explorers, Roald Amundsen and Robert Scott.* Children's Press, Inc., 1990.

Sloan, Carolyn. *Helen Keller.* Hamish Hamilton, 1984.

Smith, Linda Wasmer. *Louis Pasteur: Disease Fighter.* Enslow Publishers, Inc. 1997.

Snow, Dorothea J. *Samuel Morse, Inquisitive Boy.* The Bobbs-Merrill Company, Inc. 1960.

Bibliography (cont.)

Sobel, Dava. *Longitude, the True Story of a Lone Genius Who Solved the Greatest Scientific Problem of His Time.* Penguin Books, USA Inc., 1995.

Sprawson, Charles. "Swimming with Sharks." *The New Yorker*, August 23 and 30, 1999: 160–169.

Stapleton, Michael. *The Illustrated Dictionary of Greek and Roman Mythology.* Peter Bedrick Books, 1986.

Stefoff, Rebecca. *Nelson Mandela: A Voice Set Free.* Fawcett Columbine Books, 1990.

Stofflet, Mary. *Dr. Seuss from Then to Now, A Catalogue of the Retrospective Exhibition Organized by the San Diego Museum of Art.* Random House, 1986.

Stonaker, Frances Benson. *Famous Mathematicians.* J.B. Lippencott Company, 1966.

Sullivan, Otha Richard. *Black Stars, African American Inventors.* John Wiley and Sons, Inc., 1998.

Swanson, June. *David Bushnell and His Turtle, the Story of America's First Submarine.* Atheneum, 1991.

Taylor, Robert. *Oscar de la Hoya, Boxing Boy's Wonder.* Rourke Enterprises, Inc., 1993.

Tessendorf, K.C. *Over the Edge: Flying with the Polar Heroes.* Atheneum Books for Young Readers, 1998.

Thayer, Helen. *Polar Dream.* Simon and Schuster, 1993.

Towle, Wendy. *The Real McCoy, The Life of an African-American Inventor.* Scholastic, Inc., 1995.

Turk, Ruth. *Ray Charles: Soulman.* Lerner Publications Company, 1996.

Turner, Robyn M. *Dorthea Lange.* Little, Brown and Company, 1994.

Twist, Clint. *Stanley and Livingston, Expeditions Through Africa.* The Steck-Vaughn Company, 1995.

Uchida, Yoshiko. *The Invisible Thread.* Morrow, 1995.

Vare, Ethlie Ann, and Ptacek, Greg. *Mothers of Inventions. From the Bra to the Bomb: Forgotten Women and Their Unforgettable Ideas.* William Morrow and Company, Inc., 1988.

Williams, Trevor I. *Alfred Nobel, Pioneer of High Explosives.* Wayland Publishers, Limited, 1980.

Wymer, Norman. *Inventors.* Silver Burdett Company, 1982.

Wexo, John Bonnett. *Sharks.* (Zoobooks). Wildlife Educ., 1997.

————. *The Apes.* Zoobooks, July 1991. Volume 8, Number 10.

Woog, Adam. *The Importance of Harry Houdini.* Lucent Books, Inc., 1995.

Yount, Lisa. *Antoni van Leeuwenhoek: First to See Microscopic Life.* Enslow Publishers, Inc. 1996.

The following articles were used as references in the writing of this book. Each can be found in *Encyclopedia Britannica*, published by Encyclopedia Britannica, Inc., in 1990.

"Agnesi, Maria Gaetana" (volume 1, page 150)

"Bushnell, David" (volume 2, page 675)

"Everest, Mount" (volume 4, page 619)

"Hurston, Zora Neale" (volume 6, page 168)

"Mawson, Sir Douglas" (volume 7, page 962)

"Passenger pigeon" (volume 9, page 185)

"Shackleton, Sir Ernest Henry" (volume 10, page 683)

The author wishes to thank the following for their assistance:
- the University of Illinois Press for granting permission to reproduce the picture "My Wife and My Mother-in-law" from the *American Journal of Psychology*, Volume 42, page 444, copyright 1930 by the Board of Trustees of the University of Illinois.
- David Doubilet of Doubilet Photography, Inc., for granting permission for his story to be told.
- the Tippecanoe County Public Library reference librarians who were instrumental in the fact-checking process.

Answer Key

Great Events in World History (page 156)
Chronological Order: B, F, G, I, D, E, H, C, A

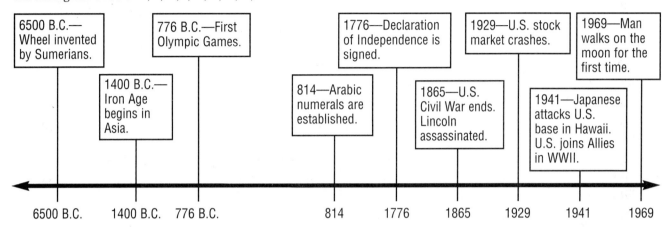

Inventions (page 157)
Chronological Order: D, H, J, A, G, E, F, C, B, I

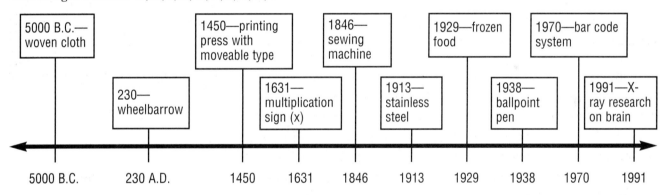

When Did Each Become a State and Join the Union? (page 158)

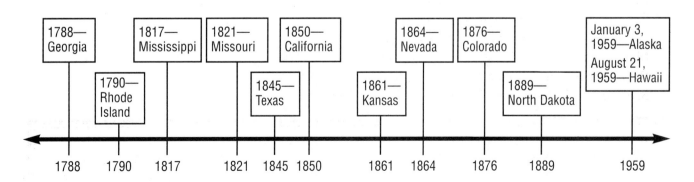

Answer Key (cont.)

Non-Capital Cities and Their States (page 159)

1	Nevada	11.	Florida
2.	California	12.	Louisiana
3	Texas	13.	Wisconsin
4.	Pennsylvania	14.	Missouri
5.	Washington	15.	Pennsylvania
6.	California	16.	Michigan
7.	Kentucky	17.	Ohio
8.	Maryland	18.	New York
9.	Ohio	19.	Texas
10.	California	20.	Tennessee

Capitals of the World (page 160)

1.	Buenos Aires	11.	Baghdad
2.	Vienna	12.	Rome
3.	Brussels	13.	Tokyo
4.	Beijing	14.	Rabat
5.	Cairo	15.	Lima
6.	Paris	16.	Moscow
7.	Berlin	17.	Taipei
8.	London	18.	Bangkok
9.	Athens	19.	Madrid
10.	New Delhi	20.	Stockholm

Rivers (page 161)

1.	I	6.	B
2.	F	7.	H
3.	A	8.	C
4.	J	9.	G
5.	D	10.	E

Who Said That? (page 162)

1. "Float like a butterfly, sting like a bee."—Muhammed Ali (Ali was a boxing champion who won the Olympic Gold Medal in 1960, as well as the world heavyweight title in '64, '67, '74, and '78. Ali would sometimes even predict what round he would knock out his opponent!)

2. "The only thing we have to fear is fear itself."—Franklin D. Roosevelt (Roosevelt spoke these words at his presidential inaugural address in 1933. The country was in a great depression, and many people were out of work and losing their homes.)

3. "Name the greatest of all the inventors. Accident."— Mark Twain (An American author and humorist of the late nineteenth and early twentieth century, Twain wrote Huckleberry Finn and The Adventures of Tom Sawyer.)

4. "Ain't I a woman"—Sojourner Truth (An escaped slave and abolitionist, Truth was a dynamic speaker. This line comes from a speech where she said, "I could work as much as a man…and ain't I a woman? I have plowed and planted…and ain't I a woman. I have borne the lash…and ain't I a woman?")

5. "Ask not what your country can do for you; ask what you can do for your country."—John F. Kennedy (Kennedy was the U.S. president from 1961–1963. He said these words as part of his inaugural address.)

6. "I've never been lost, but I was bewildered once for three days."—Daniel Boone (Boone was an American frontier settler who is best known for his exploration and settlement of Kentucky.)

7. "Men their rights and nothing more; women their rights and nothing less."—Susan B. Anthony and Elizabeth Cady Stanton (This phrase was printed in the late 1860s on the front page of Anthony and Cady Stanton's weekly journal *The Revolution*. Both women died before the Nineteenth Amendment, the one giving women the right to vote, passed in 1919.)

8. "Government of the people, by the people, and for the people."—Abraham Lincoln (The 16th president of the United States spoke these words during his Gettysburg Address, a speech given during the Civil War at the dedication of a soldier's cemetery at the site of the Battle of Gettysburg.)

9. "Man, if you have to ask, you'll never know."—Louis Armstrong (Armstrong, a great jazz musician and singer answered this when once asked the question, "What is jazz?")

10. "Genius is one percent inspiration and ninety-nine percent perspiration."—Thomas Alva Edison (Edison, an American inventor, patented more than 1,000 devices—including the phonograph and the incandescent light bulb.)

Proverbs (page 166)

1. Actions
2. Blood
3. nose
4. eggs
5. Lightning
6. company
7. hay
8. drink
9. will
10. stones
11. Rome
12. late

Index

Index *(cont.)*